BUTTERBABE

BUTTERBABE

THE TRUE STORY OF A 40-STONE WOMAN LIVING IN A SIZE ZERO WORLD

Rebecca Golden

Vermilion
LONDON

1 3 5 7 9 10 8 6 4 2

Published in 2009 by Vermilion, an imprint of Ebury Publishing
A Random House Group company

The Random House Group Limited Reg. No. 954009

Addresses for companies within the Random House Group can be found at
www.rbooks.co.uk

A CIP catalogue record for this book is available
from the British Library

The Random House Group Limited supports The Forest Stewardship
Council (FSC), the leading international forest certification organisation.
All our titles that are printed on Greenpeace approved FSC certified paper
carry the FSC logo. Our paper procurement policy can be found at
www.rbooks.co.uk/environment

Mixed Sources
Product group from well-managed
forests and other controlled sources
www.fsc.org   Cert no. TT-COC-2139
© 1996 Forest Stewardship Council
FSC

Printed in the UK by CPI Mackays, Chatham, ME5 8TD

ISBN 9780091922153

To buy books by your favourite authors and register for offers, visit
www.rbooks.co.uk

For Mom and Andrea

All my love, no matter how mean I had to be about it.

CONTENTS

PROLOGUE

The flat had wall-to-wall carpeting and he'd filled it with heavy wooden armoires and furry white throw rugs. She wore a belted trench coat, her long brown hair hanging past her shoulders. She looked at the kite in her hands then glanced pointedly out of the window at the snow. She'd never intended to fly any kites. She came to his flat with a different activity in mind.

'Morris, I want your body,' she told him.

Two weeks later, as they lay together in his bed with the carved oak headboard, he said something awkward about making an honest woman out of her. So they got married – after months of wrangling with the Catholic Church and her father. They had a baby and lived, sometimes happily, ever after.

I was born at Mercy Hospital on 14 October 1972. I weighed six pounds and was as bald as an egg. My parents brought me home to a small ranch house with a galley kitchen and two tiny bedrooms. I took my first steps in that yellow house, splashed for hours in an inflatable paddling pool and tried to dig a hole to China under the oak tree in the back yard. I broke things and learned to value others' property; then I forgot what I'd learned and broke things again. I took ballpoint pens apart and my small hands bore blue-black ink stains. I ran naked through the hall to the living room with its huge bay window and fell in a giggling heap on one of the white rugs, revelling in the softness of faux fur against my skin. I can't remember the rain, though I remember a blizzard so fierce my mother had to swaddle me in coats and scarves and tow me half a mile to the shops in an old wooden sled with metal runners.

I have pictures of the little girl in the yellow house. She sits in a pile of brown leaves, her face incandescently happy. She wears a coat with a fur hood, snow piled past her knees. She lies in her parents' huge double bed, arms stretched languidly over her head and a tortoiseshell cat draped over her chest. I know I used to be that little girl. I remember the freedom of that tiny, lithe body. I wonder what she'd make of me, of the woman who once weighed nearly 43 stone. Little girls would spot me at the library or in a restaurant. They'd stare, faces frozen with shock, pink bow mouths hanging open. Sometimes a child would make a declaration: 'That lady's fat!' Sometimes a parent would gently correct them. Sometimes aloud they would wonder, 'How did she get so big?'

I often wonder myself. Between the ages of six and eleven, I gained 14 stone. Everyone wants to know how this happened. I want to know. Over the years I've had every test and seen all the doctors. There isn't any hormonal problem or glandular issue, though each new doctor insists on blood tests to check for diabetes and thyroid disease. Whatever answer I give seems like an excuse. My whole life has been one long excuse made first to my parents, then to my teachers, my sister, my friends and, finally, to myself. I have the same conversation with myself all the time, trying to point the finger, to allocate blame. In the end, no one is to blame – and everyone is – and I need to find a better way of looking at my life. It isn't all about the weight. At least I don't want it to be.

1

RAISED BY SOCIAL WORKERS

I gained weight steadily as I moved through childhood. Children do that, of course, but after the age of six or so, I was always plump. I was chubby in an ordinary way, not like something out of a circus, but big enough to mark me out as different from other children. At 12, I started my period and gained 7 stone in less than a year. I entered secondary school weighing more than 14 stone and feeling like a freak, something the other kids felt obliged to remind me of every single day.

I ate what I liked and wasn't athletic. I used to lie in my wardrobe on a sleeping bag and read books with a torch. I went to the cinema and watched a lot of television. In college, I started drinking a litre of fizzy pop a day, adopting 'Always Coca-Cola' as a personal mission statement. I gained weight. Through college, an abortive stint in graduate school, many bad jobs and a period of disability, I gained and gained until I went to a doctor's surgery one day and found that I weighed 40 stone. Somehow, this number surprised me, caught me totally off guard.

The story doesn't start with the 40-stone woman, however, but with that 6 pound infant. Before I weighed 40 stone – before

I weighed 6 pounds – my parents had all the usual rosy fantasies about my future. They imagined their baby studying medicine or painting famous canvasses. Before I was born, my mother chose a mural for my bedroom wall, a smiling elephant in human clothes. My father helped her with the stencil, approved the colour choices and put my new cot together while smoking and cursing the inventor of the Allen key.

They had met 19 months before my birth in the dingy offices of the Lucas County Department of Health and Human Services – the local welfare department. My parents were accidental social workers. Mum had graduated from the University of Toledo with a teaching degree but loathed school-children. She spent her early twenties working her way through college while chasing exotic men across Toledo, Europe and the Middle East. After dumping her last bad fiancé – the Lebanese brother-in-law of one of her college roommates – Mum returned to Ohio to start a career.

Dad retired from the military after a 20-year career and used his business degree to land a job with the agency. A 49-year-old bachelor who'd left a long line of bar girls and prostitutes in his wake, he'd lived all over the world as a technical sergeant in the United States Air Force. Just days after retiring from the service, he wandered into the welfare department and they hired him on the spot. He spent the next 25 years there.

Dad grew up in Youngstown, Ohio, a dying industrial town on the far eastern edge of the state. His Russian Jewish immi-grant parents somehow managed to select one of the least appealing places in America as their new home. Youngstown was a city of cracked pavements and swimming pools filled with cement because black children wanted to swim. The only picture I have of my grandfather – a tiny square headshot stuck to an old ID card – shows a grim, unsmiling man, old beyond the 60 years attested to by the government bureaucrat who snapped the portrait.

My father, his older sister and younger brother grew up poor, even by the standards of the Great Depression. The family had no money for temple membership. On the high holidays, the Goldens walked for miles to attend services and had to sit in the synagogue's basement with other non-members, listening to the rabbi over a rudimentary PA system. Grandpa worked in a steel mill. He'd been conscripted into the Russian army at 13, had seen all the most exciting and exotic parts of Poland, and promptly emigrated to the first country he could find that allowed Jews to stay in school past the age of 12.

I know almost nothing about his wife, my grandmother, except that I'm named after her. We used to have one photo of her: she's short and squat and looks nervously at the camera from a crouched position next to the broken foundation of the house my father grew up in. She nearly smiles, the corners of her plump mouth turning slightly upwards; she seems to be wondering, 'A picture of me? Why would you bother?'

My mother noticed my father almost immediately after taking a caseworker position in 1970. She told me about the day they were formally introduced by a colleague: 'He had this shirt he liked to wear, some sort of oatmeal-coloured polyester thing with a zip. It had dried Rice Krispies down the front. I asked him out. I knew it would snow, so I suggested we fly kites. I got him alone, said I wanted his body and that was that.'

My mother chose her own engagement ring, a gorgeous and fanciful piece with oak leaves, small diamonds and a bright opal chip, and went to her parents' house to break the news. Her father had hated all of her boyfriends. His racism bubbled through when Mum brought the first Lebanese boy home. He was a Toledo-born Lebanese, a Catholic like all our Hungarian relations. My grandfather called him a nigger. So, despite the fact that Dad was twice her age and Jewish, she thought her father might react favourably. At least he wasn't a black guy or a Protestant.

'Are you pregnant?' Grandpa Snyir asked.

'No, but it'd be par for the course. Everyone in this family's about five months gone when they march down the aisle,' Mum answered.

On her wedding day, Mum wore a white linen dress with blue ribbon trim. Her long hair, bleached a strange greenish blonde, was pulled back from her face and hung loose to her shoulders. Dad wore a brown suit with a bright blue tie. My mother looks a little older than 25 in the wedding pictures and my father looks far younger than 49. They both look happy, if a little overwhelmed. Grandma Snyir, wearing a pink mini-dress, beams proudly at the camera, one arm draped around her daughter's waist. Grandpa Snyir looks like he's expecting the bill for a sit-down dinner for a hundred people.

A year and a half later, my parents had me.

My parents brought me home to the ranch house, the first house they ever owned. We were looking through some old pictures after my grandmother died, and I found one of my first birthday. I'm eating an entire, lavishly frosted birthday cake, digging into it with my bare hands. My mouth is rimmed with white icing, and an enormous dirty blonde wig covers my (still) bald head. 'The wig was your idea,' Mum told me. 'You loved that thing.'

When I was six, my parents sold the yellow house and made a down payment on a two-storey modern house in a new suburb.

Our new house had grey wood trim and black brick on the façade and came complete with a concrete slab porch, three huge bedrooms, a kitchen diner and a big back yard. My parents loved this house, even though its hefty price tag and the giant mortgage it required forced my mother to take second and even third jobs to support it. I loved the new house, too, as I'd always wanted a staircase to play on. My parents set about collecting furniture for the house, and took me with them to my grandmother's condo to pick up a bedroom set that had belonged to my mother in high school. The white painted bed frame, bureau and desk would furnish my new bedroom, and my father wanted to make sure I treated these 1960s castoffs with the reverence they deserved.

'If you break any of it, if you draw on the desk or spill anything on the dresser, your butt belongs to me,' he said. I couldn't see his face; he sat in the passenger seat next to my mother, and I was in the back seat by myself. He didn't raise his voice. He didn't have to. I knew he'd hit me if anything happened to that furniture. My father had no idea that children broke things accidentally. If I dropped a glass or tripped over the coffee table, he began interrogations on the spot.

'Why did you do it?' he'd ask, grasping my shoulders and staring down at me. My father had thick eyebrows and wore glasses with lenses that magnified his eyes. When he asked me about the glass or the upended table, I could never work out a satisfactory answer. I didn't do these things on purpose. At six, my body seemed comprised entirely of large, clumsy feet and thick-fingered hands. I broke things. I also took things, not realising that that might be wrong. I'd see a pile of change on my parents' dresser and grab a handful so I could practise my counting. I had no more understanding of theft than a magpie does. The coins were shiny, pretty objects, and I wanted to look at them and hold them in my hand.

'Why? Why do you steal? God damn it, tell me!' Dad was shouting again. I knew I had to explain, but at six, I lacked the ability to do so. I thought and thought and couldn't find the answer.

'I don't know,' I said, the last syllable a long, round howl. I don't remember if he spanked me for taking his change. But he did spank me often because I was always breaking rules I didn't understand. If something in the house went missing, he suspected me, and nothing I could say ever persuaded him of my innocence. Dad would find his cufflinks or cigarette lighter behind the dresser or in the pocket of his coat, but he never apologised. I explained myself again and again, so often and with such futility that I developed a queer habit of explaining even the most trivial things out loud to myself, knowing that, sooner or later, Dad would ask me why I'd screwed up again.

Mum never seemed to be in the room when Dad got angry. When the yelling became hitting and shoving, she tried to intervene. She had little patience with his excuses, but always believed his promises of change. My mother loved her husband so completely and trusted him so implicitly that she couldn't have done anything else. I know that now. I even knew it then, on some level. I want to sympathise with my mother and her predicament, but I always feel worse for the little girl with the hand-shaped bruise on her face, and for the sad, fat teenager who thought her father would beat her for hiding dirty clothes in the wardrobe.

I've spent my whole life pretending to be normal, trying to dissociate myself from these younger versions. This charade doesn't end at imagining myself much thinner than I was then or am now. It invades every aspect of life. My family is fine, I tell myself. Dad loved me. Mum did her best. I make jokes about my father hitting me; I say that one of the advantages of having an older parent is that he lacks the energy to beat you properly. My eyes are always a little brighter, a little shinier, when I say these things. And then I change the subject.

On the other hand, I don't want to make my suburban upbringing sound like something out of a Russian gulag, because that isn't the truth either. I wasn't always unhappy, I wasn't always under suspicion and, despite my father's anger and criticism, I found my own happiness. Nevertheless, those times when I had to find explanations – when 'I don't know' earned me a spanking or hard words about what a devious little liar or thief I was – had a pronounced effect. My dolls could never do anything right. They merited constant punishment, and not even my one-eyed teddy bear could offer a satisfactory rationale for his bad attitude.

Years of this inquisition toughened me up. I can find humour in virtually any situation, even manufacturing it where none exists. As a child I did this so often and so well that it has become intrinsic to my personality. What's hardest for me isn't that my father accused me, that he didn't love me enough or in the right way; what's worst is that at the ages of six, seven and eight – and, if I'm being honest, at 30, 32 and 34 – I believed everything he said about me. I believed I was innately bad. Not just a bad child, but a bad person too; a fraud, an irredeemable liar and thief. Nothing I accomplished felt earned or deserved. Joking about it doesn't change anything, but it does make me feel better: less like a victim and more like a conspirator in our old family game.

Before I was even fat, children could sense my self-doubt. At five, despite my cuteness and seeming normality, I became a target for bullies. I was the little girl who had her trousers pulled down in the playground. The football coach's son did the deed, and I stood in the dirt afterwards, clutching my corduroy trousers and crying. The same boy punched me in the face one day, bloodying my nose. The sudden violence stunned me so much that I didn't cry; I merely stood mute and surprised as blood ran over my lips. He wanted my place in line for the toy box.

For a while, our move to the suburbs had taken some of the pressure off me. Kids at school wanted to hear about the new house, and my parents were focused on their various decorating projects. My father liked to spend leisurely Saturdays watering our driveway. The oak trees in the front yard dropped mossy gunk all over the drive, and Dad would stand in front of his castle for hours, shirt up exposing his gut, shorts hanging low off his totally flat behind, proudly rinsing and repeating.

A year or two before the arrival of my little sister could throw a wrench into our fun, Mum left Dad to his driveway from time to time and took me bar-hopping with her fun friend, Maggie. Maggie lived in a charming old house in a working-class district with her German shepherd, Vince, and an enormous record collection. Maggie's house had hardwood floors and floaty white drapes. She did the whole shabby chic thing long before it was chic. Maggie had a waterbed and a massive collection of Barbies she was saving for her own future children. I played with the dolls and bounced on the bed while Vince looked on from a rag rug on the floor.

Mum and Maggie went to bars to shoot pool, and I'd tag along, eating free popcorn and taking shots with their cues when the barman wasn't looking. I'd take the pool chalk while Mum was shooting and rub my fingers in the round indentation. We'd leave with a little popcorn for the road and I'd eat it in the car, picking bits out of the bag with my blue-stained fingertips. Mum liked flea markets and antique shops, too, and once bought me an enormous jar of glass marbles that I carried proudly from bar to bar.

As a six year old, I was thin, cute and full of energy. I spent hours running in the back yard, riding my bike and swinging from the monkey bars of my jungle gym. The only hint of the weight problem to come was my boundless appetite. I could eat five or six slices of bread without feeling full. I was hungry every minute I wasn't actually eating something, and food never filled me up. This was actually a rather large hint, but my high metabolism and constant activity made it seem less obvious at the time. I also lied about food, even then. If I had three biscuits, I'd say I'd eaten one. I wasn't exactly ashamed of eating, but I didn't want Dad to yell at me for taking a biscuit he'd wanted for himself.

People wonder how a woman comes to weigh so much. I

never binged; I simply never felt full. I could eat a small pizza, and then have another meal a couple of hours later. I could eat three or four helpings at dinner and still crave dessert. I liked the taste of good food, the feel of it in my mouth. My capacity (even as a toddler) was unlimited. I didn't understand why I should stop eating. My body never gave me any cues. Even after I developed the intellectual capacity to see the connection between lots of high-calorie foods and my fat body, my ability to rationalise stopped me from any serious attempts at dieting. 'I'll lose the weight when I'm older,' I thought. 'I'll grow and then my weight will be okay for my new height.' By the time I graduated from high school and I knew these fantasies wouldn't save me, I weighed so much that I thought dieting was hopeless.

My parents had good intentions. They wanted me to have advantages they'd never enjoyed growing up in blue-collar districts where children worked as hard as adults. As a child, my mother kept house, minded her brothers and cooked while her parents worked, and my father and his siblings sometimes went without food. Before the mortgage on our suburban dream house ate all of my parents' disposable income, we used to holiday in Bermuda. We'd go with my Uncle Drew, Mum's brother, and Grandma Snyir, and I burned some of my wild energy swimming and running on the beach. I wore a white Pierre Cardin bikini (the first and last I'd ever own) and picked fresh bananas off the tree.

Sometimes I'd spend the night in my grandmother's room. In the morning, we'd stand on her balcony and watch cruise ships. Grandma played with me on the beach, helping me fill my red plastic bucket. I wore a white canvas hat with lime green eye shades inserted into the brim, and we'd make sand castles and lie in the sun while the surf slowly laid waste to their ramparts.

After the move, however, we'd take summer holidays at a lake in a neighbouring state. One spring half-term, when I was around 11 or 12, it seemed as if every other kid I knew was going on an exotic adventure except for my little sister and me. I complained to my mother: 'I work really hard. Don't I deserve a nice trip?' I thought I made a good case. I'd got at least one A on my report card, and I went to school every day even though I hated all the other kids and my scary old hag of a teacher.

None of my tales of woe cut any ice with Mum. 'Cry me a river. Your father and I have to work. If you need something to do with your week off, you can always clean your room,' she told me. Mum had a point. My room was a pre-teen hellhole of epic proportions. My clothes, toys, shoes, notebooks and jewellery were strewn across the floor. Under my bed there were some really old chicken bones from the one time during a bout of flu when my mother had allowed me to have lunch in bed. Removing them would have entailed cleaning under the bed, an area I preferred to pretend didn't exist.

Avoidance coloured so many other areas of life too. I was chubby as a little girl – in an average sort of way, no more – but I never discussed it. I stopped tucking my shirts into my jeans and – *voilà!* – no more tummy. I ate all the things other children also loved to eat. I didn't need to binge to gain weight as my body seemed magically possessed of the ability to retain fat. Lots of chubby girls diet but I never did. In addition to all my other powers of rationalisation, I had this crazy, naive idea that people should like me for my personality and shiny heart of gold. If they rejected me because of the way I looked – and I always put it that way, not 'because I'm fat' – I believed they did so because of their own superficiality and lack of intelligence.

Television and books taught me all about looking past appearances. I watched a lot of shows where the Ugly Duckling redeems herself; I spent my downtime curled up on a sleeping bag in my bedroom cupboard reading novels, including many about awkward brainiacs who eventually make good. If a kid screamed 'Moose!' at me on the playground, my fictional experience told me it had nothing to do with my belly or nascent double chin. He screamed because he was a bully, a Bad Guy, and probably really stupid.

Much as the teasing hurt, I tried to pretend it didn't matter. For the most part this meant affecting a pitying, condescending attitude towards kids who teased me. They enjoyed this about as much as you might expect and, after a while, most of the kids truly hated me – some for my body, but others for my mind. I felt alone and backed into corners all of the time, but the defensive show I put on to protect myself actually fooled some of my schoolmates. They thought I was conceited, full of myself and maddeningly obnoxious.

I thought about my mother's holiday cleaning suggestion for about a nanosecond before rejecting it. Given the disastrous state of my room, I opted for reading, lying in the grass and taking my five-year-old sister on a tour of the neighbourhood.

'This is the Hampsford Circle sign,' I told Andrea in my best official tour guide voice. 'Natives believe it to have magical powers. Isn't it beautiful? This is much better than Disney World.' Sarcasm, a natural gift of mine, quickly rubbed off on her.

'It's better than Disney World if Santa was there,' she said, perfectly aping my snotty tone.

The entrance to our subdivision had a sign that included a nameplate in green and cream. Atop the sign, two cast-concrete lions guarded the suburb. These lions, often stolen by neighbourhood teenagers, were the high point of my half-term tour.

'Here are the famous St James Woods lions. Coveted by daring thieves, these art treasures are sculpted from the finest Ohio concrete.' Andrea and I climbed onto the sign, had a little peanut butter and jelly picnic, and pretended to ride the lions for a while. I snapped pictures of Andrea attempting a wide variety of dance moves on top of her lion. Neighbours drove by, some slowing to gawk at the oddball Goldens. The sign sat in a concrete planter filled with cedar chips and anaemic looking tulips. Every car entering the *district* got a good look at us, and I didn't care one little bit. I was on holiday.

Our suburb seemed utterly removed from the city of Toledo, despite being a mere 10-minute drive from the centre. Situated on the Maumee river, Toledo now has minor national fame as a dull place with a colourful mayor. The city boasts the third largest port on the Great Lakes and a world-class museum, and is the birthplace of Gloria Steinem, but most people recognise my hometown as the place John Denver bitched about in the seventies.

Denver sang a song about how Toledo has no nightlife after

10pm, and that the only thing he could do on a Saturday night was watch cars rust. He also said that the women have a distinctly canine aspect. Despite being nearly as good a singer as he was a pilot, Denver had my home town all wrong. Toledo has all the usual plays, concerts, drunken ethnic festivals and nightclubs.

Mum and Dad seldom left home on Saturday nights, however, not even to watch the rusty Fords or wildly drying paint downtown. Instead of enjoying the nightlife, Mum and Dad spent their weekends chilling out with something they called 'Turkish tobacco'. 'We're rolling our own cigarettes to save money,' Mum told me before lighting up a carefully constructed joint. I nodded and ran off to stage marionette shows with my Barbies. I hung six or seven naked dolls by their heads from the second floor landing, which seemed like a most logical arrangement, and had them sing that goat song from *The Sound of Music*.

Twelve years later, in my first year at college, I learned that Turkish tobacco, with its distinctive odour, wasn't a money-saving technique. When I visited my parents that Thanksgiving, I had a few questions for Mum.

'The Turkish tobacco is really weed, isn't it?' I asked as we peeled potatoes for the big holiday feast.

'It's ours and you can't have any,' she said, reaching for another russet.

Later that weekend, I took my sister into Mum and Dad's room and pulled the little Tupperware box of weed out from under their bed. Andrea was 11 by then, and I thought it was time she learned about the evils of drugs, or just that our parents were completely insane. I opened the box – it made the trademark Tupperware burp – and showed its contents to my little sister.

'Andrea, this is weed. Mum and Dad were lying about Turkish tobacco,' I told her.

'Cool! I can sell it at school. I'll make a fortune,' she replied. I explained the many good reasons she shouldn't do this, and she promised to leave the drug box unmolested.

When I think back to that box of weed or to our neighbourhood holiday, I call my sister. I trust my memory, if not my interpretation of events. However, Andrea says she doesn't remember her childhood at all, that her memories start some time during her mid-teens. I envy her this convenient amnesia. She always seems to know she's in the right, at least to her own way of thinking. We're related and we grew up in the same house but maybe some day our shared DNA will kick in and I'll finally stop arguing with myself.

2

BABY OR CRIMINAL?

I don't remember when my father stopped loving me. I can't say for sure that he ever did, but I know that the last time I hugged him, I was nine years old. One day, I was about to leave with Mum on an errand. I had told her I wanted to keep her company, but I really went to avoid spending time alone with Dad. I waited in the car while Mum finished a last-minute phone call. Andrea, just two at the time, slid into the back seat. I helped her buckle the seat belt and shut the door.

Dad stood smoking on the porch, a concrete slab with square, grey-painted wood columns. I knew somehow that if I ever wanted to touch him again, this was the moment. Despite his constant anger at me – anger that I thought I deserved – I loved my father. He sometimes took me for ice cream, allowing me to choose the flavour. I always chose chocolate or vanilla, but each trip to Baskin Robbins required a fresh decision, and I treated this selection with the utmost seriousness. Dad always had a double scoop of butter pecan in a sugar cone, but he'd wait silently, patiently, while I made my choice. Then he'd order for both of us. He drove me to school sometimes. We didn't talk much in the car, but his presence seemed solid and comforting. So, after buckling Andrea into her seat, I walked around the car and stood by Dad's side for a minute before awkwardly hugging him and inclining my head so he'd know to lean down for a kiss.

'Bye, Daddy,' I said, breaking away and taking my seat in the car. I never touched him with affection after that, not at the airport when I left for college, not at my graduation, not even when he was dying.

My father gave me a china doll when I was ten years old. I'd had an unusually pleasant time at school (maths aside). It was a bright autumn day, and I played outside for hours, running in our yard, spinning in circles till I fell, lying in the grass and staring up at a cloudless sky. Normally, I spent my after-school time decompressing in front of the television. That day, the unseasonably mild weather drew me away from it, and I was still outside when my father got home from work. I watched him pull his car into the garage. When he called me, I wondered what I'd done wrong, and moved slowly as I walked back to the house. Dad stood in the family room holding an oblong cardboard box.

'Here. This is for you,' he said, waving me into the room. I picked up the box.

'Thanks,' I said, puzzled. It wasn't my birthday, nor were my grades good enough to justify a reward. But I tore through the tape, lifted the box lid and found the doll, a black-haired beauty whose porcelain skin and bright pink cheeks mirrored my own after an afternoon of outdoor play. She wore a brown suede skirt and a matching vest and had tiny boots on her feet.

I loved this doll at once, but my father brushed off my

thanks with his usual gruff stoicism. Although he never had any trouble yelling at me, accepting gratitude or affection was a different story. He had no vocabulary for those things and became bashful, like a little boy with a crush.

His gift of the doll meant more to me than it should have, so when Andrea decided to draw on her face with an ink pen, I was devastated. I reported the crime to Mum immediately. 'She didn't mean anything by it. She's only four,' Mum said, shrugging. In my eyes Andrea led a charmed existence. It helped that she was tiny, always small for her age, and had enormous, heavily lashed brown eyes. She had the sweet, open, defenceless look of a Disney fawn and the sharp, cunning little brain of a young Hannibal Lecter.

Andrea looked up at Mum with those big dark eyes. 'I'm sorry! I didn't mean to do it. I just wanted the dolly to be pretty.' A tiny tear trickled down her cheek, and Mum gathered her in for a consoling hug. She gave Andrea a brief lecture on the sanctity of others' property but my sister didn't really take it to heart. She even stuck her tongue out at me during this talk when Mum's attention was diverted by a ringing phone. This infuriated me but, at the same time, I admired my sister for getting away with so much. If she'd chosen any other doll or one of my many mutilated stuffed animals to deface, I might have patted her on the head and admired her work. But that doll came from my father, and he'd given it with something like love.

My sister had seemed like a good idea to me at first. She was born when I was seven years old. My father had tried months earlier to prepare me for the new arrival. He took me aside for a special talk, his manner so grave I worried that I'd broken something and forgotten about it.

'You know what you've always wanted more than anything? You're getting it pretty soon,' he said.

'We're going to Kings Island? Oh my God! That's so cool. Thanks, Dad!' As a seven year old, I could imagine nothing better than a day at Ohio's most exotic super theme park – the massive quantities of candy floss, hot dogs and Coke I would have, the rides I would go on while trying not to puke, the plastic souvenirs I would beg for.

Dad sighed and shook his head. 'No, not Kings Island. We're having a baby. How'd you like a sister?'

'A baby? Are we taking her to Kings Island too?' The message still hadn't sunk in – dreams die hard, and I still wanted to believe I'd be riding roller coasters and eating my own body weight in artificially coloured and flavoured treats – and Dad let it drop.

We'd had a version of this talk before. My mother had delivered another little sister for me just 18 months previously. My sister Natalie was born two months early and died before I ever saw her. I don't know how my parents dealt with this loss. The night of the birth, my father took me from my bed and carried me to the car. I drifted in and out of sleep as he drove me to my friend Ashley's house. Ashley's mum answered the door in a thick chenille dressing gown, her face tense and unsmiling. I woke next to Ashley later that morning and didn't see my parents again for two or three days. No one told me anything. Ashley and I grew tired of each other after the first 36 hours and had a loud fight over her favourite doll. Her father weighed in on the dispute by spanking me with his belt. He hit Ashley, too, and the two of us clung to each other on the bottom bunk of her bed and wailed.

Being fat always made me feel separate from other people; I wondered constantly what they thought about me, if they were judging me. But my little sister's death made me feel totally separate from my parents. This separation was literal: they suffered far away from me while I fended for myself at Ashley's house.

Ashley's mother had a dish of sweets, a pebbled porcelain bowl with a matching lid. Alone and afraid in that strange house with its weird smells and unfamiliar adults, I acted in the only way I could: I stole sweets from that dish, eating them under the covers in Ashley's room. I sucked the hard, sugary lozenges, savouring their sweet, cinnamon tang, and hid the cellophane wrappers under the bed.

My parents came for me one morning, loading my tiny suitcase into the car without ceremony. Someone told me that Natalie had died. Eventually, we visited a tiny white grave marker. Years later, I found an emergency baptism certificate for Natalie Joan, my sister for a day.

Natalie's death touched this new pregnancy. My parents observed all sorts of superstitions. When friends brought baby gifts, we had to leave them in the garage because bringing them into the house was bad luck. My mother yelled at me for opening an umbrella in the living room. We waited a few months – an eternity to a seven year old – to tell friends the good news.

My mother suffered through a long and exhausting pregnancy. Four weeks after her due date – and the night before her doctor planned to induce her – she finally went into labour. My parents woke me around three in the morning and Dad walked me across the yard. The sky was empty and black, the wet grass cold under my bare feet. My father said nothing as he shuffled along beside me with my overnight bag. Mrs Rainer, our next-door neighbour, opened the door before we could knock. She led me upstairs to the guest room and I fell asleep instantly.

'Congratulations!' Mrs Rainer woke me with news of the birth at an ungodly early hour. 'You have a little sister. She has ten fingers and ten toes!' This information excited her tremendously. I wondered how many fingers she'd been expecting. At school all of my classmates offered prayers for the new baby.

My mother phoned me two days after the delivery. 'I want to call her Diantha Jane,' she said. I knew this would ruin my sister's life. If she had a weird name like that, kids would make fun of her. Kids made fun of me, not so much because of my weight, but simply because I was the new girl at Catholic school and had shown up for class on the first day in normal clothes, my ugly plaid uniform lost in the post. I didn't want kids to tease my sister over her stupid name. I thought fast.

'I think you should call her . . . um, Andrea. Andrea Marie.' I hadn't actually had any name in mind prior to the call. I told Mum the first thing that came into my head. Later, I'd regret not trying for Pollyanna or Guinevere.

'Okay,' she said. I have no idea why Mum agreed so easily. I like to think it was my powers of persuasion, but the massive wad of painkillers she'd taken after a gruelling delivery may have been a factor. Andrea came home from the hospital a week later. She grew from a thin, bald infant into a cute, bubbly toddler while I started to develop into a pudgy, lonely pre-teen.

*

Almost from her birth, my sister became a tool in my scheme to appear normal. I thought she could help me shake off the stigma of being the freaky fat kid in school. By the time Andrea was old enough to walk and talk and deflect negative attention with her big eyes and cuteness, I'd come to the conclusion that if people could see how slim and attractive she was, they might have a higher opinion of me by association.

My sister began dancing at the age of four. For her first recital, she wore a blood red tutu and a huge white hat meant to make her look like a little Dutch girl. Not the kind of Dutch girl who sells naughty personal services out of a window in Amsterdam; more like the kind who sells you a bunch of tulips while hobbling around in a pair of clogs. Andrea started her gymnastics career at six, and would spend hours practising skips and dismounts on the bar my father installed in her doorframe.

My competitive sports – quiz bowl (a sort of team trivia game) and the school debating team – had a slightly less physical dimension. While Andrea flipped and twirled, I strengthened my buzzer finger, memorised factoids and tried (unsuccessfully) to learn the debate trick where you twirl a pen around your thumb. I went to Andrea's ballet recitals and sat through endless hours of toddler performances to see my sister's ten second solo. My mother would critique the performance in the car.

'You need to remember to point your toes,' she'd say, usually through a dense haze of menthol smoke. 'Proper extension is everything in ballet.' Despite the fact that my mother's entire dance experience consisted of waltzing a phonebook's width away from her date at the prom, Andrea took in every bit of advice, her expression solemn. I rolled my eyes and turned up my Walkman.

My sister and I lived bizarrely disparate lives. We grew up with the same parents, but not really. My father never hit Andrea; never made fun of her in front of company. As the designated criminal in the family, I bore responsibility for every childish misstep as if I'd plotted some fiendish rebellion. Andrea, as the baby, could seemingly do no wrong.

Ruining my doll was followed by a string of perfect petty crimes by my sister. At five, she broke the antenna on our new cordless phone. She took the phone outside and buried it in the back yard next to the mouldering corpses of all our dead pets. Andrea did eventually confess to breaking the phone but not before I got the blame for losing it, and the punishment. Mind you, she did own up about 15 years after the fact, the confession loosed by a subtle combination of remorse and Boone's apple wine.

My mother even cut her meat for her until Andrea turned 13. Not always – not when Andrea's school friends might have seen it – but often enough that the story still embarrasses her. I try not to tell it in front of Andrea's new boyfriends. I try, but I'm weak and it's a funny story. All of this takes on a bit of irony when you consider that my sister later spent five years in her early twenties as a vegetarian. Cutting tofu, it seems, requires relatively little effort.

I never totally supported the vegetarianism. I love to cook, and I started making dinner for the family when I was 12. I'd roast a chicken, following Mum's careful written instructions or calling her at work for advice. Later, I graduated to biscuits, cakes and breads. My father especially loved my banana walnut bread. It was one of the only things he ever praised me for. Cooking for my family made me feel important, and I enjoyed being in charge of the kitchen.

When Andrea was a vegetarian, I couldn't really cook for her any more. My vegetable repertoire was limited by my hatred of most healthy foods. Instead of trying to make something, I'd take her to a local pancake house. I'd eat three or four thick slices of maple-cured bacon while Andrea settled for banana crêpes and hot coffee. Not that she suffered in silence. She would explain in vibrant detail how pigs are tortured and killed and how large hog farms are ruining the environment.

'They pump them full of hormones and overfeed them till they can't walk,' she told me, primly sipping her coffee.

'Nonsense,' I replied, biting into a crisp piece of smoky meat. 'The bacon is its destiny. And they aren't tortured. They go quietly to sleepy death. Sleeeeepy death,' I sang the last bit and finished my bacon.

My sister worries about her weight, despite the fact that she rarely weighs in at more than eight stone. As a child she ate normally, danced and did gymnastics, but always seemed underweight. While my doctors tested in vain for diabetes and glandular problems, Andrea's asked her earnest questions about body image and what they imagined to be her secret vomiting habit. Andrea put up with it. Andrea put up with a lot of things to avoid offending adults. My sister worked hard at perfection. So, at 12, when her doctors assumed she was anorexic, Andrea nodded and smiled and calmly persuaded them otherwise, saving her anger for the car ride home.

'God! Why do they have to ask every single time?' she'd vent to Mum and me. 'Why can't they just understand that I'm skinny from the dancing and the gym and because . . . because I just *am?*' Neither of us had an answer. We were never mistaken for anorexic, given our lushly padded bodies. My mother herself had struggled with weight as a child. After a forced diet in her early teens, she entered high school with a gorgeous figure. But by the time doctors were testing my blood and patting Andrea's hand to invite puke-related confidences, Mom had had three pregnancies without losing any of the baby weight. Between the two or three jobs she worked and caring for her house and her children, she didn't have time for trips to the gym. She bore her 5 stone of baby weight all through my childhood, adding to it bit by bit till she carried over 14 stone on her five-foot-two-inch frame.

My father thought the best way to help me lose weight was to think up snide, cutting *bon mots* about how fat I was and to say them out loud in front of the largest possible audience. When I was 11, I misspelled the word 'refrigerator' at a school-wide spelling bee.

'I'm shocked!' he said in a loud voice to the audience of parents, teachers and kids. 'The fridge is her favourite place.' Mum yelled at him in the car the whole way home. He just shrugged. Eventually, he lit a cigarette and turned away from her so he could flick the ash out of the window. I sat silently in the back seat, feeling humiliated, crying quietly and struggling hard to stop before we pulled into the driveway. Tears just made Dad even angrier.

'Don't you look at me that way! And don't tell me to leave you alone,' he said to me just after we got home. I hid my face in my hands and waited for him to stop.

I was probably 10 or 11 when I realised that it didn't matter if I lied. Dad never believed me, even when I told the truth. Once I'd figured this out, I had no incentive to be honest, as lies and truth both resulted in exactly the same punishment. If I took an apple from the fridge, I'd lie about it. I lied to teachers, other kids, parents, aunts, uncles, strangers. I threatened playground bullies with my close (fabricated) ties to the (fictional) Jewish/Hungarian Mafia.

Andrea settled on different strategies to deal with school. She worked hard, got good grades and was an excellent gymnast at the age of 12 when she landed a vault without bending her knee. She continued to dance, however. As a teen, she danced with the O'Connell Studio Hot Shots alongside future celebrity and Toledo native Katie Holmes.

My sister weighed barely 6 stone in high school. As a 24-year-old, I pushed 29 stone. Not that I knew exactly what I weighed as I hadn't stepped on a scale since I was 18. That summer, after I dropped out of grad school, my sister and I applied for night work. The employer advertised for two people to work a shift together. Given my size, I knew they probably wouldn't select me on my own, so I had convinced my sister to interview with me.

We drove past factories, their chimneys belching grey clouds of pollutants into a colourless summer sky. Strip clubs gave way to gun shops and massage parlours with high privacy fences and signs advertising something called 'body shampoo'. We found the building, a tasteful grey box with a discreet black-lettered sign, and I parked my ancient Chrysler LeBaron in the adjacent car park.

I pushed open the door, Andrea right behind me. The

woman at the counter, a tall blonde with a spiky Mohican and at least ten piercings in her face, waved a casual hello and cocked an eyebrow, clearly unsure of our purpose in her establishment. Phone pressed to her ear, she saw us approach the counter and held up a finger to let us know she'd be with us in a minute.

'I'm serious, Kevin, there are two guys in there right now, cruising each other in the video booth.' She paused, listening. 'Uh huh. I'm sure. Jeff Stryker movie . . . which one? Does it matter? Sheesh! *Santa's Cummin'*, if you must know. Yup. Uh huh. Thanks, Kev. See you in a minute. Oh! Bring the mop.' She hung up the phone and turned her attention to us. 'Can I help you?' she asked.

'Er, yes,' I said. 'We're interested in the cashiers' jobs. Your ad said you needed two people over nights, and we thought we could do it together.' I tried to hold eye contact, but the many enormous dildos on the far wall begged for attention. The store, Adult Land, was brightly lit and impeccably clean. It was like a Blockbuster Video, except for all the pornography and sex toys. Copies of *Barely Legal* and *Juggs* vied for space with older, more established titles like *Black Tail* and *Hustler*. I felt a blush creeping up my neck; Andrea couldn't take her eyes off the fascinating square of linoleum at her feet.

'I see,' the counter woman said. 'Do you have any retail experience?'

'No, but I got above average scores in maths,' I answered.

We filled out applications and got the hell out of there. As I started the car, a man in jeans and a dirty vest got out of a rusty old Chevy, caught my eye and winked. Andrea and I never heard back from Adult Land. Andrea spent the summer at child land – the Jewish day camp where she'd worked as a counsellor the year before. I thumbed through the classifieds, and finally took a part-time job at a monthly newspaper.

Despite bonding over the wonderful world of porn, my sister and I never talked about my weight till I was 32 and she was 25. My desire to appear normal meant I rarely discussed my weight with anyone, even in my immediate family. By the time I spoke to Andrea, I weighed 40 stone and wanted her support as I pursued gastric bypass surgery.

'Hell, yes, you should have it,' she told me. 'I don't want you to die.' This positive response seemed to be the general consensus among my family and friends. At my size, I knew I was unlikely to have to endure well-intentioned idiots telling me surgery was an easy way out and that I should just try another low-carb diet. The spectacle of imminent death seems to clue in even the dumbest and smuggest thin people.

For the most part, Andrea makes a very convincing adult. She wears sensible skirts to work, carries a tasteful leather bag and wears brown-rimmed glasses with fashionably narrow lenses. I have a lot of girlfriends, but my sister, now far away from me in Texas, is the person I miss the most. She's always been my confidante, she has stood up for me, and I have consulted her about matters both trivial and enormous.

'Should I tell Mum about the babysitter?' I asked her. I was 13, and our latest summer nanny, Tanya, had just called me a bitch. I'd complained about having to wait at Tanya's mother's house while she went off to take a photography exam. Tanya's mother served us cold spaghetti hoops and wouldn't let me sit on her furniture. She said it was because she'd just had everything steam cleaned, but I knew it was because she thought I might break something. I weighed over 14 stone, and all of Tanya's mother's chairs were spindly legged, delicate antiques.

'So? Do I tell?' I asked. Andrea, professorial and serious even as a six year old, shrugged and gave the matter some thought.

'I dunno. Mummy says that bad word all the time but it's not nice that Tanya called you that. Maybe I'll tell Mummy. Tanya was really bad to say that.'

I changed my mind a thousand times in the two hours between our conversation and my mother's arrival home from work, eventually deciding not to say anything. Andrea wouldn't listen to any of my new reasoning. She told on Tanya, and Mum fired her the next morning.

I still look to Andrea sometimes when I most need protection. We have the same DNA and the same germs (she points this out whenever she steals a sip of my drink at the cinema). We shared a lot of the same perils with insane babysitters and our father's general incompetence at tending small children. Andrea now lives far away from me and hates talking on the phone, but I always find her when I need to and she's always the first person I call whenever I lose a significant amount of weight.

3

THAT THING WITH
THE DOG

'Give it.' DaWonda sat on the edge of my bed and used a bony elbow to prise my shoulder off the mattress. Her slim fingers, yellow at the tips from thousands of unfiltered Marlboros, snatched the letter I'd hidden under my pillow.

'"Dear Mom,"' she read aloud, '"DaWonda is mean. I don't want her to take care of us any more . . ."' She smiled. 'You know, you can tell me if we got problems. You're a big girl, almost 11 years old. Don't you think you can handle your own problems, or do you need Mummy to do it for you?'

'I don't know. Sometimes, you're not very nice.' I sat upright on the bed and tugged my T-shirt over my stomach. DaWonda draped a thin, bruised arm around my shoulder, her steely blue eyes meeting my own. 'We can work it out, Becky. I'll keep this for you.' She shook the folded letter, and went downstairs to make me cheese on toast and some alphabet soup. I didn't tell my parents about our talk. I thought I could take care of myself, and besides, I could always spell 'B-I-T-C-H' with the pasta in my soup. I'd swallow the letters and keep them inside.

DaWonda came along at a time when my parents needed more childcare than usual – during the school summer holidays. Instead of having someone to watch us for an hour after school, they needed someone for eight hours a day. Given the quality of previous sitters' homes – the flea bites we came home with from Patty's house, the cars full of redneck cousins who routinely lounged about at Darlene's – having someone come to her home to watch the children seemed like a beautiful dream to Mum.

DaWonda, in the midst of an ugly divorce from a drunken ex-con, had proposed the live-in situation. My mother agreed to this. She had the space (in the form of our never-used guest room). She also liked the idea of allowing us to sleep till the sitter got up to care for us. Having to juggle a toddler and a 10 year old while trying to apply make-up, roll on tights and create a professional appearance for a long day of visits to the filthy homes of her adult protection clients made for a rough morning. The lure of an extra half hour of sleep sealed the deal. And DaWonda moved in the next day.

I liked DaWonda in the beginning. On her first day, she gave me an extra slice of cheese in my sandwich and allowed me to choose the television show I wanted to watch. Mum and Dad went to the cinema alone, and our new live-in babysitter fed me and Andrea and put us to bed. Andrea went down hours before I did, and DaWonda invited me into her room. We sat on her bed together and she showed me her family pictures.

'This is my ex, Davey,' she said, passing me a black-and-white novelty shot of a handsome, dark-haired man dressed like a Wild West sheriff. Davey didn't smile for the camera. He rested a hand on each of the toy pistols strapped to his waist and scowled. DaWonda and Davey posed with Santa in one of the pictures. Another showed DaWonda in a white mini-dress and veil, grinning hugely and holding out her left hand to display a plain gold ring. I flipped through a stack of pictures that mapped out my babysitter's life.

'You look pretty. I really like your hair,' I said. 'Davey looks nice, too,' I added. DaWonda smirked at me.

'Davey's hot, you can say it. But that don't mean nothin'. Looks aren't anything, especially in a man. You remember that, little girl,' she said, reaching for her cigarettes. After she'd smoked, she led me upstairs and tucked me into bed. DaWonda had long, blonde hair and a body made entirely of hard edges. Her fingers had calloused tips, and her knuckles were red and raw.

Over the next few days I discovered that DaWonda had no patience for my jokes, and my odd little ways annoyed her. The children she knew would never spend a summer afternoon reading indoors. They liked to play in the dirt and turn wheelies on their bikes.

'Enough with all the questions!' she snapped at me one afternoon. I'd been glued to her side all day, hoping to make a friend, and DaWonda had had enough. 'Girl, you need to find something useful to do with yourself. Ain't no one gonna want a fat girl to marry. You need to get outside and move your ass.' I nodded, stunned, and went outside for a while. That's when I found one of my father's notebooks in the garage and wrote the note to Mum. Telling my mother directly would probably have been more effective, but DaWonda never seemed to leave us alone. I considered if I should even bother. Mum never quite managed to stop Dad from going after me, and I wondered if telling her about DaWonda would be of any use.

As it turned out, Mom fired DaWonda just two weeks after hiring her, without ever consulting me or reading my letter. DaWonda had started going to bars during her second week at our house, and one morning woke the whole family on her return at three o'clock as she tripped over furniture, swore and then vomited loudly into our kitchen sink.

As far as our babysitters went, DaWonda wasn't really that bad. Mum had a second job as the social worker in a halfway house for schizophrenics, borderline personality types and the chronically depressed, and, naturally, she employed some of these people to care for her young. By the ages of three and ten, Andrea and I had encountered an array of welfare cheats, angry rednecks and the mentally ill.

'We want a 20-piece McNugget, two large fries and three small Cokes,' I coached Mrs Davis, our new babysitter who was a halfway house graduate with many colourful tics and OCD rituals. She nervously repeated this order into the speaker at the McDonald's drive thru, paid at the window, and then drove away without the food. It took a while to convince her to go back for it.

At ten, I had developed a certain level of patience with crazy people. When I went roller-skating with some of the more drug-compliant people from the home, I was the one who negotiated our skate rental and snack buying. Unlike my skating buddies, however, Mrs Davis had a hair trigger. She babysat one evening while Mum and Dad went to the cinema. She didn't want us to leave the house. She didn't want us to leave the living room. 'You can go to the bathroom when your parents get home,' she said. 'I don't like being alone.'

Even Mrs Davis was a slight improvement over our usual babysitters, the Kidd family. I started staying with the Kidds when I was six. Andrea and I spent four summers with them. My sister learned to speak while we spent winter afternoons on the grimy plaid sofa in their dirty old farmhouse and summers in their leaf-choked pool so she began to talk like a redneck.

'I sawl a possum on the Kidds' place,' she told my mother during the drive home one afternoon. I frowned at Mum and shook my head. As a bookish, pedantic ten year old, the idea of my sister talking like one of the Kidd children offended my sensibilities.

'The baby sounds like a dumb hick,' I told Mum. 'Kids are going to tease her when she goes to school.'

'Your sister will be fine,' Mum said. 'She'll go to preschool next year. She's only three. She'll learn more of her speech from us than from the Kidds. You're just angry because of that thing with the dog.'

That thing with the dog happened when I was seven. I'd just received a new pair of roller skates and needed a place to try them out. My options on a June day at the Kidds were sorely limited. Forbidden access to the busy road that fronted the property, I opted for a long, bumpy skate in the dirt.

The Kidds' ramshackle house stood on five acres of fallow farmland. About halfway between the white-shingled structure and the property boundary, the Kidd children had erected a playhouse out of scrap wood and scavenged nails. They teased me about my big belly, and I tried to avoid them as much as possible, so I liked the playhouse because I could be alone there. I decided to head there on my skates that day.

Skating in the dirt required a certain amount of imagination. I pretended I was at Central Arena, the local roller rink, leading a conga line of crazy people to 'YMCA'. Arriving at my destination, I hiked up my blue terry towelling shorts and tried to pull my shirt over my stomach. I dragged my fingers through my tangled curls and tested my skate brakes in the dusty gravel. A dog, tongue lolling innocently from its smiling mouth, trotted out of the playhouse to greet me.

'Hello, doggie!' I said, reaching out to pet it. The dog, a large collie mix with a brushy yellow tail, cocked its big head at me. Ignoring my hand, it stood on its hind legs and threw its heavy paws over my shoulders like a cheerful drunk greeting an old friend.

'Awww, you want to hug me. There's a good boy,' I said. I'd never really owned a dog. Given my dearth of canine experience, I didn't know that dogs don't hug children, and the dog and I landed on the ground. Lying there, while the collie mix snarled at me and tore at my scalp with its fangs, I did the only thing that made sense. I screamed, which enraged the dog, but also brought the oldest Kidd girl running. She pulled the dog off, and I ran to the house, blood streaming down my face and staining my cotton T-shirt.

Mrs Kidd saw the blood on my shirt, swore loudly and turned off the television. She grabbed my arm, dragged me into her small, dark kitchen and rummaged furiously under her rusting kitchen sink for supplies. 'Here we go! First aid kit.' She emerged clutching a dusty grey box, its red cross faded to a dull, mottled fuchsia. Mrs Kidd opened the kit and pulled out a roll of dingy grey medical tape. 'Hold still. I know just how to do this. One of my favourite shows is *General Hospital*.' Mrs Kidd worked hastily, using the tape to stick my scalp together, but, despite her efforts, the bleeding continued, and she decided to seek professional advice.

'The child is approximately seven years old,' she told the accident and emergency nurse on the other end of the phone. Sally Kidd, greying, gaunt and missing a tooth in the front, rested one hand on a prominent hipbone and took a long, cleansing drag on her Virginia Slim.

I had no idea which soap had taught her the word 'approximately', but I knew somehow that she hadn't used it correctly. 'No,' I thought to myself. 'I'm not approximately seven. I am exactly seven.' The dirty tape crisscrossing my scalp itched, and I put a hand to my head.

'Don't even think about it, missy!' Mrs Kidd glared down at me. 'Them's sterile.' I did as she told me and sat quietly in the kitchen chair. I wanted my mother to come and get me right away, but Mrs Kidd didn't call her and I wasn't allowed to touch the phone. I sank back into the chair, tucked my knees under my chin and rocked back and forth. I couldn't think of anything else to do. I asked for the time, and tried to work out the number of minutes till Mum would come for me. My head ached, but I was too tired and too anxious to cry any more.

When my mother picked me up that day, I hoped she'd tell Sally we weren't coming back. As I stood in the hall with baby Andrea, waiting, I caught most of the one-sided conversation Mum had with Sally Kidd in the kitchen. 'I'm not paying you to watch soaps. If I wanted my kid to get mauled, I'd drop her at the pound. This is the last time.' Mum wasn't yelling, but her tone was full of outraged authority. Sally tried to mumble an excuse, but Mum cut her off. 'I don't care who you thought was watching her. If you let another animal near Rebecca, I'm pulling my kids right the hell out of here.' I couldn't believe I had to come back to the Kidds' house at all, but at seven I had already learned that there were many things I couldn't control, that all I could do was endure these things quietly while hoping for something better.

The drive home took us from the Kidds' dilapidated three-storey to our brand-new suburb just across the road. Narrow ribbons of pavement cut white lines through a hastily installed ocean of dark green turf grass. From the window of Mum's Chevy hatchback, I watched a neighbour's sprinkler move in large, unhurried arcs, the water shimmering in the late afternoon sunlight. We pulled into the driveway, and Mum juggled the day's mail, an infant and a wounded seven year old between the car and the house.

The next evening, a Saturday, my mother went to a pre-christening meeting at the church. My sister's baptism, planned for the following morning, would bring a loud gaggle of relatives into the house. My head ached at the thought of it. I lay on the red shag pile carpet in our family room, half aware of the *Love Boat* repeat playing on our battered 19-inch television. My father sat on the sofa, reading the paper, a lit cigarette clamped firmly between his thin lips.

'Dad? Can I have some juice?' My throat ached and it hurt when I tried to angle my neck towards the sofa.

'No. You don't need the sugar and you're sure as hell not messing up my kitchen. Shut up and watch your show.' With that, Dad went back to the sports section. I lay back down on the floor, staring intently at the long, curling threads of carpet, each one the colour of old blood. Sweat ran down my forehead into my eyes. Moving my hand to wipe it away seemed like too much of an effort. The air conditioning, set to a sub-arctic temperature, should have cooled me down, but my skin burned as I lay shivering on the rug. I wanted to ask Dad for help, but I knew somehow that I shouldn't. He'd think I was lying about being sick, then he would yell at me and the thought of noise or movement made me dizzy with nausea.

Mum arrived home, cheeks slightly flushed from the heat. 'Father Bob wants us to stand together, so you'll need to hold on to Becky while they sprinkle Andrea. Becky?' Mum crouched next to me and felt my forehead with the back of her hand, her wedding ring cool against my skin. 'Morris! She's burning up. Go and run a cold bath.'

My mother helped me up the stairs and into the tub. Floating in the cool water, I stared up at the smooth, white ceiling. A small piece of blue and silver wallpaper had come loose at a corner, revealing a tiny triangle of yellowing dry wall. Mum brought me a glass of orange juice and knelt beside the tub to help me drink.

'Your temperature's pretty high, 105. Does your tummy hurt?' she asked.

'No. My neck does, though,' I said, struggling to swallow the sticky sweet juice.

Mum drained the tub and helped me into a clean night-gown. She woke me every two hours so I would drink more juice and take baby aspirin. In the morning, my fever hadn't broken, and at 5am we went to the accident and emergency department. In a white room full of bright lights, my family doctor diagnosed an infection from my dog bite. After the doctor cleaned out my scalp wound and applied a fresh dressing, we went home to prepare for the christening.

My mother tried to be gentle as she arranged my hair over

the dog bite. 'You want to look pretty for your sister's big day, don't you?' she asked. This was a purely rhetorical question. I actually wanted to spend the big day in bed asleep. Instead, I put on my best dress, a lavender floral pinafore with puffy sleeves and a pleated bodice, and went to church.

My recovery took a week or so. I swallowed penicillin syrup, the cherry flavouring barely disguising the smoky, bitter taste of the drug. My mother bought me a set of Wonder Woman underwear as a get-well present, and, once I felt better, I abused this gift by wearing it outdoors to play.

'Becky, those are under things. They're not a costume.' Mum had heard about my semi-nude public exploits from a neighbour and thought that a logical explanation would be enough to lure me back into more appropriate play clothes.

'I'm not Becky. I'm Wonder Woman. I can wear whatever I want,' I told her, trying in vain to snare her with some sewing thread I'd fashioned into my very own Lasso of Truth.

'Nice try, sweetie. I'm Wonder Mum, and I do your laundry, and I say you're wearing proper clothes outside,' she told me.

My father managed to document the Wonder Woman phase. As a teenager, I was mortified by the pictures he'd snapped of me cavorting on our jungle gym, hanging upside down from the monkey bars in glorified knickers and a matching training bra. My dimpled stomach and chubby thighs stood out in stark relief against the dark blue polyester. I vowed never to wear synthetic knickers again.

Whether you're a fat child, a fat teen or a fat woman, you learn to avoid the camera. I spent years trying to hide behind other people, furniture and even a Civil War cannon so that amateur photographers couldn't get my torso in their pictures.

Even at that age, in the pictures my father took and put in our family albums, I saw myself in a way that horrified and repulsed me. I saw a fat, dirty child hanging upside down in cheap nylon underwear, making a sloppy show of herself. Looking at those pictures filled me with shame, and I destroyed all of them, tearing them into tiny pieces and flushing them down the toilet.

During summers, Andrea and I spent weekdays with the Kidds and weekends with our father while Mum worked additional jobs to keep us safely in the suburbs. In addition to grabbing the odd shift at the group home, my mother worked as an estate agent and spent Saturdays showing houses to obnoxious couples with unrealistic expectations.

With an infant in daycare and a seven year old about to enter a second year of private school, Mum had houses to sell and schizophrenics to socialise. Dad's childcare skill set consisted of turning on the television and retreating into his bedroom to watch football. Dad had become a father for the first time at 50. At 57, caring for an infant and a seven year old sorely tested his patience. I spent a lot of time outside, riding my bike, playing cowboys and Indians and exploring the many construction sites that littered our half-built suburb.

Two months after the dog got me, a new boy moved in across the street from us. Ryan Milhone had red hair and freckles. He let me ride his bike, and offered to tend my bruises when I skidded off the pavement and banged my crotch on the crossbar. 'That's okay,' I told him. 'It's not like I've got a wiener there or anything.' I said this very seriously, making sure to use the correct anatomical term. 'Why don't I get Charlie from across the street? He'd probably do better with a boy's bike than me.' Ryan agreed and I trudged up the Martins' steep driveway. Charlie Martin's mum had died when he was five and I was six. He and his four brothers lived with their dad and could do pretty much anything they liked. King, the Martin's enormous German shepherd, had a special greeting for guests, and I always tried to brace myself whenever I visited. So I squared my shoulders and took a deep breath as I rang the doorbell. The door opened, and King barked and slobbered and strained hard against the choke chain as two of Charlie's older brothers struggled to restrain him.

'Hi, guys,' I said, nervously eyeing the dog. 'Is Charlie home? There's a new kid . . .' I broke off and turned to run as King shook off his young masters. I got halfway down the steep, hilly front yard before the dog pounced. I put my hands over my newly healed scalp and screamed. King ignored the head and went straight for my chest, nosing my T-shirt aside and grasping my ribcage in his huge, powerful jaws. 'Get him off, get him off!' I yelled, as two more Martins came barrelling out onto the grass. The brothers got King off me and somehow managed to wrestle him into the house.

'You're not supposed to run, you know,' the oldest boy told me, 'and the screaming doesn't help, either,' he added, slamming the front door. I lay on the lawn for a few minutes before running home.

'Dad!' I screamed, my voice carrying upstairs to the master bedroom. 'King got me. I'm hurt!' My father emerged from the inner sanctum, tattered old jean shorts riding low and revealing a generous slice of plumber's crack. He pulled his shirt up over his gut and sleepily scratched his belly button.

'Another dog got you? Christ! Maybe you should stay in the house when your mum's out.' He shook his head in disgust and retreated into his room, firmly closing the door. I stared at the closed door for a minute, wondering what I should do. My shirt clung to the bloody wound in my side. My side hurt. I wished my mother was home. Dad stayed in his bedroom; I could hear the match on television through the closed door. I sat on the floor for a minute and tried to work out a plan. Our next-door neighbour was a doctor. Maybe he'd know what to do.

I found Dr Berger watering his lawn. He wore white shorts and a red polo shirt, his blond hair carefully feathered into the latest yuppie style. 'Hi there, Rebecca. What can I do you for?' he said, smiling.

'Dr B., King bit me!' I howled, tears and snot flowing freely. I sat on the Berger's front porch while the doctor went inside to fetch supplies. I felt relieved that I'd found a responsible adult.

My mother pulled into our driveway as Dr Berger applied the final bandage. King had left deep bite marks on me, front and back, each small, bloody wound haloed by a purplish bruise. Mum took one look at my torso and called the police. Despite the police report, King only left our neighbourhood some years later after attacking a two year old. The toddler's parents and the Martins reached a sort of canine plea bargain that sent King to a farm the Martins' cousins owned in Kentucky. King moved hundreds of miles away, where he could threaten some other unsuspecting neighbourhood.

People like the Kidds, DaWonda and, most especially, my father provided me with early lessons in the importance of self-reliance. I spent my childhood making plans and preparing. I never knew who I'd need to ask for help, or if help would even be available. I learned to wait out bad situations, mostly by retreating into a book or my head. I discovered that, if you wait long enough, your mother will pick you up from the incompetent sitter's house or you'll figure out which neighbour to approach for a bandage.

Other lessons I learned from my childhood were to avoid big dogs, and that underwear stays under my clothing (hence the name). The scars on my scalp pale in comparison to other, deeper marks. Some, like my surgical scars, are visible, tangible. Others mark part of me I try to keep hidden. An angry dog is an obvious threat but, as I moved from Catholic school to public school, I learned that other children were the real danger. They could hurt me without touching me at all.

4

MOOSE ON THE LOOSE

'The moose, the moose, the moose is on the loose!' chanted children all around me in the school gym. It took me a minute to realise that all the shouting was directed at me.

By the age of eight, I'd already begun at my third school. In kindergarten, I'd gone to an expensive private day school with a strong liberal bent. Assignments could be done if and when I wanted; playtime happened whenever I liked; and if I felt like leaving the playground and wandering over to the library in the high school building, I did, no permission necessary. I next attended a Catholic school. That first year, at six, I learned that abortion was when 'mummies kill their babies'. The next year, I had Sister Mary Mackie. Sister's stories all ended the same way.

'I knew a little girl who liked to lean back in her chair, just like you do,' she told a classmate who'd been poised to tilt. 'She fell on the radiator and I had to call an ambulance.'

'Oh, I see you're thinking about swinging from the hooks in the cloakroom,' Sister said to me. I'd only been toying with the thought, furtively eyeing one of the large – one might even say 'fun-sized' – coat hooks, but Sister's eagle eye missed little.

'I knew a little boy who liked to do that. He got a hook through the throat and I had to call an ambulance.' I decided not to swing, and felt oddly reassured that Sister was on such intimate terms with the local emergency services.

Because of chronic overcrowding in the lower year groups, the school allowed us to use the playground only once a week. My classmates and I still had playtime every day, however. In spring and autumn, we spent most of the time chasing each other around the school car park. During the snowy, freezing winters, we huddled together against the school's brick façade and counted the minutes till maths class.

The boys wore white shirts, dark formal trousers and clip-on ties that they ripped off the minute the dismissal bell rang, hastily stuffing them into their desks before bolting for the door. Girls wore exceptionally ugly yellow and brown tartan pinafore dresses and white blouses with Peter Pan collars. In the winter, the school graciously allowed us to augment the short dresses with dung-brown polyester trousers that had an unfortunate tendency to unravel in the crotch. I tried not to bend over too much.

My parents began to worry that the small Catholic school couldn't provide all the academic challenges I needed. Also, the school charged money, so Mum and Dad decided that I should attend Main Elementary public school, a redbrick box erected sometime during the Great Depression. The school had served the children of Ohio farm families for three generations before Sylvania turned into a nouveau riche suburb, its woods torn out in favour of McMansions and its farms dismantled into half-acre lawn plots. The influx of new students had led the school district to house some classes, including our year group, in portable trailers and to send children to lunch and playtime in shifts.

The kids at Main thought I was a giant weirdo, and weren't shy about telling me so. Until that moment in the gym, they'd done so on a one-to-one basis, limiting their comments to whatever weird thing I was actually doing at the time. This was new, this group effort. It took me a few minutes to realise that every child in the gym – all six hundred spoiled suburban rugrats – was chanting. It hit me then: I was the moose.

I remember crying and yet trying not to cry. I didn't want the other kids to know I could hear them, that they were getting to me. I tried to tough it out, pulling my book up to hide my face. I'd never actually seen a moose, except for Bullwinkle, so the strange epithet confused me. I had no idea what had started all the other kids – especially the tiny group I thought might be my friends – yelling at me, pointing at me, laughing at me. It occurred to me that I'd done something to deserve this treatment. Had I eaten too quickly at lunch? Maybe I'd worn a T-shirt one size too small. Blaming my situation on my behaviour or my wardrobe let me off the hook for actually *being* fat. As a nine year old, I had no idea how I could lose weight. I knew I didn't want to eat less. The way I looked still seemed more or less normal to me. I had a round little belly and a hint of double chin, but my mother bought clothes for me in the children's department and my T-shirts and jeans looked just like everybody else's.

I sat on the floor of the school gym, book bag in my lap, and waited for the cue to get up and walk to the bus that would take me home. The other kids lost interest in me after a few minutes, but their words still echoed in my mind. The kids at this new school clearly had little use for me, and as I sat waiting, trying to blend into the heavily varnished blond wood floor, a new feeling came over me.

I lacked the useful obscene vocabulary of an older child. My parents had tried not to swear in my presence since I'd overheard my father's stunned response to the result of the 1976 presidential election and spent the next month telling every strange adult I met 'Bullshit! Carter won!' This sad lack of profanity made it hard for me to put my feelings into words. But my hands bunched themselves into white-knuckled fists. I knew then that I hated my schoolmates, even though my abruptly truncated Catholic education had stressed the importance of turning the other cheek. I got on the bus and silently prayed to Jesus to smite my enemies.

When I got home, I went upstairs to my room and pulled the dictionary off the bottom shelf of my bookcase. I found two entries for 'moose': 1: a ruminant mammal (*Alces alces*) with long legs, widely palmated antlers and large, sloping shoulders. An inhabitant of forested areas of northern North America, Asia and Europe, the largest member of the deer family. 2: proper noun, Loyal Order of Moose: a member of a national benevolent and fraternal order.

I knew I hadn't joined an order and, after looking up 'benevolent', I knew that word didn't describe me, especially given the vivid fantasy I'd just had of Jesus magically setting Keith Schroeder's head on fire. It was Keith, one of the lead gym chanters, who came up with 'moose' as a nickname for me. Keith's little brother ratted him out later. Danny Schroeder, a chubby boy himself, alternately liked and despised me, depending on which way the school's fickle social wind was blowing. During one of our friendly periods, Danny apologised for his brother's role in my school-wide infamy. I hated Keith, but he was two years older than me and huge. I couldn't stand up to him and he found myriad creative ways of torturing me for two more years before he headed off to junior high school.

The Schroeder boys lived in the house directly behind mine. When I was seven, I saw their father lose part of his index finger to the lawnmower. A year later, Mr Schroeder moved out of the house and Mrs Schroeder's 24-year-old boyfriend moved in. The boyfriend liked to pretend the boys didn't exist, and the boys tried hard to avoid him so Keith and Danny spent a lot of time in the street outside their house.

A lot of the kids who took the most pleasure in hurting me seemed to have some ordinary tragedy in their lives. I could have commiserated with Keith. When I was nine, I thought inanimate objects had feelings, and tried not to show special favour to my teddy bear so that the other stuffed animals wouldn't be hurt. Despite my foolish, tender heart, however, I despised Keith. Calling me names and hitting me with a broom handle when I tried to cross the street in front of his house had killed any sympathy I might have had for him.

The moose definition baffled me at first. I lacked antlers (palmated or otherwise), and didn't inhabit the forest, not even on holiday. But, from the picture, a little black-and-white drawing, I could tell that a moose was a big, hulking thing. I felt ashamed then, without fully understanding why I should.

I thought about telling my parents the day the teasing started. The playground code of silence only went so far with me – all in all, I've generally preferred tattling to taking crap from other children. Then I thought about the dreaded inquisition that would follow.

'What did you do to make them mad at you?' my father would ask.

'I don't know,' I'd whine, shrugging and looking at the floor.

'Yeah, right – "I don't know-oh-oh",' he'd drawl, imitating my whiny tone. 'You did it, whatever it was.'

I decided not to say anything. My parents couldn't make the other kids like me, but my father could make me feel even worse about the situation than I already did. I wondered if he'd call me moose, too. Maybe he'd do it in front of company. So I took the teasing for months before my parents found out about it – and they found out from my teacher.

Even though my father never took 'I don't know' as an answer, I really had no idea why the other kids had selected me as the school pariah. I had a hard time making appropriate conversation with my classmates. I knew I could be obnoxious but I'd tried to make friends. I'd worked hard at entertaining. On the first day at my new school, my mother dropped me off and I took a seat at a worktable with a couple of other kids. Ian and Charlie had been in the same class as me the year before. Charlie wore glasses and barely looked up as I took the chair opposite his. Ian offered a hand for me to shake, an oddly adult gesture for a little kid. He had blue eyes and curly black hair. He told me our teacher was supposed to be very pretty and very strict, but he hadn't quite figured out how those things could go together.

'I already know someone in our class. Jenna Gladstone. She lives down the street from me,' I paused, leaning in for the kicker. 'Jenna already has boobs,' I whispered, giving the word several extra O's in my pronunciation. Ian laughed. Charlie looked up from his comic book, utterly confused. I heard an

'Ahem' from the doorway and looked up to see a tall, blonde woman in a red sweater, black checked skirt and black leather boots. Mrs Leeds, our new teacher, invited me out into the hallway for the first of many special talks.

'You're Rebecca, aren't you? I just met your mother in the car park. We have rules in Mrs Leeds' class, Rebecca. One of them is that we don't gossip. Do you understand that?' She spoke in a light, sweet soprano, her black eyes glinting. Her friendly tone didn't quite match her expression. I felt awkward and shabby next to her. I tugged at my pink knitted T-shirt with a tiny heart in the centre, and nodded vigorously.

'I'm sorry. I won't do it again,' I promised, utterly solemn.

'Good! I'm glad we spoke. Go back to your seat,' Mrs Leeds said. I started towards Charlie and Ian. 'No, Rebecca. Not there. You'll sit in the back till class starts.' Mrs Leeds pointed to another worktable, far away from the boys. 'You need to be alone for a few minutes so you can think about our talk,' she added, smiling brightly. I took a chair at the empty table and watched as Ian and Charlie had a whispered conversation. Ian looked my way and shrugged. We both knew there was nothing to be done, but Ian seemed to imply that there were no hard feelings.

Apart from that comment about Jenna's boobs, I hadn't done anything to the kids at school in the three weeks I'd been there, so I couldn't understand why they took so much pleasure in crushing me. It never occurred to me that you could enjoy someone else's suffering. The book characters I liked the most never teased anyone. But then I never saw any of the kids who laughed at me with a book that hadn't been forced on them by a teacher.

The kids who picked on me spent playtime running and screaming and cutting earthworms into little pieces. Unlike storybook characters, my classmates didn't understand the universal truth that it's what's on the inside that matters. At nine, I still believed this, much as I believed in Santa Claus and the Easter Bunny. A little extra baby fat, big bones, a slight paunch – these things had nothing to do with my mind or my spirit.

I told myself that the kids at school were probably all stupid, mean and common. So I decided to pity them. I also pitied myself rather a lot, especially during the many playtimes, lunch periods and Saturday afternoons I spent alone.

While most of my teachers had admired my love of books and my advanced (and as yet non-obscene) vocabulary, Mrs Leeds was very different. She took an instant dislike to me. Most teachers express their hatred for pupils by marking their papers a bit lower, or by denying them a part in the class play. Mrs Leeds made her feelings known by insisting I be tested for mental retardation.

My weight set me apart, but so did my grooming. My hair was a giant tangled snarl most of the time and I rarely wore socks that matched. To Mrs Leeds' mind, a messy kid who asked too many questions couldn't just be unfashionable. A girl like that must have something wrong with her. I took the test, and I can only hope that the contrary results stunned her. Mrs Leeds continued to take me out into the corridor for spittle-spewing talks about my attitude. If I talked back to one of the boys who screamed 'Moose!' at me in the playground, she'd tell me that mouthy little girls didn't make friends. For calling an older child a pervert, I got a special talk and the privilege of sitting in the corridor alone while the other kids enjoyed the class Valentine's Day party. Afterwards I found that the tissue box I'd decorated with paper hearts and red glitter held exactly two cards. One was from Ian, the only kid in our class who didn't hate me. The other came from Mrs Leeds, who signed it with love.

My corridor chats with the teacher continued into early March. Mrs Leeds would lean over me, bringing her angry red face close to my own. 'You're not trying hard enough, Rebecca,' she said one day, black eyes boring into me. 'All the other girls follow directions. Why can't you? I just don't understand it. I wish you'd take more pride in your appearance. How hard is it to comb your hair before school in the morning?' She waited. 'Well? Answer my question!'

'I don't know,' I said. 'I'm sorry.'

'Don't be sorry. Try harder. I've had enough of you today – pull your desk into the corridor and wait till the bell rings. I don't want to look at you any more this afternoon.'

I have naturally curly hair and a tender scalp. My mother tried to wrestle my curls into submission, but combing out the snarls hurt so much that I'd be a weeping, shaking mess afterwards. On some days, neither of us could face it: Mum let me brush my own hair, and I left the worst tangles untouched. The next day at school, my hair hadn't improved, and Mrs Leeds had me out in the corridor before the morning bell rang. She yelled at me, but I tuned out the words. Usually, I'd start crying when she yelled, and that would satisfy her. This time, I found that I could go somewhere else in my head, and Mrs Leeds couldn't follow.

'Rebecca!' she screamed at me, snapping me out of my trance. 'You will pay attention when I speak to you!' She grasped my upper arms and shook me: 'You [shake] will [shake] listen when I'm talking to you [shake].' My teeth clicked together, and I nodded mutely, tears spilling down my face. The hand-shaped bruises on my arms finally got the message across to my parents and my mother met with the headteacher the very next day.

'But what do I do about my teacher?' he asked. Mr Jones, a sweet, affable man, hated to offend anyone. 'There will be all sorts of questions if we remove Rebecca from that classroom. It could really embarrass Mrs Leeds.'

'Mrs Leeds has a mother,' Mum told him. 'Let *her* mother worry about that.'

I spent the rest of that school year in another teacher's classroom. Meanwhile, Mrs Leeds turned her attention to an effeminate boy who carried strawberry-scented lip gloss in his back pocket.

Mrs Leeds stayed at the school for years afterwards. Sometimes I'd run into her on the staircase and, if we were both alone, she'd glower at me and I'd squeeze past her, averting my eyes and clinging to the railing. I still thought she was pretty. I felt bad that I'd let her down and wondered if she might have liked me if I'd tried harder with my hair or if I hadn't said anything about Jenna on the first day. It didn't occur to me until later that Mrs Leeds' problems had nothing to do with me, that I wasn't to blame.

Mrs Leeds wasn't my only problem at that age. I was probably the worst girl in the history of Brownies. Mrs Christie, our Brownie pack leader, voted for Ronald Reagan twice and used to tell us that when the Russians attacked, she prayed that she and her family would be among the first to die.

Life after the bomb wouldn't be worth living, so they wanted to perish together by the family hearth, preferably while kneeling in prayer.

It was fine with me if the Christies died first in the coming nuclear holocaust. Coral Christie, as much of an outsider as I was, wore her hair in stick-straight braids, got straight As and thought people on welfare were lazy, heathen scumbags. She told me so one day at playtime. We were nine, and she spoke to me once in a while out of Christian charity.

'It's true,' she told me, making eye contact much longer than necessary. 'Mother says they all have a baby and pierced ears before they're even 16.' Coral wasn't allowed to pierce her ears until high school. She'd gone deathly pale when I'd shown her my own desecrated lobes; Mum had got them done when I was two. She'd thought babies looked cute with earrings and had no idea that, if Coral were right, it would automatically make me a pregnant whore immediately following puberty.

Coral's mother, Mrs Christie, led our Brownie pack with all the charm and efficiency of a female General Patton. The pack met in the cafeteria after school, and I'd joined thinking I might make some new friends. Knowing of my pierced ears and dismayed by the continuing presence of my mismatched socks, mysteriously Jewish name and tangled hair in her otherwise spotless little corps, Mrs Christie made Brownies as difficult as possible for me.

There were 21 of us in the group, and Mrs Christie divided us into pairs for most activities. Given my status as the school freak (I ranked slightly above little Dougie Baer with his lip gloss and pronounced lisp, but he wasn't an actual girl and couldn't be a Brownie), this meant that 20 other girls paired off while I did the 'fun' activity with the assistant leader. Mrs Schoolcraft – busty, big-haired and made up like Dolly Parton on Halloween in a Bangkok drag bar – was sweet and well intentioned, but she wasn't an actual Brownie and I resented having to explain the instructions to her every time we made a craft item like a Mexican God's Eye or created a list of camping essentials.

Mrs Christie thought Brownies should teach girls all the essentials of life. Hosting the perfect tea party, baking cakes and making craft projects out of brightly coloured thread ranked high on her list of necessary skills. To this end, she enlisted the help of Mrs March, the mother of my sworn enemy. Dana March had long spindly legs and arms and straight, shiny brown hair. She had a gap-toothed smile and a coterie of pretty friends. She ruled the social set in my school year and I'd hated her with a passion ever since my second week at Main when she stole my best friend. I'd met Lexie Rainer a year before I started school at Main. Her family moved in next door to us when we were both seven, and I liked her so much I forgave her when her mum started dragging me to church with them. My parents told me to ignore the big-haired fundamentalist preacher and keep quiet. Free babysitting is free babysitting, and they relished the alone time on Sunday mornings.

Though she always pretended to like me to my face, Dana told Lexie that she'd catch fat germs if she hung out with me, and Dana and Lexie literally left me behind one day, riding off on their bikes together so fast I couldn't keep up. When I finally caught up with Lexie and Dana at the Marches' house, Mrs March invited me in and made it very clear to Dana that the three of us would play nicely together or there'd be hell to pay in the form of no television for a solid week. Dana included me that afternoon, and, although Dana and I didn't see eye to eye, I became smitten with her mum.

Mrs March stayed home and baked biscuits when she wasn't shopping for sweaters and having her hair expertly highlighted at the most expensive salon in town. She greeted Dana every afternoon with a plate of biscuits and a wet kiss that left an artful pink lipstick stain on her cheek. I asked my mother, whose tights had ladders and whose self-permed hair was plain brown like mine, why she couldn't stay home like Dana's mum.

'I like my job. You like living in a nice house. If I had to lie around the house all day, I'd go crazy,' she told me one night as she tucked me into bed. 'Laura March is a big phoney and her daughter is a brat. But don't tell her I said that,' she added. Then she tickled my feet, kissed my forehead and turned out the light.

Unlike my mother, however, Mrs Christie had nothing but admiration for Dana's mum and had chosen the Marches' house as the venue for the social event of the school year: a formal Brownie tea, complete with bone china cups and silver stirring spoons. Mum bought me a new dress for the tea party, together with patent leather shoes and white tights. She spent the better part of two hours combing out my hair. It hurt, but she tried to be gentle. 'Beauty is pain,' she told me, reaching for a smoke. 'Remember to keep your legs closed,' she added.

The Marches' two-storey faux-Tudor house had a formal entrance ('We call this a foyer,' Mrs March told me, giving the word the full French pronunciation), a lot of white shag pile carpeting, and many decorator-chosen brand-new antique reproductions. All we had at home were plain old antiques. I took a tiny biscuit and perched on the edge of a blue damask sofa.

'Not too many, dear,' Mrs Christie said. 'You don't need the calories.' Mrs Christie wore a large straw hat with a green feather. She herself ate at least five tiny biscuits and loaded her tea with cream and honey. Before going on a carb-free diet a few years later, Mrs Christie would top out at more than 21 stone. I, however, concentrated on keeping my knees locked tight and preventing biscuit crumbs falling on the carpet.

After two hours of clenching my thighs and watching other people eat, I was thrilled to ride home in my mother's messy hatchback. The shiny shoes left blisters on my heels, and the lace collar on my dress itched unbearably. I decided to quit Brownies – beauty hurt too much to be worthwhile. I didn't need to be beautiful, and keeping my legs together, while not always a bad idea, wasn't as important as having cramp-free thighs.

All of this happened so long ago that I barely remember the snide remarks I made to Mum about 'foy-ayyys', white carpets and Dana March's buck teeth. I would have entered our house through the garage, immediately torn off the shoes and tramped across our rust-red family room carpet, sliding on tights-clad feet into our warm yellow kitchen.

Despite all of the trouble that followed – and my slow, inexorable inflation to a weight of nearly 43 stone – I actually like to think I would have eaten a couple of biscuits then, right out of the packet. When I imagine this rebellion, I try not to think of my father walking in on me, snatching the packet of biscuits out of my plump hands and shoving me roughly out of the room.

Maybe I got away with it, though. Maybe I ate the biscuits all by myself, and whispered a tiny (first) 'fuck you' to the girls and ladies of Brownie Troop 666, to Mrs Leeds and even to the man who designed those tight, shiny shoes. I could say that to everyone else in the world (if only in my head) but never to my father, at least not when I was eight. He left me behind a little more every day as I grew fatter and angrier, but I still loved him then. And at that time I hoped he loved me, too.

5

THE QUARTER GAME

Dad and I played the quarter game all the time when I was five and we lived on Penn Road. 'How many quarters?' Dad would ask.

'Lots!' I'd reply. Then, offering the challenge, 'Three.'

Dad nodded, totally serious. Challenge accepted. Game on. Dad rifled through his change and found five quarters. He let me hold the coins, which were still a little warm from his pocket. I handed them over one by one. 'One, two, three,' I counted as he took each one in turn. Dad signalled for another coin. He wanted to break the record. 'Really?' I asked. He nodded, and I handed over the change. Dad had done it. He'd managed to fit four quarters into his nose. More impressively, he'd got all of them into a single nostril. Pride overwhelmed me. Dad was the best.

I loved the quarter game. I had my job – coin handler – and felt that I was taking part in something of huge historical importance with my Dad. Dad seemed like the tallest, strongest man in the world when I was five. I thought he could lift our house off its foundation and carry it down the street.

When we visited Mum's former college roommate in Beirut, Dad carried me on his shoulders as we toured ancient ruins and modern shopping bazaars. Aunt Pat, an honorary relation, had married Nizar, a dashing Lebanese army colonel. Before the wars in the 1980s, Lebanon had a sunny, cosmopolitan sensibility. Not that I paid too much attention to the country at the age of six; I was too busy throwing screaming temper tantrums because there wasn't any peanut butter.

During our two-week stay, Mum and Dad often left me in the care of Uncle Nizar's family housekeeper, a cheerful 18 year old named Fatima. She led Pat's two sons and me on long walks to the park. She put me on a makeshift leash, knowing my tendency to wander, and would tie me up to a swing while she went and flirted with all the handsome French soldiers. I remember cedar trees, graceful yet squat, and the honey-sweet taste of baklava.

Back home in Toledo, a new school year started and Dad and I quickly established our routine. My father drove me to kindergarten at my hippie liberal private school, and we'd stop for breakfast at a diner sometimes as a special treat. It wasn't all perfect between us though, even then. The same funny man who stuffed change in his nose for my amusement yelled at me for taking ink pens apart. He called me destructive, and would sometimes spank me.

Dad turned 50 two months after I was born. My father's own childish offences had been punished with a slap or a punch, and he learned early on not to make mistakes. Dad learned to be a father while he was raising me, and, more often than not, he learned from mistakes.

'Daddy, what do cigarettes taste like?' At six, I had no idea how disgusting cigarette smoking really was. It was 1978. My parents, grandmother and lots of family friends smoked, and I wondered what I was missing. Cigarettes surrounded me. If I carelessly bumped into my grandmother, I'd burn myself. She'd kiss the tiny red welt and offer sincere apologies, and I'd remember not to get too close, till the next time. A childhood spent in smoke-filled cars, in the smoking sections of restaurants and in houses that smelled of burning tobacco killed the romance of cigarettes for me. Growing up, I never thought smoking was cool – it was just another lame thing my parents did to annoy me. But at six, all I felt was curiosity, and Dad was there to educate and inform.

'Here,' he said, handing me a lit Benson & Hedges. I took a drag, inhaling deeply. The taste, like a freshly filled ashtray, only bitingly hot, didn't exactly flood my mind with images of macho men on horseback or bikini-clad models elegantly puffing on the beach. I threw up, violently and completely, and never wanted to smoke again. Perhaps this wasn't a mistake, and Dad meant to dissuade me from forming a bad habit, sparing me the joy of smoking through a hole in my throat. But the little smirk he gave me, and the way he ignored my discomfort makes me wonder.

All the time I thought of myself as an ordinary little girl, my father saw me as something else: a messy creature beyond his understanding of acceptable (adult) behaviour. He had no idea how to handle spilled milk and endless childish questions. Maybe this was because he'd never actually been a child himself in any real sense. My father and his brother worked as children. They went to school, but they always had little jobs because of the family's desperate poverty.

After his first stint with the Air Corps, my father attended New York University. He saw Marlon Brando on Broadway in *Cat on a Hot Tin Roof* and finished his business degree in Youngstown before going back into the service. He stayed in the military for 20 years, never advancing past technical sergeant in an air force that listed his race as 'Hebrew' on official forms.

Dad was hardly typical for a man of his generation. He shopped for groceries (though he often went off the list in ways that infuriated my mother); he cooked, he did laundry and vacuumed. He never expected his wife to look after the house for him. Aside from the expensive camcorder Dad once bought without consulting my Mum, I was the only thing my parents ever fought over. My development surprised and confounded my father. The cute, happy little girl became a sullen, angry pre-teen – a fat pre-teen with no friends and a spotty academic record. The school made me take maths and PE, and both had a tendency to ruin my Grade Point Average.

'Leave me alone!' I shouted. Eleven years old and boiling with hurt and frustration after a long day of playground bullying, the last thing I wanted to hear was my father's opinion of my eating habits.

'Don't tell me to leave you alone. Don't ever say that. And don't blame me when you're too fat for anyone to marry you,' Dad made his point and slammed the bedroom door. Football season had just started, and he had a game to watch.

I avoided my father as much as possible. I'd read curled up in a sleeping bag emblazoned with the Cracker Jack popcorn and peanut snack logo. Dana March had made a special point of teasing me about this during my last official act as a Brownie.

At nine, I'd reluctantly agreed to one last weekend trip to Camp Libbey, a rustic campground about half an hour away from Toledo. I'd never had much fun there before, but someone promised s'mores – sandwiches made of chocolate, crackers and toasted marshmallows – and I still held out hope that I might make one friend among my brown-clad sisters.

'She can't be away from food, like, ever,' Dana told Coral Christie. Coral, holding out totally preposterous hopes of popularity, quickly agreed.

'Seriously! Maybe she'll try to eat caramel popcorn right off her sleeping bag. Hey, did you know she got her ears pierced when she was two?' I overheard them in the toilets. Crouched in a cubicle, I silently prayed that they wouldn't go looking for feet. That night I crawled into the sleeping bag that I'd chosen because I loved the bright colours and warm, flannel lining, and quickly fell asleep. I missed the s'mores that time, but felt pretty good about my decision to resign my Brownies commission.

My father picked me up the next morning, and we barely spoke during the drive home. Nothing I did seemed to please him. He made fun of me in front of his friends. One particular friend never knew what to do in these situations. The best response I got from him, a sarcastically amused sort of derision, was only slightly better than a slap or a screaming insult.

'She's working on being the fattest kid in school,' Dad told her, pulling out a line that reliably earned him nervous laughter from his pals. From her perch on a swivel chair, our friend tried to steer the conversation to any other topic.

I went to my room, closed the door and opened my latest book. A fan of Judy Blume, I wondered what kind of paradise my life would be if Mum and Dad got a nice, suburban divorce.

Despite my father's many flaws, we never had that conversation. Like the girl who dates losers hoping her career advice will turn them into functional adults, I thought I might eventually find a way to turn Dad into a storybook father.

Whenever I spent time alone with Dad, I never knew what to say. Car journeys were the worst. Dad had trouble hearing out of his right ear so, if you needed to say something to him, he'd snap the radio off and stare at you like whatever you had to say had better be important. I'd stammer something. He'd shrug or grunt and turn the radio back on.

Most adults liked my jokes. My teacher that year seemed to like me slightly more than the other children. Mrs Sharp had huge blue eyes, curly brown hair and a kind smile. When I missed the bus accidentally on purpose to avoid Keith Schroeder and his large posse of moose-yelling bully boys, she didn't seem all that upset.

While we waited for my grandmother to come and get me, Mrs Sharp took me into the staff room to see our class hamster. Pinkie had given birth just hours before, and was in seclusion in the hope that a quiet, child-free space might deter her from eating her young again. Mrs Sharp pulled the cover off Pinkie's hamster cage, and we peered inside, hoping for the best, fearing the worst. All was well, mother and babies nestling cosily in the cedar chips. The little ones nursed, and Pinkie didn't look even remotely hungry. We put the cover back and waited for Grandma.

'You won't tell any of the other kids you got to see Pinkie, will you? We don't want to hurt anyone's feelings.' Mrs Sharp didn't want anyone to think she had teacher's pets, though I knew I was her favourite.

'I won't tell,' I promised. 'Do you think I could name one of the babies?' I asked.

'We'll see. Assuming they make it.' Mrs Sharp had lengthy experience with classroom rodents which made her a pragmatist. We pondered the miracle of birth and the larger miracle of undigested offspring for a few minutes before going outside to look for my lift.

My grandmother had just retired from her job at the hospital, and often filled in for my parents when it came to transportation. Grandma had worked as a nurse and then a nursing manager for nearly 40 years. She missed work, and picking me up or entertaining me after school took her mind off the hospital. Grandma lived a quarter of a mile away from us in a new development so sometimes I'd talk the bus driver into letting me off at the entrance to Grandma's neighbourhood so I could stay with her and watch television till my parents got off work.

My grandmother's flat had a big, sunny kitchen. We'd watch television in there while Grandma's kitten, Chessie, played inside a paper grocery bag or stalked birds through the window. I'd try to talk Grandma into playing the piano for me, and sometimes she'd give in. Grandma's hair had turned from blonde to silver since our last trip to Bermuda. She wore it in a loose perm, the bright curls framing her long, angular face. She always wore pink lipstick and she liked long beaded necklaces. She wore clip-on earrings because, in the 1930s, nice girls in her small rural town didn't pierce their ears.

Grandma didn't expect me to entertain her so I never had to play the clown. She was Mum's mum but, with such an age gap between my parents, she was only a year older than my father.

They had little in common, however. Growing up, Grandma and her older sister had wanted for nothing. Despite the Depression, their father had prospered, and she had an idyllic childhood.

For me at home, things weren't so sunny. After my latest doctor's appointment, my parents decided that the best way to correct my growing weight problem was to padlock the refrigerator at night. Dad screwed the hasp into the side of our large, off-white fridge, and snapped the lock in place with a satisfied smirk. 'No more snacks for you,' he said.

Even without the actual padlock, which my parents kept in a drawer during the day, the shining metal hasp stood out in stark relief against the fridge's pale paint. The few friends who visited would surely notice this addition, I thought. If anyone at school found out, I could never go back there. I went to my room and cried. Food was the last thing on my mind. I wondered if I could ever trust anyone enough to invite them home.

I threw myself into my riding lessons, spending hours at the stable. One day after my lesson, I came home to find my father in my bedroom, trying to reroute the cable in an attempt to improve the signal to the television upstairs. He worked at the wiring through a hole in the wall, and I lay on my bed, reading and trying to pretend he wasn't there. The phone rang, and I moved to answer it. When Mum was out, Dad sometimes let the machine pick up so that estate agency clients could leave messages, and, just as I'd hit the on switch to the brand-new cordless (the old one having recently vanished into its shallow grave in the yard), Dad shouted at me not to pick up.

'Hello?' I said. I couldn't just hang up. It was a family friend and I breathed a sigh of relief. 'It's for you,' I said, handing Dad the phone. I lay back on my bed and picked up my book. Dad spoke very briefly and hung up. Focused on my novel, I didn't hear him approach. Something sliced the air, cracking hard against the back of my leg. 'When I tell you not to answer, you don't answer!' Dad yelled. He held my riding crop, a foot-long plastic stick wrapped in black tape, and shook it in my face. 'Don't you give me that look!' Dad hit me again, this time on the shoulder. The crop then landed hard against my legs and back. I lost track of time. The situation seemed unreal, like it was happening in a book or to some other girl. Dad was shouting, but I stopped hearing him. I thought about the riding stable and the book I'd been reading. I thought about the spelling test I needed to study for, about my sister in her new pink leotard, about anything outside that room. Dad wore himself out after a few minutes and went back to his cable project like nothing had happened.

'I can't help how I look at you!' I said, coming back to myself. 'What am I supposed to do? Put my eyes out?' I jabbed at my closed eyes with a finger. 'There you go! No more looking,' I said. Red spots formed behind my eyelids. Dad didn't answer. When I opened my eyes, he was gone.

Dad lost control again a few weeks later. We'd rented our basement room to a college student. Alejandro, a friendly Venezuelan with a large stock of sweets, who didn't mind if I helped myself when he was out but Dad caught me snooping and didn't believe me. He called me a thief and chased me into the living room. Furious that I'd run from him, he slapped me hard across the face, leaving a red mark shaped like his hand.

My messy room, an affront to someone who'd grown up with none of my material advantages, proved a huge source of contention between my father and me. When I was 15, for an inspection, I'd shoved all the dirty clothes, crumpled papers and old stuffed animals into my wardrobe, sloppily made the bed and declared the room clean. Dad swore as he opened the wardrobe. I knew he would hit me again. I reached towards a table lamp, my mind hatching some half-baked plan of self-defence. Dad saw my hand move and shoved me into the wardrobe. I fell into a heap of books and laundry, and cowered there as he feigned a kick.

'You'd hit *me*? I'm your father! Stay down!' I sat in the wardrobe for an hour, too stunned even to cry. My mother overheard him. She tried to make my father understand he'd done something wrong.

'She took a dive,' Dad said. 'An 18-stone object doesn't just fall like that. It wasn't that bad.' He mumbled something about cleaning the gutters and went out of the back door, leaving my mother alone at the table. Mum shook her head sadly, watching him go. She'd tried to referee our fights for years and it exhausted her.

A few years later, just before I started college, my parents, sister and I travelled to Cape Cod. I'd got into Boston University, and the Cape would be our last family trip before I started. My parents sat me down for a special talk shortly before we left. They knew how much I weighed, having spoken with my doctor. I didn't know it myself because I always backed onto the scale to avoid seeing the number, but my parents were shocked and worried and wanted me to try dieting over the summer.

'You weigh 26 stone,' Mum said. 'You need to think about your future. I'm afraid for you.' A few months earlier, she'd taken me to a new doctor who prescribed amphetamines, but these hadn't worked, and this short-lived attempt at a pre-college diet also petered out just before we hit the road.

At the shore, my sister ran up the long, sandy pathway to the beach, turning cartwheels in front of the white-capped surf. I followed slowly, and peered out at the cold, grey ocean for a while as she chased waves and looked for seashells. I found a piece of sea glass, a smooth green semicircle, and decided to go and stow it in the car. The path from the beach, with its ankle-deep sand, proved a huge challenge for me. My weight made me sink into the soft sand, and I struggled for almost an hour to climb the one hundred feet to the car park. Each step exhausted me. I pulled myself along, stumbling, crying and ashamed as other tourists watched my struggle. When I finally reached the car, I felt tired and pathetic. I climbed into the back seat, and tried to ignore the smoke from my father's cigarette. He sat in the front passenger seat, waiting for Mum and Andrea to finish their sightseeing.

'Twenty-six stone is a lot to haul up the beach,' he said, noting my heavy breathing.

I don't know if it was the physical exhaustion, or if 18 years of humiliation had worn me down, but I'd finally had enough. 'Why do you hate me? Why? I love you. You're supposed to be my Dad! You're supposed to love me too,' I cried, clutching a souvenir T-shirt to my hot, sweaty face. Dad said nothing, a sad little smile the only sign that he'd heard what I said.

The first night I spent in Boston, I ordered a medium pizza and two litres of Coke. I felt free from my parents, from my home, from my past, and to me that meant I could eat whatever

I wanted. I already weighed so much, why bother dieting, I thought. Losing 10 pounds would hardly make a difference. At that distance, my father finally stopped sniping at me. I'd talk to him on the phone from Boston because my mother insisted on handing the phone to him, and he'd grunt his reply, but we never really talked about anything important.

When I was 22, I learned to drive so that I could get around in the college town where I'd be attending postgraduate school, and Dad even gave me some fatherly advice. 'Don't think you have to pass anyone,' he said. 'Your grandfather never passed a car unless it was stopped.' Dad wanted me to drive safely and to be sure to check the oil. I told him I would, thanked him for the advice and drove away.

My father had emergency surgery during my third month as a postgraduate student. I drove home as fast as I could. My father pulled through. 'I always loved you,' he told me as he lay in his hospital bed, weakly gripping my hand. I nodded as if I understood, but I didn't really believe him.

He recovered from his surgery, but died of a complicated series of illnesses and organ malfunctions nine months later. It's hard to explain. When people ask how he died, I can't just say 'cancer' or 'heart attack'; I have to launch into a five-minute explanation. My father's death, like his life, was full of complications.

I think about my father at Christmas and on his birthday. I think of him and wonder what kind of relationship we would have had if he'd lived a bit longer. Sometimes, when I count out change for a coffee, I look at the dates on the coins. The quarter game continues, and sometimes I win.

6

MOOSE ON FIRE

'Boom, boom, boom, boom!' Patrick Gianelli followed me down the corridor, adding sound effects as he went. 'Wide load approaching!' Patrick shouted. Kids turned to stare as I walked down the hall, Patrick close behind me. I was 12 years old and three weeks into a new year at McCord Junior High. Patrick – another fat kid with something to prove – had taken to following me after French class.

As he beeped and boomed behind me, I remembered the heavy book bag on my shoulder. I seldom visited my locker, and my book bag contained every textbook in my curriculum. The bag weighed over a stone. I tested its heft on my shoulder and thought about all the saliva-coated balls of paper he had hit me with in French class. I swung hard and fast, catching him totally off guard.

The black Esprit tote slammed into the side of his head with a satisfying 'thwack'. His glasses flew off, shattering against the terrazzo floor. He lay dazed and moaning in a chubby little heap in the hallway, and I walked on to English class, unconcerned.

Patrick never reported me. We avoided each other, which was easy, given that the school was a sprawling seventies compound.

My mother bought me make-up and took me for a good haircut before school started. I had acne, greasy hair and a round, pendulous stomach that rested on my lap like a freshly risen lump of pizza dough and, as much as I lived inside my head, I couldn't deny that my body was a disaster. No amount of make-up could fix my bad skin. No matter how clean it was, a T-shirt the size of a tent would never enhance my figure. I didn't want to get up early to fight these particular lost causes and I gave up on the beauty regime after the first two days of term.

I slept till 7am every weekday, rolled out of bed, threw on an outfit from the floor and caught the school bus outside my house at 7.15. Boys on the bus still called me Moose but I kept my headphones on and listened to Duran Duran or National Public Radio all the way to school.

I entered McCord for my seventh grade year in 1985. Ronald Reagan – elderly, with badly dyed hair and orange in the face – led the free world while his red-suited wife urged all us kiddies to 'Just say no' to drugs. My new deputy head, Mr Dorffman, even wrote a song in Mrs Reagan's honour. The song urged all of us to join the school's anti-dope club, Healthy Youth, and to trade drugs for hugs. Once a month or so, students would shuffle into the school gym for an anti-drug singalong:

I love life, that's the truth.
I've sworn off weed for Healthy Youth.
That's all I want to be!
I'm psyched, psyched, psyched,
'Cause I'm pot free!

I had problems with the concept of Healthy Youth. I considered cigarettes and alcohol to be drugs and, as my parents consumed both, I felt hypocritical and so dropped out. Besides, the 'Hugs not Drugs' T-shirts wouldn't fit me, even in the largest size they made. Though I avoided the scale, I was wearing a size 24 by this time, and probably weighed about 18 stone.

Halfway through the school year, we had a special assembly. Nancy Reagan had just said yes to McCord Junior High's anti-drug programme. The First Lady called the school to wish all of us happy, drug-free lives. She also sent a glowing letter of praise that the deputy head framed and hung in the school's main office. Whenever I did something to merit punishment, I'd sit in the office waiting for my turn with Mr Dorffman and I'd read the letter. Reading it made me crave something to take the edge off, but I couldn't quite put my finger on what that might be. Perhaps a McDonald's quarter pounder with cheese would do the trick. I'd count my pocket change and think about how I could talk my sister's babysitter into taking me to the drive thru.

Mrs Cardboard Tits, the school dinner lady with the unpronounceable Slavic name we'd all gleefully bastardised, lectured me about my slackerdom in the drug war one day in the cafeteria. As usual, I ate alone, and this attracted her like a shark to its prey.

'Rebecca, all the Healthy Youth kids miss you. Why don'tcha go back? Hugs not drugs! That's the plan,' Mrs Cardboard Tits smiled expectantly.

'I'd like to, Mrs C, but my parents drink and smoke, and I'd feel funny wearing the T-shirt around them,' I answered, casting a longing look at the piping hot slab of cafeteria pizza on my tray. I wanted to dig in, but thought it'd be rude with Mrs Cardboard Tits hovering over me. I also wanted to pick all the cheese off, eat it, and then devour the sauce-slathered pizza crust. This isn't really the sort of thing you want to do in front of an audience, especially when the audience is a 50-year-old woman with size FFF breasts and a hairnet.

'Think it over, Rebecca. I'm sure your mum and dad would never want you to do the pot.' She had a point. They certainly wouldn't want me dipping into their stash. I gave Mrs C a polite nod and turned my attention to the pizza. I bought lunch every day, a flat, rectangular slab of sausage pizza, a pile of greasy French fries, a small carton of grape juice and a tiny box of chocolate milk. In high school, this lunch expanded to include a can of Coke. With the use of the high school drinks machine, I had at least three Cokes a day.

At both schools I looked forward to lunchtime. It wasn't so much that the slice of pizza, the greasy fries or the Coke meant anything to me in themselves; it was the escape from the tribulations of the day that I enjoyed. From six o'clock in the morning till noon, I wandered through junior high and high school on tiptoes trying to avoid the many traps and snares set by my classmates. A pack of thin girls laughing as I passed them in the hall meant that I'd reach over my shoulder and find a 'wide load' sign taped to the back of my shirt. Even the people who tolerated my presence, who were not exactly friends, found ways of separating themselves from me. My fatness and strangeness affected them the way a contagious disease might. No one wanted what I had, not even people who enjoyed my company and laughed at my jokes. The minute someone popular or athletic drifted by, my non-friends melted away from me.

At lunch, though, I could sit and eat and enjoy the quiet space in my head. The food I chose had balance: fat, calories and salt in proportions I found faintly intoxicating. Everything I drank contained outrageous amounts of carcinogenic dyes and high-fructose corn syrup. By the time I started high school I weighed over 21 stone and knew from all the books I'd read that diets fail. The books also warned of the dangers of yo-yo dieting – that even if I could lose some weight, I'd gain it all back. Most of the other kids ate a similar lunchtime diet, I rationalised, and few of them were seriously overweight. So I staked out a peaceful lunchtime, eating what I liked. In addition, my father didn't approve of the pizza and fries, a fact that increased their appeal.

People talk about comfort food. I never took comfort in any specific food. I took comfort in choosing whatever food I liked. Making these choices felt like independence and freedom. Pointing to a slab of French bread pizza as I walked through the lunch line, meeting the sceptical eye of the woman with the plastic hairnet who offered it up, paying for it all with money my parents blindly doled out each day – these things made me feel like I had some degree of control over my life. I could take my tray to a table, sit, eat and feel at ease, if only for half an hour.

As I finished my pizza slab that Mrs Cardboard Tits had delayed, I snuck a glance at my old lunch table. I'd started off the school year eating with Renata Singh, but Lisa Schwartzman, a friend of Renata's who'd gone to a different primary school than the rest of us, seemed to decide my presence was lowering the tone of the table.

'So, let's watch Rebecca eat, shall we? Fun! Like watching maggots eat a dead bird. Oh, I see a little pizza cheese dribbling. Perhaps she needs a bib?' Lisa had time for the running commentary as her own lunch of a Diet Coke and three crackers didn't take long to eat. She'd sit uncomfortably close to me, as if we were great friends, and make her comments in a fake sweet voice. Renata didn't defend me. I took it as long as I could but, after two weeks, I knew I'd have to eat somewhere else.

The transition took a couple of days. The first time I walked into the cafeteria knowing I'd have to eat alone, I stopped in the doorway and surveyed the crowd of kids lined up to buy hot lunch, the cluster of jocks in one corner and the cheerleaders at an adjacent table wearing their red and black uniforms. I didn't see any place where I'd fit. I left the cafeteria and spent my lunch break in the ladies' toilets. I sat in the handicapped cubicle and read a book. The next day, I packed a sandwich and took it into the toilets.

'Miss? You okay? I've seen your shoes under the door for half an hour.' One of the school janitors knocked on the door of my cubicle. I came out after a minute or so, and threw my empty paper bag in the bin. 'You can't eat in here. It's against school rules. It's not clean, neither,' the janitor told me. She wore a flowered smock over a McCord T-shirt and a pair of stained khaki pants. I nodded and left the toilets, wondering how I'd get through the next year and a half of school. The next day, I got in line, bought my pizza and found a table by myself. No one bothered me, though I'd occasionally hear laughter from Lisa's table. She and Renata always seemed to be looking my way, whispering and laughing. I'd turn my gaze back to the pizza, trying hard to think of anything other than my status as a canteen untouchable.

Because the plots of the books I read always seemed to hinge on outcasts triumphing over adversity, I constantly over-estimated my classmates' humanity. After my expulsion from the lunch table, I tried to sit with Edye and Renata during a school assembly. Lisa wouldn't have it, and ended up leading everyone in a chant to a popular rap tune of the era:

'The moose, the moose, the moose is on fire! We don't need no water; let the motherfucker burn!'

I slunk out of the gym and hid in the toilets. I had an angry little speech prepared for the janitor, but she had other things to do that day, so I had the privacy necessary to enjoy a really good cry. I wanted to do something nasty to Lisa, but couldn't really think of anything appropriately violent. Boys like Patrick Gianelli were relatively easy. I'd say something sarcastic (or break their noses with a bag full of textbooks), and they'd slink off and make their nasty comments out of earshot. Lisa practised a softer, more insidious form of warfare, and I had no idea how to defend myself from it. She made me feel totally unfeminine, like a fat, neutered thing, and any reaction that underscored my supposed lack of femininity, such as punching her snotty face in, would only prove her point.

A bona fide social outcast in a man's plaid shirt and baggy

jeans, I carved out a niche for myself among the other geeks, burnouts and untouchables. I joined the school veterinary club so I could hang out with Tim Riley, a nascent homosexual and fellow chubby kid. Tim lost his baby fat in high school and starred in all the school musicals, but at this stage he was still another despised fat kid. Vet club met once a week with our sponsor, Dr Esplin. He'd talk about different creatures and their medical needs, and sometimes we'd take a field trip to his surgery. 'If anyone is squeamish, let me know now,' Dr Esplin said. A little cluster of vet club geeks stood around the table in a semicircle. We all wore masks and scrubs, and stared intently at the patient, an enormous St Bernard lying anaesthetised on the table. The dog's tongue hung out of her slack mouth, and a large, clear tube lay between her jaws. She took regular, deep breaths, but otherwise remained utterly still.

Dr Esplin cut into her belly, and a smell of blood – a heavy, iron-rich tang – made the room spin all around me. Dr Esplin's assistant noticed me struggling for balance and guided me swiftly out of the room. Later, when I was feeling a bit better, I had to do something to retrieve my tough girl rep. 'Can I keep the dog's uterus?' I asked Dr Esplin. He'd put it in a mason jar of formaldehyde, and it looked like a huge wad of overchewed pink bubble gum. I thought I might offer it as a gift to my favourite teacher, Mrs Cobau. She taught biology, and had shown no mercy at all to the dead frogs and formaldehyde-soaked earthworms she'd made us dissect. When wit failed to win people over, I resorted to gifts and I thought the dog uterus might have some value to her as a classroom display. Mrs Cobau told jokes and all the kids liked her. If I could obtain this gummy pink treasure for her, surely I'd be her favourite. I craved approval. Other kids seemed like a lost cause, but I never gave up trying to please my teachers.

Dr Esplin was obviously confused by the request, but couldn't think of any good reason not to grant it. Vet club met on Fridays, and I wanted the dog uterus to stay fresh till I could present it to Mrs Cobau first thing Monday morning so I took the organ home and stowed it in the fridge.

Andrea and I sat together at the kitchen table. My sister opened her rucksack and carefully extracted a pink notebook, a neatly labelled folder and a razor-sharp pencil. She laid out a pristine sheet of lined notebook paper and began writing with such tense concentration that you'd think she was outlining her doctoral dissertation in astrophysics. 'This year is much harder than last year,' she told me. 'Way more homework, and I have to copy it out when I'm done 'cause there's points for hand-writing,' she added. I frowned. I did my own homework on the bus on the way to school, and the idea of doing a second draft of it seemed ridiculous to me. But Andrea seemed to enjoy the work, and her grades – even at the age of eight – reflected the effort. Much as I would have liked it if we'd attended the same school at the same time, I felt a bit of relief at not having to compete with her academically.

My mother rustled around in the kitchen preparing the dinner. Then she opened the refrigerator door and screamed. 'What the hell is this thing?' she demanded, spying my vet club treasure.

'A dog's uterus,' I answered. 'What does it look like? Duh!'

My mother struggled for words. 'I . . . want . . . it . . . gone!' she spat.

I couldn't see the problem. It wasn't as if I'd put it on top of the chicken or anything. It was merely chicken adjacent. I looked at the jar, nestled on a shelf in the fridge next to dinner, and shrugged. My mother constantly badgered me about my grades so I knew exactly which buttons to push. 'I'm giving it to Mrs Cobau on Monday,' I said. 'It's for science class.' She cleared a space around the uterus and warned my father not to put any of our food too close to the jar.

On Monday, my mother drove me to school early. She'd had an uncomfortable weekend with the dog's lady bits on ice next to her perishables and wanted the jar and its contents out of her house as soon as possible. I turned up for first period science class half an hour early and found Mrs Cobau alone in her classroom, hard at work marking a stack of quizzes.

'Good morning, Mrs Cobau,' I said. 'I brought you something special. It's from the vet club, sort of, but mostly it's from me.' I held out my treasure, expecting praise and glory and an A grade. No such luck.

'What the . . . er, what is that, exactly?' Mrs Cobau, petite, with black hair and eyes, stared into the jar with an expression somewhere between horror and total confusion.

'It's a dog's uterus!' I said, smiling. 'I thought you might want it, you know, as a biology thing.' I shook the jar gently, and the pink, slimy mass twitched. Bits of biomatter swirled in the clear formaldehyde as the uterus resettled itself.

'Rebecca, I appreciate the thought, really I do, but I can honestly say that I've never had any need for a dog's uterus. Thank you for thinking of me, though.' She smiled brightly. 'You'll need to find another . . . er, home for it, I think.' She nodded politely and went back to her marking.

Grudgingly, I took the jar back home and returned it to the fridge.

'What the fuck?' my mother had worked at the welfare department for nearly 15 years and had developed the sort of obscene vocabulary that would make a battle-hardened Marine blush. Mum peered into the fridge for another second or two before angrily slamming the door. 'What happened to Mrs Cobau?'

'She didn't want it. I don't get it. It's a dog's uterus. It's perfect.' I was completely taken aback by my favourite teacher's lack of appreciation for the treasure. When I'd asked the vet for it, I'd had to out-manoeuvre Tim Riley for the prize, and Tim had called a couple of times over the weekend, begging me to reconsider. 'Call the Riley boy and give it to him,' Mum commanded.

'But Muuuum!' I wailed. The uterus was mine, and I didn't want to give it up. We had plenty of room in the fridge, and it wasn't as if anyone would accidentally cook it. The formaldehyde would deter even the most clueless chef (dad) from grilling the thing.

'But nothing. Call him!' Mum wouldn't take no for an answer. I called Tim and he came for the uterus immediately. I made the handover at our front door and, just like that, the organ departed. I watched it go with regret, knowing that seventh grade would never get any better.

In addition to biology, English, maths and history, I also studied art. I've always liked to draw and paint. In my liberal kindergarten, our art teacher let us do whatever we liked. I made my mother a heart-shaped pocket vase and, through application of six different colours of glaze, created the perfect shade of road kill organ meat purple. For my father, I made a head-shaped paperweight, also glazed purple. Little balls of clay formed the eyes, and the large, beaky nose gave the thing an uncanny resemblance to Dad.

When I was 12, I signed up for a full year of art class. I shared a table with Tim, Renata, and Doug Webber. Doug took art because he thought he might see naked people. He wrestled for McCord, and had all the intellectual gifts of a well-shaped block of concrete. He thought art would be easy, and made our class memorable by constantly talking about his groin. 'My pubes are really curly,' he told me one day as we were sketching still life: a pile of hammers, screwdrivers and awls. I tried hard to concentrate on the hammer head; I wanted to get the shading just right. 'Moosie, I'm talking to you. My pubes? Curly? Seriously – they actually tangle down there. Wanna see?' He crowded me, and I could smell his post-lunch hot dog breath.

'No, thanks. Maybe you should show Mr Pritchard? I nodded towards our teacher, who sat at his desk totally engrossed in the *Toledo Blade*. I think he'd appreciate seeing your *kielbasa*.' I'd moved on to sketching an awl. Doug snorted and scratched his crotch.

'You'll change your mind. The ladies always do,' he smirked.

'*Ladies*? Dude, you're like, 13 years old. What ladies?' I asked, incredulous.

'All of them,' he said, raising one heavy blond brow. Doug's hammer looked like it had a serious case of scurvy. Misshapen, with a soft-looking head, it meandered across the page, ending abruptly at one corner. He peered at it, frowning, and started adding little curly hairs just above the handle. 'My unit is just like this,' he said, thrusting the paper in my face, 'only much bigger.'

I wanted to seem tough and knowing, but I wondered if the thin girls felt as uncomfortable as I did when boys like Doug talked about sex. Some of the girls in my class actually had boyfriends. The closest I'd ever come to having a boyfriend was kissing one of the Kidd boys in the back of his mother's rusty Buick when I was eight. My chubbiness also ruled out most clothes of the pretty or girly variety. I wore my flannel shirt, jeans and an oversized T-shirt almost every day.

Our headteacher, a whip-skinny 40-something who favoured short business skirts, pearls and three-inch heels, called me into her office one day to discuss my lack of fashionable wardrobe choices. 'Your classmates and a few of your teachers have complained about how you dress,' Mrs Roth said, giving me her patented look of concern. 'Rethink the plaid and see if you can't find a pair of socks that match.' I knew how I looked, and I realised that other kids had a fairly low opinion of me. Mrs Roth wouldn't say which teachers complained, and back in class I found it hard to concentrate. Could it be Mrs Cobau? I dismissed this out of hand. Mrs Cobau – funny, smart and totally cool – would never have a conversation with Mrs Roth unless she absolutely had to, I imagined. She surely wouldn't seek her out for something as frivolous as a talk about my clothes.

Could it be one of the male teachers? Maybe it was Mr Hoover, the teacher with the bad breath and roving hands. I'd stood in front of him after a class presentation one day, and he'd gripped my shoulders and rubbed up against me, clutching even harder when I tried to pull away. This disgusted me, but I didn't take it personally.

My mother noticed my long face that night at dinner, and I told her what Mrs Roth had said to me. 'You could start to vary the wardrobe a little, but it sure as hell isn't that skinny witch's place to talk to you about it,' she said. Mum called Mrs Roth the very next day. 'Maybe you should worry less about one student's clothing and more about the people you're supposedly supervising,' she said. 'The guy who's all hands? Maybe you could make him a priority.'

Mrs Roth sputtered something, and my mother kindly offered to put her thoughts in a letter to the school board. Mrs Roth never talked to me about my clothes again, and I felt slightly better, though I began to view all but one of my teachers with wounded suspicion.

Years later, it occurred to me that none of my teachers had said anything to Roth about me. She herself had this picture of a perfect student body, and I was the cockroach in her yogurt. I played this role fairly often during my childhood in the suburbs. Years later, I read Anne Lamott's book *Operating Instructions*, in which she quotes a friend of hers, a Jesuit priest, about being different. The gist of it was this: if you're at all different from other people, you're supposed to stay at home; if you do show up, you're supposed to have the good grace to feel ashamed of yourself. I think my lack of shame annoyed people like Mrs Roth and Mrs Leeds. I ruined their pretty picture, and I didn't even have the sense to hate myself for it.

I felt sad when kids ostracised or teased me. I felt confused

when my gifts of dog organs were rejected. I felt . . . something
. . . when Mr Hoover rubbed up against me. I felt humiliated
when the headteacher told me my clothes weren't up to scratch.
I ached for acceptance, and dreamed of having one good friend.
But, despite all of this, I never actively hated myself. I knew I
could write well, and that my jokes made people laugh. I took
care of my sister, and my grandmother loved me. My mother,
despite her own criticism of my personal style, stood up for me
when it mattered.

I had a few things going for me. I thought that one day I'd be
thin. I didn't actually diet or exercise to achieve this goal, but I
hoped for it and fantasised about it. Thin or not, I knew that
junior high school wouldn't last forever. I had slightly less than
two years of hell ahead of me. I read my novels, listened to my
Walkman and tried to stand up for myself when I could. And I
ate whatever I liked.

I'd go home after a day of catcalls, whispered taunts and
mean, girlish laughter and order a small pizza with bacon
and mushrooms. I had an hour or so alone in the house before
my sister got home. I'd sit by myself in front of the television
and eat the whole pizza, hiding the empty box in one of the bins
in the garage.

Every bite of pizza was an act of defiance. My body was
nobody else's business. If I wanted to eat pizza, no one – not my
father, not the kids at school and certainly not my headteacher
– could stop me. This strategy saved my life and ruined a large
portion of it, all at the same time. Much as I claimed my body
and resented anyone who dared express an opinion of it, I often
felt strangely disconnected from my physical self. I lived in my
head, noticing my body briefly whenever I caught a glimpse of

my reflection, or was forced to visit a doctor or step on a scale. The only times I specifically sought an awareness of my body were the days and nights I spent riding horses. In the riding ring, I sat up straight, held my head high and focused on moving forwards, moving faster, and on jumping anything that got in my way.

7

MY EQUESTRIAN CAREER

Horse people talk about the glue factory all the time. 'You're going to stick a lot of stamps if you keep it up,' Moira said. She was riding one of the old school horses, a relatively docile mare named Daisy, and Daisy had decided she'd rather go back to her stall than canter. Moira would have none of that: she tapped Daisy with her crop, just once, gently, and Daisy moved from a slow trot to a slow, grudging canter.

The indoor riding ring at Blue Bonnet Farm was an immense structure with a metal roof and a dirt floor. At the centre of the riding track was a circuit of jumping obstacles ranging from simple poles a few inches off the ground to huge cross-tie fences about four feet high. I walked my school horse in a circle, breathing in all the usual stable smells: fresh hay, fresh manure and freshly turned earth. Then I coaxed my horse into a slow trot and concentrated on moving up and down in sync with the horse's gait as we rounded the corner closest to the door.

I was riding Dexter, a coal black quarter horse with a white blaze on his nose and three white socks. Dex trotted and cantered easily. He had a lot of wild energy and I couldn't always keep up with his demands for more speed. Sometimes Dexter wanted to jump, and I'd hold on for dear life as he suddenly veered off the track, hurtling towards the cross-tie fences. I'd pull him up short; he'd snort and do an awkward little dance as he tried to reconcile the walking pace I was forcing on him with the gallop he'd just dropped from. After Dexter settled, we'd go back to the track like nothing had happened.

Blue Bonnet provided lessons to a lot of kids in my suburb. You got a different mount every week, and at 12, in the middle of my *de rigueur* horsey phase, I preferred Dex and his quirks to old, slow Daisy. Daisy wouldn't jump. She drove me crazy with her stubborn slowness. After our first agonisingly slow walk around the riding ring, I entertained thoughts of animal cruelty. If I'd had a driving licence I would have driven her to the glue factory myself.

'Whoa, girl, whoa!' I shouted. One day Daisy had decided to cut the lesson short and walked me straight into the stalls area. She stomped off the riding track and exited the training area through an enormous set of double doors leading to a long corridor. Her stall, complete with fresh oats and water, lay just off this corridor, and Daisy wanted to go home and eat. Despite my best efforts with the reins and my crop, she carried on towards her stall, and I had to lie across her broad shoulders to avoid the low ceiling. I couldn't smack her. The last thing I wanted her to do was run with me indoors and in that position. I waited for Moira, my instructor, and she held Daisy's lead while I shimmied off her back.

'Stupid nag,' I grumbled. 'No carrots for you, paste pot.'

Daisy huffed and puffed a bit, and the whiskers around her broad, thick lips quivered. 'Oh, fine. Here. But you're only getting one.' I tendered the carrot and she chomped the whole thing, including the leafy green top.

My parents thought of riding as a form of exercise for me, something my new diet coach had also recommended. Our neighbour, Deirdre, a registered nurse, offered her services one day. 'I'm taking some classes to update my nursing skills, and you could be a big help to me, Becky,' she said, pouring me a glass of apple juice. 'I need to plan a diet for someone, and then weigh them every week to see if my diet really works. But it's really important that the person follows the diet – I could get a really low grade and no credit for the class if they don't lose any weight,' Deirdre explained.

Deirdre obviously couldn't practise this diet herself. At five feet nine inches, she weighed about 9 stone. Deirdre exercised regularly, playing tennis at the country club with her brother. She had a beautiful tan in the summer, and her lightly browned, perfectly muscled shoulders contrasted neatly with the white sleeveless shirts she favoured. With her long brown hair and blue eyes, she reminded me a little of Wonder Woman. I was nine years old, and Halloween was only a few short weeks away. I didn't want to go on a diet, but I agreed to the plan and faithfully followed the menu Deirdre prescribed. I visited her once a week to stand on the medical scale in her kitchen. Deirdre took notes on my progress for her school report.

That Halloween, I dressed as a witch. I wore pointy-toed boots borrowed from the back of my mother's wardrobe, a black hat, green face paint and a shawl Mum found under some old bathing suits. Before I could go door to door begging for sweets, though, I had to stop at Deirdre's so she could weigh me. I rang her doorbell and waited for a few minutes, but no one answered. I stood on Deirdre's front porch, a wide, wooden structure that she'd decorated with a pair of cast cement geese dressed in yellow raincoats, and watched as groups of children canvassed the block. They walked together in pairs or in larger groups. Some wore shop-bought costumes with cheap plastic masks, while others had carefully crafted their own disguises. I wanted to trick-or-treat, too, and wondered where Deirdre was.

I rang again, and after another couple of minutes or so, Deirdre opened the door and waved me inside. I followed her down the entrance hall to the kitchen, and had to stop short to avoid bumping into her when she stumbled. She grabbed the wall for support and directed me to the scale. The hallway had been dark, but in the brightly lit kitchen Deirdre's strange condition became immediately apparent. Her hair fell awkwardly across one shoulder in a strange, off-centre ponytail, and smears of brown mascara underscored her bloodshot eyes. She smelled like some apple cider Mum had thrown out because it had been in the fridge too long. I stood on the scale waiting, but Deirdre didn't move from her seat at the kitchen table. She took a sip from a tall glass filled with amber liquid, and shook her head at me.

'I don't need to write it down,' she said. 'Your weight, I mean. I don't need it for school. Your mother thought you'd try harder if I told you that, but it's wrong to lie. You either want to do it or you don't.' Deirdre took a huge gulp of her drink and waved me towards the door. I took my empty pillowcase and left, closing the door softly and carefully behind me.

My haul of sweets at the end of the evening impressed my mother. I never told Mum what Deirdre said about the diet. After Halloween, I made excuses to avoid the weekly weigh-ins, and eventually Mum stopped asking me to go for them. I had never looked at the number when Deirdre weighed me – I had already taken to backing onto the scale. After this failed diet idea, the recommendation of horse riding as exercise appealed to my mother, and I rode horses on and off for about four years.

After a year or so, I'd taken all the classes Blue Bonnet Farm offered, and had grown tired of the school horses and their sad routines. Mum found a place for me at a small private stable where school horses like Daisy and Dexter were quickly replaced by the love of my young life, a chestnut quarter horse named Bear. The nickname suited him. He had endless patience, and a solid, quiet nature. I loved him from the milky fur between his huge black eyes to the tips of his silver-shod hooves. Bear loved the sugar cubes and apples I brought him, and enjoyed me brushing him and picking pebbles out of his hooves. He tolerated me riding him, and always did exactly what I asked – never more, never less. If I urged him into a trot, we'd trot until I decided on our next move. He cantered on command, and slowed to a walk when I tugged the reins. He never went any faster than I asked or tried to take me over any fences I hadn't planned on jumping.

Bear was owned by the trainer, Sheila, a short, squat woman in her early forties with a day job as a counsellor at a local homeless shelter. Sheila also worked with the stable's resident 'princess'. Tiffany won every show she entered and had indulgent, adoring parents who seemingly bought her anything she liked. A willowy blonde with a hard little mouth, Tiffany got away with murder. At 14, she had a 21-year-old boyfriend, and none of the adults we knew seemed to think this was at all inappropriate.

'That's how you need to sit on a horse, Rebecca,' Sheila said as we stood at the rail of the outdoor ring and Tiffany passed us for the third or fourth time. 'You've got a different body type, so you're not going to look as pretty doing it, but you can learn a lot just from watching Tiffany,' she added. I didn't have Tiffany's natural grace, but I loved riding. It allowed me to fully inhabit my body without the usual self-consciousness. I felt free, quick and powerful. For the first time, I thought of myself as graceful.

As Tiffany took jump after effortless jump, Sheila watched her star pupil with awe-tinged pride. 'I'd cut you in half to get another one of her,' she half-whispered to me, never taking her eyes off Tiffany.

Sheila pushed a fringe of grey-brown hair off her damp forehead and waved Tiffany over. 'Great work, Tiff. Lovely seat.' Tiffany nodded, looking bored. In the short time I'd known her, Tiffany had displayed about one and a half facial expressions, and 'lustful' probably wasn't the one she wanted to share with our chubby, plaid-swaddled riding instructor.

Sheila drove me home, her battered grey saloon rattling hard all the way. She punched the buttons on the car's ancient radio, finally settling on a station playing an old Patsy Cline song. 'So, what're you going to do this summer?' she asked me. Summer was months away, but Sheila and I had little in common except for horses and excess cellulite, and she really had to stretch to come up with topics for conversation.

'Probably go to the pool a lot,' I said. I loved to swim. The weightlessness of immersion gave me a sense of freedom within my body I couldn't find anywhere else. Over the summer, I knew I'd spend a lot of time floating in pools all over Toledo.

'Maybe I'll watch for cute boys, too,' I added. I shared this confidence with Sheila, giving her an ingratiating smile and leaning forward, hoping for some small show of approval. Tiffany talked about nothing but cute boys and horses, and Sheila always laughed and offered stale dating advice while the two of them groomed horses or rubbed oil into a saddle.

'Aren't you a little young to be crotch watching?' she asked, frowning slightly. It suddenly seemed vitally important for me to know all the words to 'I Fall to Pieces', so I stared straight ahead and listened to the radio, and we completed the rest of the ten-minute drive in silence.

Much as I loved the stable, I still hated school. Riding meant nothing there and I rarely discussed it. I wanted to keep that special time to myself, keep it away from the other kids. They'd just make jokes about me breaking the horse, I thought. When I mentioned riding to my gym teacher, he laughed at my suggestion that this was exercise. 'Maybe for the horse,' he said. 'If you want extra credit for home exercise, you've got to run or join a sports team. Sitting on a horse is active, maybe, but I can't count it,' he added, shifting his hands in the pockets of his nylon mesh shorts. He blew his whistle, signalling an end to our conversation.

Riding requires a fair amount of work. My gym teacher didn't understand that riders never just sit on a horse. Most of the time I rode, I trotted. When your horse trots, you 'post' – you move up and down in the rhythm of the horse's gait using your leg and thigh muscles. You hold your body upright, arms stretched forward. When you finish after an hour or two, you lead the horse to its stall, remove its saddle and brush it's coat. You pick out the hooves and brush the feet. You provide food and water. You clean the saddle and put it away. Riding seemed like a fair amount of exercise to me, but I had no whistle and no tiny pairs of mesh shorts, so my opinion lacked the academic weight of a fully qualified gym teacher's.

So I didn't talk about riding at school. I kept my head down and tried to blend into the walls and the floors. By the time I was 12, the teasing and constant humiliation had ground me down. I felt like nothing, like nobody. I skipped school whenever I could. I even thought about dying. My teacher that year, a horrible old woman with tuna breath and the looks and demeanour of one of the less glamorous Disney witches, harped on constantly about my appearance. I hated her and I hated my classmates, and I hated myself for my own total powerlessness. The only thing that made me feel like a person was climbing aboard a horse and moving forward, moving so much more quickly than my chubby, stubby legs could ever do on the ground.

As the year wore on, I found myself spending a lot of time observing Tiffany. Her horse Snow had the stall right next to Bear, and we often had lessons at the same time. Snow was a tall, blindingly white creature with a gentle face and lovely manners. I wouldn't have traded Bear for Snow, of course, but I couldn't help liking her. I was a 13-year-old girl, after all. I'd sneak Snow the occasional sugar cube knowing that she'd pick me over Tiffany if she could. At the very least, I felt Snow would appreciate me for protecting her from Tiff's idiot boyfriend, Tate.

'You want it? Huh? Stupid horse.' Tate held an apple out of Snow's reach. Every time the mare gave up on it, he dangled the fruit again. She'd reach, stretching her long, elegant neck, and Tate would yank the apple away from her at the last minute. He laughed, mouth wide open, revealing large, crooked teeth. Tiffany sat on a hay bale, carefully applying a thick, shiny coat of pink lipstick, adding a bit around the outside of her mouth to give her thin lips a little boost.

'Oh, Tater. You're so silly,' she said, eyes glued to her compact mirror. Tiffany closed the lipstick with a snap and stuffed it into the left cup of her brassiere. She whisked a little pressed powder over her pale cheeks, closed the compact and stuffed it into the right bra cup. I was only about six months younger than she was, but the two of us were worlds apart. Despite my own burgeoning figure, I resisted wearing a bra. I found them uncomfortably confining, which left me to store my own Bonne Bell lip gloss – which I liked mainly because it tasted like bubblegum – in my pocket.

'Lookie what I got!' Tate said, dangling away. Snow blinked once or twice and made another attempt at the treat. Tate yanked it away from her, giving Tiff a quick look to see if she was paying attention. I decided enough was enough. 'If you show her the apple, you have to give it to her. Otherwise, you're just being a big, mean jerk,' I told him. I narrowed my eyes and shook a finger at him so he'd know I meant business.

Tiffany yawned and rubbed at a spot on her boot. Tate frowned, struggling mightily to process this new information. 'Whatever. Here, stupid horse.' He let Snow take the apple, and she polished it off in the usual one and a half bites. Tate had the good grace to look a little ashamed of himself. Tiffany didn't register this exchange at all. She moved from lipstick to boot polishing to a very thorough study of her pink-painted fingernails. She gave a delicate yawn, stood up and approached the stall. 'That's my Snowy girl, pretty pretty,' she cooed, before giving the mare a kiss on the nose.

Much as I despised Tiffany, I knew she was the normal one of the two of us. Tiffany looked like everyone else, and dressed like all the other thin, pretty girls. She knew which clothes were 'in', exactly how much make-up to wear and which shoes matched her outfit. She had a boyfriend who drove her to school. Her grades were good enough without being intimidating. I saw her tease her horse and kiss her boyfriend with tongues. I saw her lean against a stall and let Tate stick his hand under her shirt. I felt superior on many levels. I also knew I'd trade places with her in a heartbeat, if such a thing were possible.

I tried telling myself that it was better to be smart than pretty or popular. Then I'd think, *It's not like you know that for sure.* Television had given me the queer idea that it was somehow better to be a good person than to be a beautiful one. The problem with that, I thought, was that I wasn't especially good, either. I actively wished for terrible things to happen to kids who teased me, or to thin, popular girls like Tiffany who epitomised things I would never be. Whenever Tiffany took a big jump, I hoped she'd fall off and break an arm or (through some miracle of physics) suffer a disfiguring facial injury. It was the same when my father yelled at me. I sometimes wished that he'd die, and then I'd feel my own inward ugliness, something bone-deep inside me that I knew I could never change.

After a ride one day, having carried out the usual routine of brushing, hoof scraping and the offering (and happy acceptance) of treats, I sat on the barn's dirt floor and enjoyed the stillness of the large, empty space. Bear stood quietly in his stall, the apple I'd provided a distant memory already. Tate walked in, leading Snow. After parking her in her stall, Tate stood next to the white mare and clumsily worked at the buckle of her halter. He ran a finger between the leather strap and her cheek, tugging gently and then a little harder. Nothing happened. The halter stayed in place, the bit firmly fixed between Snow's teeth. Tate pulled a scrap of paper out of the back pocket of his jeans and frowned at it, lips moving as he read. He shook his head, crumpled the paper, and threw it in the dirt.

'Rebecca? Do you know how this thing comes off? Tiff had to go to the mall, and I told her I'd fix Snow before I went to work,' he said. 'She gave me this note with directions and all, but I don't really know what the hell half of it means,' he added.

I sighed. 'Sure, Tate, I'll do it,' I said. 'For Snow,' I added, a touch snottily. I walked over to the stall and grabbed the harness just behind Snow's ears. I eased it down an inch or two, and the mare spat out her bit.

'Cool!' Tate said. 'Do you know how to brush her? 'Cause I kinda told Tiff I'd do that, too.' I showed Tate how to operate the curry comb and the other brushes and picked out Snow's hooves myself.

Tiffany's parents paid for her lessons but rarely put in an appearance at the stable. My father had virtually no interest in my riding but he'd still drive me out to the stable. It was a long silent trip. Although he never actually shoved me out of the moving car, he left as quickly as possible and only ever watched one lesson. He came to my horse shows, grudgingly plodding along after my mother and sister as they walked round the riding ring to the bleachers.

For my first event, my mother and I had spent hours the weekend before shopping for horse paraphernalia. I picked out a navy blazer with silver buttons and a pair of cream jodhpurs. I had to lie down on my bed to get the zip up, and my new riding boots pinched my toes. Despite this, and the fact that my helmet smashed my curly hair totally flat, and the chin strap did an excellent job of emphasising my nascent double chin, I liked wearing these clothes because they made me feel pretty and athletic.

Horse shows gave me the rare chance to be the star of our family. Andrea dressed up for the occasion in a dress and tights, her patent leather shoes an interesting (if slightly ridiculous) counterpoint to the dull matte finish of stable dirt and horse manure. My father brought his camera and took pictures of me exercising Bear in a field before the show, and of me with my sister. My mother looked on proudly as I rode, cheering when I entered the ring and started trotting.

For this first show I rode Bear in careful circles around the arena, trotting as instructed, and slowing to a walk at exactly the right moment. I sat stiffly upright, trying to mimic Tiffany's effortlessly perfect riding posture. I posted as Bear trotted, rising up and down in the stirrups with every beat of his front hooves. When the judges announced the results, I'd won.

'Good job, Becky,' Mum said, hugging me. As we waited for the awards ceremony, Dad snapped pictures from every conceivable angle. The camera, a professional-grade Nikon I'd been expressly forbidden from ever touching, totally obscured his face. The shutter clicked as my mother, sister and I smiled brightly in the dim light of the indoor show ring.

The ring announcer called my name, and I stepped forward to accept my blue ribbon. My face felt tight and I realised I was smiling – smiling for myself. I felt light, happy and giddy. I'd never won anything before, not in a contest that required special skill on my part. I wondered if the popular kids at school felt this good all the time. I stared at the ribbon in my hand, felt the shiny blue satin for a second, then turned and scanned the crowd for Mum. 'I won!' I said, running across the arena to her.

'I know!' she said. 'I saw you! Good job, honey.' Mum hugged me. Dad looked off into the distance, his eyes shaded by sunglasses. I looked at him for a second then grabbed Andrea for a hug. She endured this briefly before wriggling free.

I kept the blue ribbon for years afterwards, through high school and college. The simple rosette of cheap blue fabric with two long, trailing legs finally went missing after half a dozen house moves, but I don't really need that souvenir to remember the day. I have one of my father's pictures, a poorly focused action shot of a dark-haired girl in navy riding a compact brown gelding.

Horse shows, my first taste of competition, slowly lost their appeal and I went to the stable less and less often till my parents finally decided that they would no longer pay for lessons. I gave up riding during a summer heat wave, but soon found another way to compete and to prove I was as good as other kids. I joined my junior high school trivia team and never looked back.

8

BOB WEARS CROTCHLESS LEATHER PANTIES

September 1985. I'd paraphrase the Ben Folds song, 'One Angry Dwarf and 200 Solemn Faces' but I wasn't 47 inches high. I was probably 47 inches *wide*, but I avoided the tape measure and tried not to think about the ladies size 24 jeans I was slowly but surely wearing the crotch out of. My thighs rubbed together and the denim thinned out. At the age of 12, I taught myself to sew so I could fix the ragged, white-rimmed holes.

I wore white leather Reeboks, my only fashionable accessory, and was still hauling all of my textbooks around in my black Esprit tote. I skulked through the school corridors, staying close to the walls and trying hard to blend into them. Every time the bell rang and I had to walk from one class to another, I clutched my book bag to my chest and avoided making eye contact with anyone.

On the way to class one day, I saw a flyer advertising quiz team trials pinned to the bulletin board outside the gym. I memorised the date and time of the trials, and pushed the locker room door open with my shoulder. The dimly lit dressing room with its dull green floors and yellow walls echoed with high-pitched laughter. I found a locker far away from the other girls and changed into shorts and a T-shirt. I hid my body behind the locker's open door, and dressed quickly, rolling my plaid shirt into a ball and dropping it on top of my jeans at the bottom of the locker. By the time I finished, most of the other girls had assembled in the gym. I clambered up the glossy pine spectator stand and sat by myself.

Mrs Blunt blew her whistle to get our attention. 'Listen up, women! I know this year is hard. I don't envy any of you. You should know I'm here for you.' She paused to adjust the green rubber band fastening her steel-grey ponytail. The girls in my class affected bored poses, slouching on the benches or furtively eyeing the clock. 'This is also a very special time for all of you. Your bodies are changing. You're growing breasts and menstruating.' Mrs Blunt paused for the nervous laughter. 'Believe me, I know all about periods and boobies and whatnot. If you ever have a bra malfunction, just come to me and I'll give you a safety pin, no questions asked. I also have a box of period supplies you're all welcome to borrow.' I wondered if she really wanted her period stuff back after we'd borrowed it and decided to keep extra pads in my book bag so I'd never have to find out. We finally moved on to the gym portion of class. Afterwards, I repeated my awkward dance in the locker room, hiding behind a locker door while I shimmied back into my jeans.

On the bus ride home, I thought about the quiz trials. I made a special point of watching a quiz show that night, beating my mother to most of the answers. Most of the kids trying out got better grades than I did, and being on the team meant that

I'd have to sit in front of an audience and answer questions but, at bedtime, I mentioned the trial to my mother, and she offered to call my grandmother and arrange a lift home afterwards.

'Sounds like a good thing for you to do,' Mum said. 'If you're going to be on a team and represent the school, maybe you should think about letting me take you to the salon for a nice new hairstyle. You're beginning to look like a Shetland pony with all that hair in your face.'

'Muuuum!' I howled, offended. We always said goodnight in the hall, now that I was too old for tucking in. My mother's cotton gown clung to her round belly and large breasts. She tugged at the material and it fell loose with a little popping sound as the static electricity dispersed.

'If you lose a little weight, if you really try, I'll buy you all new clothes,' she said. She smiled down at me expectantly.

'Maybe I'll try. Maybe I could start after Christmas,' I said, not really meaning it. Over the years, all the fake and half-hearted promises made a liar out of me. My standard reply to any request I found unreasonable or unpleasant was either 'I guess so' or 'Maybe'. What I really meant was 'no', or, more to the point 'hell, no', but I still couldn't say the words. After years of living under my father's thumb, I had stopped saying no, at least out loud.

'After Christmas, then,' Mum said brightly. 'You wait and see, honeybunch, we'll have to keep the boys away with a shotgun.' She ruffled my hair and sent me off to bed.

I forgot to start my after-Christmas diet. Mum forgot, too. Maybe she didn't want to fight with me about my weight. After work, after the second job, dinner for four, a pile of laundry, a ride to the stable and then a trip to gymnastics for Andrea, my mother barely had the energy to stumble up the stairs to bed. Both of us generally left the weight issue alone, though my mother made periodic attempts to prod me into dieting or brushing the snarls out of my hair or caring about my appearance.

'Do you think you'd like to go to Weight Watchers with me?' Mum would ask.

'Maybe. I guess so,' I'd say. I never went.

I hated admitting I was fat. I didn't want to talk about it. In junior high, I wanted to pretend to be normal as much as possible. The quiz bowl seemed like another way for me to pretend. If I won games, everyone would know how smart I was, and the weight wouldn't matter. I lay awake thinking for a long time that night.

Quiz team trials were held in the library, a large, open space with tall windows and blond wood tables. I faced stiff competition. My school stood in a moderately wealthy suburb favoured by upwardly mobile Asian doctors and engineers as well as newly minted Jewish accountants and lawyers. Many of my classmates had learned through years of conditioning to value education, or, more specifically, the things you could buy if you went to a good college and became a lawyer, doctor or accountant. Their parents had had dreams of Harvard and Princeton for them while viewing their ultrasounds, whereas my mother had smoked menthols for two.

'What are *you* doing here?' Ethan Silverberg sneered at me. He wore his wallet on a chain and a pair of high-top Converse All Stars. Ethan stood four foot ten, weighed about 5½ stone and would probably have snapped neatly in two if he'd even tried to lift a basketball. I made sure the school librarian wasn't looking then made an obscene hand gesture. We found seats on opposite sides of the room and waited for the tryout to start. A hundred and twenty of us packed the library that day. After completing a written test, we took turns playing practice games, testing out our skills with the school's buzzer set.

'For ten points, this president married Lou . . .' *Buzz!* I rang in, interrupting Madame Clark, our French teacher and team coach.

'Herbert Hoover?' I answered nervously.

'Correct!' she said. Madame Clark continued down the list of questions. Seven other students held buzzers, but none of them had a chance to ring in. Our group completed a set of ten questions. I answered nine of them correctly. I rarely made the honour roll. I failed miserably at maths, and had to take the remedial pre-algebra class with all the burnouts and aspiring drug addicts. My socks still didn't match and I smelled like week-old cheese (a robust Emmenthal, I imagine). I was only half Jewish, and my dad didn't even go to temple. Still, I knew where Hadrian's Wall was, and I was only too happy to share this vital knowledge with anyone who would listen.

When the team list was posted, my name was at the top. Our team went undefeated that year. We cherished the five minutes of fame allotted to us in the middle of a school assembly honouring the soccer team. As we stood at centre court enjoying our moment of glory, I tried to high-five Tye Shultz, a teammate whose family background was as academically suspect as my own. Tye's parents, long divorced, cared more about screaming public fights than their only child's GPA.

'Rebecca – ot-nay ere-hay,' Tye said under his breath. He'd developed a lot of affectations and constant use of pig Latin – in which he'd split a word and use the syllables backwards – was actually the least obnoxious of them.

'The soccer guys are doing it, and they didn't even win all of their games,' I pointed out. We watched as the cheerleaders spun and kicked at centre court, loudly demanding that the assembled crowd show school spirit. I stifled a yawn and shifted from one foot to the other. We'd been standing at the sidelines for a good ten minutes, and my feet hurt. 'Seriously, Tye, if the stupid jocks can be proud of winning half their games, why shouldn't we celebrate a little?' I asked.

'The upid-stay ock-jays are atching- . . .' he paused for a moment, giving me a panicked, searching look. '*Way*,' he finished.

I understood. As the only female quiz team member, I probably wouldn't be beaten to a pulp or stuffed into a locker by the soccer team, many of whom were glowering in our direction. Todd Helmuth, the team's co-captain, made a throat slashing gesture at Tye. Then he made the 'I'm-watching-you' gesture, aiming a V of two stubby fingers at his eyes and then at us.

'Great. Thanks a bunch, Uh-becca-Ray,' Tye said.

The next year, my quiz team didn't do quite as well, but sitting in front of an audience and demonstrating my intelligence made me feel almost normal. The team accepted me as a peer, if not a friend. The following year when I changed schools, I joined the high school team. In addition to the usual trips to other schools for games, the team performed on a regional television show. To me the host Bob, despite being barely out of college, looked uncannily like Dr Bunsen Honeydew from *The Muppet Show* and had a high-pitched tenor which only added to his Muppet-like quality. He favoured plaid suits with leather elbow patches and brightly polished shoes.

During the second or third practice of the year, the team held tryouts to see which four players would represent the school. Initially, this idea excited me. If I played well, everyone at school would know. I watched a lot of television, and the idea of fame appealed to me. Halfway through the practice, I led my teammates.

As we moved through questions on helium, Henry VIII and Shakespeare's comedies, my mind wandered. I thought about the studio where the show was filmed. Studios have bright lights, and I'd probably sweat a lot in the heat. Television also meant a permanent record of my physical appearance, of me taking up twice as much space as the teammate sitting next to me. I knew the capital of Mongolia and could name both of Lincoln's vice presidents, but I had no idea how to stare into a camera lens and look as if I belonged. At the end of the round, I had fallen to fifth place. I wouldn't face the camera for another year.

My team lost the show that year. The game wasn't even close. Our team captain – a six-foot-four-inch genius named Niels White – blew a crucial starter question, putting victory out of reach once and for all. After that, team practices lost that spark of hope.

'For ten points: is a zebra black with white stripes or white with black stripes?' Niels read.

I buzzed in: 'White with black stripes?'

'Correct,' Niels said, turning to the next question.

'How can you tell?' asked Laurence Wong, a 13 year old who had skipped two school years. At five feet tall and weighing just five and a half stone, he looked like a fragile, bespectacled elf, but if you crossed him he'd find some very clever way of making your life difficult. Laurence's parents wanted the best education for him and thought America would offer their son opportunities he might not find in China so, when Laurence was five, they sent him to live with a wealthy uncle in Sylvania. Uncle Wong, a medical doctor, had spent the Second World War in Taiwan, developing a competitive edge while learning to hate the Japanese and their many well-aimed bombs, and he honed his nephew's competitive nature by waking him up at 2 am to scream at him for not being respectful enough.

We feared Laurence Wong more than we loved him, an arrangement that worked well for all concerned. Laurence appeared to be one cruel word away from killing all of us, but he had a decent sense of humour and had led the school to a bunch of debate titles. Luckily, his uncle didn't own any firearms, so Laurence concentrated on getting perfect grades and annihilating our quiz team opponents with his brain alone.

Niels pondered Laurence's question and shrugged, thumbing through the packet to find the next starter question.

'No, seriously, how can you tell that it's white with black stripes?' Laurence asked again.

'You look at its pubes,' Niels finally replied. This made as much sense as anything else I learned in high school.

I had learned about Laurence's uncle because he told the story to Meg Hall. The three of us shared an uncomfortable bench seat in the minibus on the way to a debate tournament in Canton. Laurence didn't speak for a good hundred miles, and

Meg couldn't stand the silence. A transfer student from a prison town in Kansas, Meg carried an extra 3 stone proudly. She had a barrel chest and straight hips, greasy brown hair and a face full of angry red pimples. Meg wore old plaid shirts and dirty jeans and bragged about her boyfriend in Leavenworth.

Despite her trollish bad looks, there was something compelling about Meg. She got excellent grades in every class. As a newcomer to speech and debate, she performed a prose and poetry reading about Vietnam with a studied solemnity that won high marks from the judges. I read selections about cute kitties and how we name them. I knew how terrible the pieces were and how ridiculous I sounded, but I didn't care. I just wanted to go to speech tournaments, especially the ones that got me out of school.

'Spill it, Wong,' Meg said in the minibus, giving Laurence a friendly elbow to the ribs. Laurence looked at her for a minute and then shrugged. He told her about his late-night visit from the uncle, and Meg clucked sympathetically.

'I don't care about winning any more,' he told her. 'I don't care, but if I don't win, my uncle gets pissed off, and there's yelling . . . it's not good,' he said.

'Lie to him. Debate, don't debate. Win, don't win. But tell him you won, and he'll probably leave you alone,' Meg advised.

'I've never considered lying,' Laurence said, 'but it makes a lot of sense. Thanks a lot, Meg. Lying! Of course.'

I hung out with Meg and Laurence during speech and debate trips, and spent hours in school vans with the quiz bowl team. No matter how well I got along with my teammates, however, this familiarity never translated into friendship. I never saw them outside school, and none of them ever wanted to sit with me in the cafeteria. I made invitations, but no one ever wanted to come and watch a film at my house. I invited 18 people to my 16th birthday party. No one said yes.

While quiz bowl didn't improve my social life, I still enjoyed the game and relished the opportunity to prove myself. So the following year, I found myself behind the podium being filmed for television. There, I was astonished to learn that Bob apparently wore crotchless leather panties. This information, helpfully carved into the plywood lectern, explained a lot about the man and his penchant for plaid.

The set, a two-tiered platform with lit nameplates and built-in buzzers that looked like doorbells, allowed two teams of four players to face the camera simultaneously. One team sat on folding chairs on a riser at the top of the set, while the other sat below at floor level. Technicians wheeled cameras into position and fitted us with microphones. None of us was ready for a close-up. Acne, braces, cellulite and a wealth of poor fashion choices abounded on both tiers.

Laurence took the seat next to mine and pointed out a pair of Asian students on the other team. 'Look sharp, Rebecca. Yellow peril,' he told me, without a trace of irony. I nodded, game face tightly in place. I used to have a videotape of that appearance. On tape, Laurence looks pale and nervous in a blue blazer and red tie. I wear a sweater in a drab grey green, the exact colour of fermented cat puke.

I can't remember if we won the game. Unlike many of the guys I've played team trivia with over the years, I don't have a stack of notebooks full of meticulously kept quiz bowl records to catalogue my every blown question. I do, however, remember that we won a lot of games that year, and that Bob allegedly loved wearing red lace teddies and patent leather spike heels.

'Way to go, Golden!' I felt a large palm smack the centre of my back. Doug Webber grinned at me. 'Nice work on TV. Go Cougars!' Doug offered his hand for a high five, and I hit it, happy if totally confused by my sudden elevation. One of the cheerleaders even decorated my locker before our second taping. Although I still spent weekends alone watching Woody Allen films on our new VCR, school seemed a little less grim, if only temporarily.

I found the quiz bowl team less than a week after arriving on campus at Boston University. My teammates liked my play but hated me. Their contempt stung but I wasn't really surprised by it. A 29-stone first year who shared her feminist views at the drop of a hat was unlikely to find broad popularity among a group of guys whose hobbies included fantasy baseball and beer.

My university team played in the inaugural Beaver Bonspiel that year. It was at the Massachusetts Institute of Technology, and their rodent mascot (considered nature's engineer) gave the tournament its title. The MIT guys assigned team names to all the competing schools, and got the university copy shop to make a sign for each team to carry. Keeping with the beaver theme, each sign bore the name of a rodent. I handed our 'Hamsters' sign to Jack Shay, a first-year law student who would eventually spend more than a decade picking up degrees at BU. Jack, a tall ex-football player whose hobbies included bottled beer, pitchers of beer and watching BU Terriers hockey, smirked at the red-and-white sign and shook his head. 'At least we're not the Lemmings,' I told him.

We didn't win the tournament. I remember that we won several rounds, lost a whole lot more, and that the weather that weekend was particularly grey and wet. I opted out of the team lunch – no one invited me, anyway – and went to the Coop bookshop. I grabbed a sandwich and hit the Coop's music section where I bought an Elvis Costello CD my friend Max had been pushing.

The biggest collegiate tournament of the year, Penn Bowl, required a six-hour drive in a 15-seater minibus. The entire team would miss every class on Friday (a major sacrifice we of course only undertook for the greater glory of BU) and assemble in the student union to wait for Theo Alexiou, another law student, to show up with our rented transport. Jack always sat in the front passenger seat for the leg room, while tiny, bearded Theo drove, so we ended up referring to them as Mum and Dad. Theo didn't seem to mind the pairing, though he always made a special point of switching radio stations every time Elton John came on.

'You know, dear, we never talk any more,' Theo told Jack, changing lanes suddenly to cut up an old lady in an estate car.

'That's it,' Jack replied, 'separate beds!'

I've been to Philadelphia at least seven times. Since all of these trips involved quiz tournaments, I've never seen the Liberty Bell, eaten a cheese steak or even bought a nice, tasteful vial of souvenir crack. By the time I made my first trip to Penn Bowl in late January during my first year, the guys on the team still hadn't warmed to me, though I'd struck up a friendship with another woman on the team. Audrey, a six-foot-tall Colorado native with short black hair and brown eyes, liked to argue politics with me and never took my tortured liberal act too seriously. As the only women on the team, we usually shared a hotel room on trips, and by the end of the year we were solid pals. Aud walked with me through west Philly on the way to campus from the hotel. As we walked, we giggled our way through the rap theme to Will Smith's old television show *The Fresh Prince of Bel-Air*. It wasn't terribly convincing. At my college fighting weight, I didn't look like I spent a lot of time playing 'B-ball', and I was far from cool. We were always well behind the rest of the team because the extra weight I carried slowed me down considerably and Aud walked slowly so I could keep up with her.

Every group has a goat – a kind of scapegoat everyone talks about when they're out of the room. It's almost unbearably awful to be this person, and to know full well that you are. Every group that included me chose me for that role: my Girl Guide troop, my unit at summer camp, the children's theatre group I joined, the writers' floor in my college dorm and, naturally, the male part of the college quiz team. I say this, but I know it isn't that simple. All the things I tried to do to fit in made me seem even more awkward and ridiculous than if I'd just shut up and kept my head down. I wanted people to like me. I wanted respect and recognition, and I created a bold, obnoxious persona, thinking this would help. I made stupid jokes and tried to insinuate myself into private conversations.

'I don't know why the guys lied,' I wrote in an e-mail to the self-proclaimed official curmudgeon of college bowl, hoping she'd understand. 'If they didn't want me to go to the tournament, they could've just told me.' My BU teammates had attended a pop culture tournament the weekend before. I'd been specifically excluded, though I'd caught on to the plot well ahead of time. My feelings were hurt, and I felt stupid and pathetic. I also felt angry. I'd been on the club's A team for four years. I'd helped the guys achieve whatever success we'd enjoyed as a team, and they still didn't like me.

The curmudgeon, a 39-year-old biology postgraduate student who played on Western Michigan's quiz bowl team, wrote back the next day: 'If they don't like you, they don't know what they're missing. I'd be on a team with you any day.' The curmudgeon, whose real name was Julie Mellinus, first e-mailed me after reading a post I'd made on a college bowl website. After our initial exchange of e-mails, Julie and I wrote to each other frequently. Julie had lived in Boston for ten years, had played in a rock band called Video Free Europe, and moved to Michigan after seeing David Attenborough speak. There and then, she had turned to her husband and told him she wanted to do a PhD in evolutionary biology. Rick shrugged, nodded, and a year later, they moved to Kalamazoo.

Part of the problem between the team and me was that women were a rarity in quiz bowl. Most of the people who played were male, and many had rudimentary social skills. Asperger's syndrome was not uncommon among them. One of the guys even had theories about women and why they wanted to marry 'dicks with wallets'. My feminist sensibilities, very close to the surface when I was 19, were duly offended. I felt the need to speak out, and I did so with all the righteous rage of a younger, fatter Andrea Dworkin. The guys gave me a lot of blank looks.

'What's the hair you've got across your ass?' one asked, scandalising me so thoroughly that I couldn't formulate a reply. I spent a lot of time feeling scandalised by my teammates. Some of it was probably justified, but looking down my nose at them and lecturing them about gender equality never won me any friends among them either. I felt very fortunate to know Julie, if only via e-mail, and when she asked me to join her team for a summer tournament, I leapt at the chance.

A lot of college quiz team players continue playing after they graduate, and a number of open tournaments had sprung up. I'd graduated from BU, and had a long summer at my parents' house in Toledo ahead of me before I was scheduled to start graduate school. Julie had friends on the University of Michigan team, and we met in person for the first time in June at summer practice for a tournament called the Philadelphia Experiment.

'Rebecca? I thought it might be you!' A tiny woman with glasses and short, reddish hair waved to me. I'd never described myself to Julie, nor had I ever sent pictures. My enormousness sometimes shocked new acquaintances, but Julie's open smile and the huge hug she gave me told me I'd found a friend. When Julie hugged me, I felt relief, surprise and gratitude. She knew I was fat and she didn't care. I hoped I could be as good a friend to her as she'd been to me simply by hugging me in public. As we walked into the practice room together, I had to choke back tears. I shook it off, focusing on the practice, on ringing in and answering questions.

Ten years later, as I prepared for gastric bypass surgery, Julie and I set out for another masters' tournament together. Since the summer tournament in Philly (in which we'd done fairly badly), Julie and I had become closer friends. When my mother made me crazy, I could always get in my million-year-old Lincoln Continental and drive three hours to her house in

Kalamazoo. I'd make a pot of soup, we'd have drinks, and things always seemed a little easier. The day in 2001 when terrorists attacked the Twin Towers and the Pentagon, I drove to Kalamazoo. Julie, Rick and I passed around a bottle of coconut rum. The next morning, Rick found out that one of his medical school friends had died aboard the Pentagon plane. Over the years I've spent a lot of time at Julie's house. I feel safe there on her 20-year-old sofa, surrounded by plastic insects and the cheerful clutter of people who don't 'get' decorating.

Julie and I put a team together for the pop culture tournament that week before my surgery. We'd come in second at the event the year before and now we wanted the coveted trophy. The two of us, buoyed up on coffee, adrenaline and whatever mimics the spirit of athletic competition in ageing trivia geeks, were willing to drive five hundred miles to get it.

In the world of team trivia, questions about popular culture are referred to as 'trash' because of their lack of serious academic weight. After college, I'd helped start a business with a bunch of other quiz bowlers: we wrote question sets and ran tournaments, all of them centred on pop culture. The guys in charge of our little group created the acronym 'Testing Recall About Strange Happenings' (TRASH) for our new (no-money-making) venture.

Long before TRASH arrived on the scene, though, Charlie Steinhice, a tall, dark Mormon convert (and diehard Liberal Democrat), started running an annual pop culture tournament. Trashmasters became Charlie's *raison d'être*. Winners at this Chattanooga tournament traditionally received a treasure trove of silly prizes along with a prized brand-new toilet seat. And I wanted it. Not that I could really do that on my own. I was a good player (a quiz team guy would no doubt chime in here to add 'for a girl'), but solidly middle of the pack in terms of skill with the buzzer; Julie played at about the same level. Our teammates, James Quintong or JQ (sports guru) and James Dinan or JD (awesome trash generalist), would do the heavy lifting.

The four of us comprised a team I'd named 'Duggar Vasectomy Fund'. Funny team names are a tradition at Trashmasters, and I took my inspiration from a cable documentary I'd seen about the Duggar family and their huge brood of children. When we formed the team in December 2005, the Duggars had just welcomed baby number 16. Driving around downtown Chattanooga on our way to the tournament, Julie and I naturally ended up discussing the Duggars' matching gingham dresses and their dubious decision to leave family planning to a higher power. Julie couldn't believe that the Duggars had 16 children, let alone 16 children whose names each began with the letter J.

'We should send them a do-it-yourself home vasectomy kit if we win,' I told her.

'What's in a do-it-yourself home vasectomy kit?' Julie asked, signalling for a turn.

'A bottle of Jack Daniel's and a claw hammer,' I replied. Julie had trouble steering for a minute or so after that. She convulsed with laughter, probably at the mental image of Mrs Jim Bob whacking her husband in the balls, and narrowly avoided the SUV stopped at the lights in front of us.

'Remember Charlie's rules,' our genial quiz master said at the tournament's registration meeting the next morning. 'Winning beats losing, losing beats getting stomped, and getting stomped beats not playing.' Most of the players knew this line so well, we could (and usually did) finish it along with Charlie before heading to the university classrooms where we'd play the day's first rounds.

Charlie went out of his way to accommodate me that year. Despite losing 3 stone through near constant exercise and carefully keeping a food journal in the six months preceding surgery, I still weighed 38 stone. Charlie made sure all my games were on the first floor and that my team never had to switch buildings between rounds.

Carrying 29 extra stone – up stairs, up hills, even while walking through indoor hallways – exacts a toll on the body. My knees and feet had ached constantly. By the end of a day of sitting and answering trivia questions, I usually felt such bone-deep tiredness that I would have curled up on the floor to rest between the last two games if I'd actually been able to get up again. I felt less of this tiredness that year. I felt better than I had in years; the exercise helped my stamina, and I tired less easily than I had just a year before. But I also got a boost from the good company of my fellow trivia geeks and the fact that my team won every single game.

As we made our way to the room for our final round, I noticed several of my former BU teammates, including Jack and Theo, filing into the room ahead of us. They still played together, always giving their Trashmasters team a name that inserted the word 'gerbil' into a current film title, such as 'A Gerbil Runs through It', 'The Gerbil Reloaded' and 'Good Night and Good Gerbil'. That year, The Thin Red Gerbil had lost one game, and so had Soul Truck, the team we were about to play. If we won the round, we would win the tournament. If we lost, Soul Truck would have a better record than we did, and that would force a playoff among the three teams. My ex-teammates hadn't come to cheer me on, but to check out the competition.

The round didn't start well for us. I could go into excruciating detail (without a doubt, one of the guys has detailed records in a spiral notebook somewhere), but I don't remember the exact score. I know that Duggar Vasectomy Fund trailed significantly at the halfway stage, and that every correct answer I gave would count. With JQ and JD leading, the team mounted a comeback. The guys answered three or four questions in a row, naming long-forgotten (by me, anyway) football players, dead rappers and films starring Jim Carrey. After the nineteenth question of the 20-question round, we trailed the other team by ten points, the margin of a single starter question. If we got the last one, and scored any points at all on the bonus question, we'd win the round. If Soul Truck answered correctly, we'd lose.

The moderator began reading a list of actors, starting with obscure character types before naming more notable film stars. When he said 'David Warner', I knew. I hit my buzzer, and all eyes were on me. 'Jack the Ripper?' I said, a question and an answer all at once.

'Ten points,' the moderator said. 'Bonus. For five points each, name the Defence against the Dark Arts instructors from all six of JK Rowling's Harry Potter books.'

Julie and I actually said 'Yes!' in triumphant unison before exchanging bruising high fives. We'd both read the Potter books, and we knew we'd just won the game. We named the relevant wizards (and witch), and that decided it. We'd run the board at Trashmasters, winning not just that game, but the whole tournament. My old teammates watched all of this, probably amazed that I'd won the game. None of them congratulated me, but I didn't need their approval. I'd had my moment in the sun, and Julie went home with a brand-new SpongeBob SquarePants toilet seat.

As the medical team wheeled me into the operating theatre a week later, I thought about the tournament and my quiz team friends, especially Julie who, with Rick, had also helped me during a health crisis the year before. I counted backwards from one hundred at the anaesthetist's request, certain that I'd live to play another Trashmasters. As I drifted off, I thought of my friends and teammates who were counting on my survival; of my mother and sister who were waiting in the recovery room. I felt loved, and also like a winner for the first time in my life. I even thought about Johnny, one of our old tenants, and the advice he'd given me during the time he'd lived in our basement and become a sort of older brother. I thought about all these people, and I knew I would live – knew I desperately wanted to live – because of all the things I still wanted to do.

9

YOU'LL FIND IT WHEN IT SMELLS

Ignacio moved in the day we met. I couldn't resist. With his dark good looks and limited knowledge of the English language, he seemed like the perfect man for me. He'd just turned 21, and the 13-year age difference had the added allure of a good scandal in our uptight little suburb. Given the fact I was about eight years old at the time, it would have caused a scandal pretty much anywhere.

My mother met me at the babysitter's house one day, and Ignacio was waiting for us in the front seat of her car. Mum introduced us as I climbed into the back seat. 'This is my daughter, Rebecca,' she said. 'Ignacio's going to be living in the basement for a while,' she told me, speeding up to make the lights.

'Hola, señorita,' Ignacio said, turning to face me over the seat back. He smiled brightly, clearly unaware of the kind of household that awaited him. I had no idea what he'd said to me, but I didn't care. I already had a mad crush on him, but I kept my feelings deeply hidden. Ignacio had huge brown eyes, like the round bottoms of Hershey's kisses. He wore his black hair in a cute, boy band-esque mullet. I wondered what our babies would look like. Then I wondered what we'd have to do to make the babies, and decided that kissing might be involved.

My parents, ever on the lookout for ways to ease the financial burden of their enormous suburban mortgage, had decided to rent the basement out to college students. For two hundred dollars a month, the new boarder would have a large bedroom and the use of our kitchen. My mother threw in dinners with the family as a special bonus, and Ignacio learned to appreciate fish sticks and leftovers like a real American.

Ignacio didn't last long. Perhaps my constant staring disconcerted him. The basement lay fallow for a time, and I held a sleepover party there for my ninth birthday. Nancy, a college friend of my mother's, brought her twin daughters, Amie and Aziza. Nancy had married a minor member of the royal family of one of the Arab emirates. Her daughters were my age, and couldn't get enough of the one thing billions of dollars of oil money wouldn't buy them in their Muslim homeland: crisp, smoky, forbidden, delicious bacon. We took them to the Original Pancake House and they each ordered eight slices of thick-cut bacon and nothing else. The twins and a few lukewarm friends from school attended my birthday, and we danced to Michael Jackson on the radio.

'Dance with me, Becky!' Aziza demanded. I spun in circles, shaking my hips and waving my arms. Amie joined us and we twirled, bare feet gliding easily on the soft, leopard-spotted carpet. Mum and Nancy came downstairs with a bowl of popcorn and a jug of lemonade and returned a few minutes later with my father's turntable and a stack of old records Mum had saved from her days of studying Arabic and dating exotic men.

'I have a special treat for you girls,' Mum said, flipping over one of the albums with a flourish. 'I've got Fairouz!' Aziza and Amie shrieked and clapped their hands. I looked at my American school friends and shrugged. Mom put on the record and the room filled with a honey-sweet soprano. I had no idea what Fairouz was singing about, but the languid, sinuous flow of the music enchanted me. Soon, all of us were dancing, trying to imitate harem dancers from old films we'd seen on television.

'That's not how you do it,' Mum said. 'Like this – you need more hip action.' I watched, awestruck, as my mother twisted from side to side, throwing out her left hip, then her right, stomping her feet and turning her upraised arms gracefully to the music. The other girls imitated Mum, forming a semicircle around her while Nancy stood by the stairs and clapped along with Fairouz's singing. When Amie and Aziza left the country, I cried for days. Mum never brought out the Fairouz album again, and we never danced together after that.

The rec room's fallow period ended when Taco moved in. He arrived from Venezuela speaking two words of English ('hello' and 'toilet'). A shy, chubby boy, Taco (whose real name was Tomas) came along with my parents when they rescued me from Girl Guide camp. I wanted nothing more than to get the hell out of the woods with all their stupid nature and boring trees and return to civilisation. I craved air conditioning and cable television the way some people crave black tar heroin. I'd hiked and eaten things cooked with actual fire. I'd made crafts out of green twigs and handled live snakes. After a week I'd had enough. I wanted cartoons, a McDonald's happy meal and clean sheets.

When my parents finally arrived, I was actually glad to see both of them. Mum and Dad helped me drag my luggage through the woods to the camp car park. A stocky teenager with skin the exact colour of cinnamon toast sat in the back seat of the Chevy thumbing through a Spanish/English dictionary.

'Who's that weird guy in our car?' I asked my mother.

'Shhh! He'll hear you. That's Taco. He rented the basement. And he's not weird . . . that I know of . . . just Venezuelan,' Mum told me. She threw my suitcase in the boot of the car while my father grabbed a quick smoke. We all got in, and Taco stared at me, mouth slightly ajar. He smiled then, and stuck out his hand for me to shake. 'Hello, toilet!' he said, grinning broadly.

'You can call me Rebecca,' I told him, extending my hand in return.

'Eh?' he said, frowning. 'No, uh, unnerstan'.' He caught Mum's eye in the rearview mirror. 'Toilet?' he repeated.

'Yes, Taco, we'll stop for toilet soon,' she said. Taco seemed to get the gist of what she'd said and relaxed against the black vinyl seat. We stopped at a restaurant, where I happily reacquainted myself with Coca-Cola. Taco ate his burger quickly, taking large bites. He kept the chewing to a bare minimum, pausing occasionally to throw in a fry or two. Taco obviously enjoyed his food, not to mention a thick wedge of apple pie with ice cream, two or three Cokes and a chocolate shake for the road and was initially thrilled by the idea of dining with us *en famille*. He soon took issue with the food Mum served at home, though.

'No steak?' he asked after a couple of weeks with us. A steady diet of cable television and long, confusing conversations with my parents had helped with his language skills. 'Ebry night, at home, ees steak,' he explained.

'That's nice,' Mum said. 'Here, you eat what I make. It's that or you can cook for yourself,' she added, smiling.

'Qué?' Taco said.

'No steak. Not every night. Leftovers tonight. Or you use that . . .' Mum pointed to the stove. 'Use that, make steak. Buy it at the grocery.' She grabbed a supermarket leaflet off the fridge and waved it at him.

'Steak from here,' Mum shook the flyer. 'You,' she pointed at Taco, 'cook there,' she pointed at the stove again.

'Hokay, Mother. I eat leftover,' Taco said. Taco had taken to calling my parents 'Mother' and 'Father'. As far as I was concerned, he was welcome to them. I still hadn't forgiven them for sending me to the camp in the first place.

Taco bought a set of weights and spent hours every day pumping iron in the basement. His face lost its round sweetness, and he became more conventionally handsome in a sharp-boned, dangerous sort of way.

Taco's English pronunciation often left a lot to be desired. 'I wan' go to see the bitch,' he told my mother. 'I miss the bitch. I wan' roll all over the bitch.' Taco helped himself to a huge glass of milk from the fridge while my mother mulled this over.

'I see. What will you do with this bitch?' Mum asked. I sat at the kitchen table, ostensibly doing my maths homework. While I couldn't have cared less about how fast two trains would go while passing each other on the way to Des Moines and Albany, I was dying to know about the mysterious bitch. I wondered if Mum would explain to Taco why we don't use that word in company, just as she'd told me not to use her favourite word ('fuck') at school.

'What I do?' Taco thought for a moment. 'I swim. I lay in sun. I roll in san'. I try maybe surf.' He chugged the milk remaining in his tumbler and started to pour another large glass.

'Stop right there. Half a glass. I'm going to need some of that for coffee in the morning,' Mum commanded. 'Okay. So you want to go to the beach, right?' she added, putting the milk back in the fridge.

'Si. The bitch. Where you think I go?' Taco asked, puzzled.

'Oh, I knew what you meant,' Mum lied reassuringly. 'So which beach will you go to?'

'I drive to Florida with my friends Eduardo and Carlos. We drive, we go to the bitch, we come back,' Taco explained. 'We go for the weekend.'

Mum didn't try to dissuade him. Miami is a good 24-hour drive from Toledo, but this exhausting itinerary was a major improvement over Taco's previous travel idea. A couple of weeks before the bitch talk, Taco had been to a local ski shop and bought a thousand dollars' worth of equipment. 'I drive to Alaska for ski. I do it in one weekend,' Taco told us. It took both of my parents several hours, an illustrated road atlas and a phone call to the university geography department to persuade Taco of the impracticality of driving six thousand miles in a weekend. He returned the ski stuff and settled instead on his new plan to roll on the bitch.

Taco had one dream in life, and it had nothing to do with his studies. After his muscles developed and actual three-dimensional women became interested in him, attending class fell to the bottom of his list of priorities. Taco plastered the basement with posters. Though some were of semi-nude blonde women with vapid, pouty mouths, the vast majority depicted fine German cars. 'My papa, he is buying me a porch,' Taco told me. 'You be good girl, maybe one day your papa buy you porch, too.' He gestured at the poster of a glistening ruby red 936 Turbo.

'Oh, a Porsche?' I said. 'Yeah, I don't think so. But it's cool that your dad wants to get one for you,' I added, trying to keep my eyes off the naked woman on the coffee table; Taco sometimes left *Hustler* open so he wouldn't lose his place.

Taco felt enormous gratitude towards his papa for the promised sports car. He began collecting bottles of wine as a gift for his father. He'd find two or three interesting vintages a week, storing the bottles on top of the faux-stone bar in the basement. The clammy, semi-humid room apparently provided an ideal climate for the very best in Ohio and Michigan varietals.

Taco's collection would eventually number a good hundred bottles of wine, some of it the cheap local stuff, some of it very good and very expensive. But, by the time he'd put the finishing touches to his father's gift, tragic news arrived from South America: Taco's father had received a copy of his son's latest report card and decided not to buy the Porsche. The dream was over. Taco cursed his father and retaliated the only way he knew how (well, the only way that wouldn't result in him being dropped from Papa's will). Taco drank the entire wine collection in a single week.

My bedroom was on the second floor of our house and had a little flap cut into one wall. This flap gave access to a laundry chute to the basement. We'd throw our dirty clothes down the chute, and then retrieve them from a wooden collection box next to the washing machine. At the end of Taco's week of wine un-collecting, I woke at around 3am to a very strange smell from the chute. I couldn't quite identify the odour, but it smelled like the oven after cake batter had been spilled inside it.

'Mum? Wake up. There's a weird smell from the basement.' My mother moaned and tried to roll away from me. 'Mum! Wake up! I think something's burning.' This got her attention. She leaped from the bed and ran to my room. After a quick sniff of the laundry chute, she grabbed my father and the two of them ran downstairs.

Taco had decided he needed mood lighting for his final wine binge. The polyester scarf he'd draped over a table lamp was smouldering when my parents arrived on the scene. Dad took care of the fire, and Mum screamed at Taco, who lay on his bed in a stupor brought on by two whole bottles of syrupy Ohio wine. He moaned apologies, but my mother had had it. She gave him notice, and he moved out a few weeks later.

When Taco moved out, my sister cried for a week. Andrea loved Taco. He had carried her on his shoulders and taken pictures of her to send back to his parents in South America. He kept one of these pictures in a silver frame on the dry bar. In this snapshot, my sister wears a fedora and a white nightshirt. At three, her face still has the round softness of babyhood. Her brown eyes, huge and luminous in the pale moon of her face, follow you from the frame. She holds an unlit pipe in her unsmiling mouth.

By the time I came home from college one summer, Andrea had long since grown out of liking the tenants. She was 15, and resented having to explain the presence of various foreigners to her school friends. Neither of us had jobs that summer. Bored senseless, we took to snooping. Andrea beckoned me into Desai's room one day. Desai came from Malaysia with a huge stash of barely legal schoolgirl porn and a dream: working towards his MBA and his goal of running his father's business (into the ground). He rarely spent time in the house, practically living at the university library where he met with his group project teams.

'Okay, so I found a totally skeezy porno mag,' Andrea told me as she flopped onto Desai's bed. I sat beside her.

'So what's new there? You know how much the guy loves topless Japanese girls in kilts,' I said.

Andrea leaned over the edge of the bed, pausing in irritation to flip her waist-length princess hair out of her field of vision. When she sat up, she held a black plastic grid full of shiny brass bullets. 'I don't know where he keeps the gun,' Andrea said. 'Should we tell Mum?' My sister didn't seem at all perturbed by this. She looked at me with a sort of practised nonchalance, an expression she perfected during her years of teenage non-rebellion. Andrea never smoked, drank or slept around. She got perfect grades. But she could give a dirty look that would fill you with shame, even if you hadn't actually done anything wrong.

'If we tell her, we have to admit to going through his stuff. You want to take the hit for that?' I asked. 'Besides, you didn't find a gun or anything. What's he going to do, throw the bullets at us?'

'Good point,' she said. 'I'm not saying anything. He's moving out next month anyway. He probably won't kill us in our sleep between now and then. Not with exams to study for, at least.'

Andrea replaced the bullets and we stayed out of Desai's room. I'm pretty sure he never shot anyone, but it's not like I kept him on my Christmas card list after he moved. Part of renting to students is that they become strangers again the minute they move out. We lived with these people, some of them for years, and never heard from any of them once they left.

Our final tenant in the suburban dream house was Shin, a college student who'd served in China's national army. Shin never drank and had no visible porn. He never left his room. Only the smells of the meat he stored in the cupboard and of burning rice from his hot plate hinted at his presence in the house.

My father died shortly before Shin moved in. I was 24, had lost a copy-editing job in Illinois and had moved in with my mother and Andrea while I looked for work in Toledo. Winter meant Christmas and my father's birthday. Mum needed to get away from all the inconvenient memories and the three of us went on a cruise. While my sister and I lay on deck chairs watching Cuba slide by, Andrea's cat Maya was hard at work at home. Shin let the cat play in the garage periodically while we were gone, because otherwise she'd sit by the garage door and miaow for hours. We returned home to the news that Maya had slaughtered a vole, the only small rodent foolhardy enough to find its way into our garage, and had brought the carcass to Shin for his approval.

'What did you do with it?' Mum asked. She'd just parked her luggage in the hallway and had planned on taking a hot shower to recover from our long and uncomfortable flight home and the three-hour drive from the airport in the snow. I'd taken up half of some stranger's plane seat, and the woman had expressed her displeasure by elbowing me hard in the ribs every five minutes or so. Shin didn't even say hello, nor did he help with a single bag.

'Kitty kill rodent,' he repeated, utterly expressionless.

'What did you do with it?' Mum asked again. 'You know, cats hide their kills. If Maya brings you something . . . er, dead . . . you need to throw it out right away,' she explained calmly.

'You'll find it when it smells,' Shin said, turning on his heels and going straight to his room to cook some cupboard-aged meat.

Mum found the vole before it started to smell. She picked up a brown leather shoe the next morning and noticed its unusually heavy weight. Peering inside, she found the freshly decapitated gift Maya had left especially for her.

Shin's brusque manner and mispronunciation of some English words caused other problems. 'Why? Why they kick me out of Taco Bell?' he asked me. Shin had asked the counter girl at the local Mexican franchise for a fork. Not an unreasonable request. Except that his accent made it sound like he'd asked for a fuck, and that's not something on the menu at any Taco Bell I've ever visited.

The day we met, Shin had asked me a number of uncomfortable questions, and I had never really warmed to him after that. 'Why you so fat?' he asked, staring openly at my body. My mother changed the subject and I quickly excused myself from the room.

At 24, I never talked about my weight to anyone. Not my sister, whom I'd grown up with. Not my college roommate, who'd been one of my best friends for more than five years. I never even talked about weight with my grandmother, who as a registered nurse might actually have had decent advice for me. Bringing up this subject in such a blunt way had poisoned any goodwill I might have had for Shin, and his poor dead animal handling skills killed the rest. I hoped he asked for fucks all over town, primarily from burly rednecks with long criminal records.

Not all of the tenants were foreign. One of them, a postgraduate student in chemistry, came from the exotic land of Iowa. Johnny moved in the year I turned 13 and we bonded right away. Despite the age difference (he was 24), we shared a love of snarky humour and a disdain for my parents. I rolled my eyes at every lame, ingratiating comment Mum made over dinner during Johnny's first night in the house. My parents didn't notice but Johnny caught my eye and smirked.

The padlock on the fridge was one of the first things that brought us together. After my parents went upstairs to watch television in bed (8pm on the dot every night), Johnny would remove the lock to make a late dinner or grab a snack. Aside from that first family dinner, Johnny preferred to cook for himself. I'd snatch the lock, one of the first acts of my nascent teenage rebellion, and he'd neglect to ask for it back.

Johnny became a surrogate older brother. I'd sit on the basement stairs and talk to him about my stupid teenage problems, and he'd offer obnoxious advice. At 15, I begged my mother to get me tickets to see Sting. The ex-Police front man had just put out *Nothing Like the Sun*, which I bought in vinyl and played so many times that I started to think I, too, might be an Englishman in New York. Mum gave in after two solid weeks of whining, begging and insincere promises to clean my room and raise my maths grade. This left me with a dilemma: who could I take? Mum didn't feel like sitting through the concert. She'd heard enough Sting coming from my bedroom record player to last her several lifetimes. She told me to find a friend, and she'd drop us at the concert and pick us up afterwards. I made some phone calls.

'Laurence? It's Rebecca from quiz bowl,' I said. I'd never called Laurence Wong before, and my nervousness was obvious.

'Yes?' he said. Laurence wasn't going to make this easy.

'Sting is coming to Detroit. You told me once that you like him,' I said.

'And?' Laurence said.

'IJustThoughtYou'dLikeToKnowGoodbye,' I said, spitting it out in record time and slamming down the phone. I tried a girl from my English class, and gave up after she told me she had a wedding to go to. I hadn't actually told her when the concert was. I told Mum she'd have to go with me. Mum mulled it over for a couple of days and then recruited Johnny.

We had a great time at the concert. Despite my mother's terrible driving directions, we made it on time and quickly found our seats in the nosebleed section. The seat immediately next to us stood behind an enormous red-painted column. 'I wonder what they charge for that one?' Johnny joked.

Just a year later, I found myself struggling harder at school than ever before. I took honours courses whenever I could, as kids in those classes were too busy trying to get into Harvard to pay me any unwanted attention. My lack of maths ability, however, forced me into the regular, non-honours geometry class with all the burnouts, losers and junior sociopaths.

Ed Ciali, the middle child of a huge pack of trailer dwellers who attended school in my district, sat immediately in front of me. 'Hey, fat bitch, what up?' he'd ask at least once a lesson. My parents and teachers always told me to ignore guys like Ed, and I did, but ignoring him only made him more determined to get my attention. After weeks of grabbing my notebook and spitting into it, calling me whatever names his limited vocabulary permitted and knocking my pencil out of my hand so he could comment on the size of my rear when I bent to pick it up, Ed decided to up the ante. 'If I pricked her, do you think gravy would come out?' he asked one of his pals in the class. 'Let's find out!' His hand moved, hard and fast, jabbing a ballpoint pen into my arm. The wound was small and hardly bled. I blinked back tears and tried to move away from him but the one-piece desk/chair combination was tight around my midsection, and the wall was directly behind me. I couldn't escape. I pushed my chair against the wall, but Ed kept touching me. His hands slapped my sides. I closed my eyes and took deep breaths through my nose as fingers tapped against the skin on my cheeks and forehead.

The bell rang, and I stayed in my seat for a couple of minutes before my maths teacher told me to move along to my next class. I spent the next hour, the last period of the day, in French class with Madame Mininger. I couldn't really focus on the lesson. I listened to Madame as she conjugated irregular verbs. The words she spoke in her Midwestern American French accent seemed to hang in the air like the bright bubbles in my parents' holiday champagne.

At home that night, I talked to Johnny as he stood in the

kitchen, waiting for a potato to bake in the microwave. 'It's all too hard. The kids at school hate me. My dad . . .' I couldn't finish that thought, not then. 'It's just all so bad. I don't want to do it any more. I don't want to live with it.' I tried not to cry but failed. I'd read a book once about a little girl who cried without making any noise. I envied her the skill.

I didn't tell Johnny about Ed stabbing me. For all he knew, I was crying over typical school bullshit. 'Whatever you do, wait on it,' he said. 'There are so many things you haven't done, things that are great. Going away to college – far away – is one thing,' he said. 'If you ever get a chance to swim in the ocean, that's good, too. Oh, and sex. Sex is great. You should definitely do that before you kill yourself.' The microwave timer went off. Johnny collected his potato and went downstairs to eat in his room. I shouldn't have felt any better after that conversation. Nothing Johnny said was especially kind or comforting. Still, things seemed a little less desperate. I felt like I had a friend.

Johnny's advice about college stuck with me long after he moved out. As a high school senior, I filled out applications to local colleges in pencil, hoping they'd reject me. I had to fight with my parents for months before they even began to consider more distant choices. I had to lie, wheedle, pout, scream and cry, but my parents finally agreed to let me go to college in Boston. Despite the huge student debt load that resulted, I never regretted that choice. Whenever my father yelled at me the summer after high school graduation, I closed my eyes and thought about New England. I didn't stop there. I imagined all the places I'd travel to one day – Europe, South America, Australia. My father couldn't touch me any more. Whenever he tried, I closed my eyes and planned out my escape.

Johnny moved out during my junior year of high school, and I worked hard at completing the list he'd given me. I took suicide off the table, and never seriously considered it again, not even when I weighed nearly 43 stone. The ocean beckoned and I wanted to travel and have a whole lot of sex, some of the thoughts that came back to me as I thought on Johnny as the anaesthetic took hold for my surgery. I learnt from the other lodgers too. Taco taught me that the best revenge sometimes happens at a great remove from the people who've hurt us, and need not be anything they even know about. Shin taught me not to proposition strangers at fast food restaurants.

Success and happiness are like the dead vole. You'll find them if you're meant to, and hopefully not because of the stench.

10

FOKKERS ON THE RADIO

I only saw the one kangaroo. It paused at the edge of the forest, and then veered away towards the trees as the train passed by. We travelled past banana plantations, the trees heavy with ripening fruit. I could barely make out spiky jade treetops above a thick haze of fog, but the fog burned away slowly as we made our way north from Sydney. The things I saw through my window – the trees, a river, even that shy kangaroo – had an odd grey tone in the pale morning light.

The train moved at a leisurely pace, snaking through jungle and over bridges as we moved up the coast. My seatmate had moved as soon as we left the station. 'You'll want the space to yourself, I expect,' he said, his tone pleasant and matter-of-fact. The carriage had plenty of free seats, and he might have moved even if a thin girl had had the seat next to his. I nodded and looked away, taking in the view of the strange country I'd spent months planning to visit. Our little house in Glebe, a southwestern suburb of Sydney, had become familiar. Even the 20-foot palms lining the road I took to class every day had begun to seem commonplace. With its little fruit shops and the high density of college students on the streets, Glebe could easily have been a neighbourhood in Boston and I craved somewhere a little more exotic. I didn't want to make this train trip to Byron Bay alone, but I was unwilling to forego the holiday just because I didn't have any friends.

Strictly speaking, this wasn't entirely true. I had my house-mate, a sweetly incorrigible Belgian trust fund kid named Jean-Claude, but he moved in an entirely different social universe than I did, and spent the break in Western Australia, cheating on his Sydneysider boyfriend with an American sailor he met on the beach. Our other housemates, a Disney-worshipping Jehovah's Witness and a redheaded guy from New York, annoyed me and I felt thrilled to be away from them for a week. I felt little affinity for the other American students in my programme. They came to Sydney for the beaches, the freely flowing beer and to have record-setting amounts of sex with each other and with any local foolish enough to spin the STD roulette wheel. I came for no better reason than that I wanted to say I'd gone. Or, rather, to prove to myself that I could go halfway across the world, that the weight couldn't stop me.

When I'd chosen to attend college in Boston, I'd made the same sort of statement. Moving to a new city a thousand miles from home had frightened and exhilarated me, but I'd got the hang of it with the help of some new college friends. During my first year at BU, I took an analytical history class. The class of ten students sat grouped around an oak library table in a tiny turreted room. The history building was once a private residence, and I imagined that our classroom, with its tall window overlooking the Charles River, once served as some spoiled rich girl's bedroom.

The guy sitting next to me looked a little like John Lennon. He wore round granny glasses and had sideburns, like Lennon in the late sixties after he started letting people take naked pictures of him. After class, he introduced himself to me as Max, and he walked with me towards my dorm before peeling off towards his flat. That night, he called about the reading assignment and we stayed on the phone for eight hours. Max and I talked every night after that. He had a girlfriend, a senior named Darcy he'd gone to high school with. Not that I considered this a warning for me. I never thought of Max as a romantic prospect. I never thought of myself as attractive enough to draw that kind of attention, and I took it for granted that men wouldn't look at me as anything other than a friend.

Max had a great sense of humour and could do impressions. 'Rebecca, I can't believe that Landes guy. He kept asking me "Didju do the reading assignment . . . Did-*Jew* . . . ". I think he's an anti-Semite,' Max said, his Woody Allen spot-on.

'Firstly, great Woody,' I told him. 'Secondly, Professor Landes is Jewish, so I don't think he meant anything by it.' I lay on my back in the hallway outside my dorm room. It was 2 o'clock in the morning. Max had called around 11, we hadn't run out of important things to discuss and I didn't want to wake my roommate. In addition to the impressions and his views on our homework, Max had a near encyclopaedic knowledge of twentieth century literature and all kinds of music. When I knew him, he was in his Elvis Costello phase. He also spent most of that winter rereading all of William Faulkner and Vladimir Nabokov.

I also made friends with another student in that class. Leigh Anne sat across the table from me. Her wire-rimmed glasses were perched at the end of her tiny button nose; she wore her long hair in a thin bun at the top of her head and scribbled furiously whenever Professor Landes opened his mouth. Her analyses of the readings always made perfect sense. She could distil the heart of meaning from even the densest history tome in just a few words.

Leigh Anne walked home with me after class one day. She wore a green knitted hat with a large pom-pom on the top. We walked down the broad pavements, carefully avoiding the slick piles of yellow leaves dotting the path. Leigh Anne shivered and pulled her coat a bit tighter. 'It's so cold here,' she said. 'I can't wait to get back to Pensacola for Christmas.'

'It's only in the forties,' I replied, kicking some leaves out of our way. 'It's not cold – it's brisk. You Floridians are such winter wimps. It won't really be cold till at least the end of November,' I said, mostly to the pom-pom. At five foot seven, I towered over Leigh Anne. We walked slowly for another few minutes. Leigh Anne picked up the thread of conversation when she noticed I was a bit winded, a kindness I really appreciated. After the isolation I'd felt in high school, having friends who tried to help me with my weight-related difficulties rather than shunning me for them was a relief. We said goodbye in front of her dorm, and I walked to my own feeling good about history, college and my new friends.

After sharing a dorm room with Leigh Anne in my second year, I decided to save some money by moving off campus. Leigh Anne couldn't be persuaded to make the move with me. She liked not having to cook or do a lot of cleaning, and the dorm suited her fine. By the autumn, I'd moved into a ramshackle flat in Allston-Brighton, a neighbourhood in the heart of Boston's student ghetto. I'd found the building after an exhausting summer-long search. Unable to afford Boston's pricey rental market as a lone tenant, I scoured the *Boston Phoenix* for roommate ads, made appointments, and spent the better part of two months looking at rooms no one would rent to me. I felt I made a good impression, despite my size and the worn, ripped clothing I often wore. I didn't have money for clothes that fitted me – and fat clothes are extremely expensive – and had to make do with what I had. I mended my skirts, my jeans, my underwear – I even mended my ugly bathing suit, which didn't actually fit and required the addition of a T-shirt to hide the fact that the straps and top strained against my stomach, revealing half my torso and creating cleavage Anna Nicole Smith would have found indecent.

One appointment took me so far away from campus, I thought about backing out after the second bus transfer. I fell getting off the bus and my knees bled as I struggled back to my feet. A pack of teenagers wearing baggy shorts belted across their hips so as to reveal the tops of their underwear screamed with laughter at the sight of me. I walked half a mile to the house and rang the bell, trying to smile as the door opened. The tour lasted about five minutes. After another hour of walking and buses, I dragged myself across the threshold of the flat I was temporarily subletting and collapsed on my bed. I called Max, hoping he'd offer a little sympathy.

'Hello,' Max answered on the first ring.

'Hey, Max, how's it going? Any luck with the job search?' Max had graduated in May, but a history degree has little practical application, and he'd been trying to avoid temp work for the last six weeks.

'Christ, Rebecca, you know it doesn't work that way. You think they just hire you at an interview? Give me a break.' Max seemed more bored with me than angry. I wondered if I'd fallen out of his personal top ten, and, if so, why. Max had to quantify everything. He had lists of his top ten favourite songs, books, films – everything really. He had two friends in the world apart from me: his girlfriend, Darcy, and his best friend Harrison. In Max's friend top ten (well, top three) Darcy was first and Harrison second. Max kindly informed me that I was number three, but a solid number three – like *Abbey Road* to Darcy's *Hard Day's Night* and Harrison's *Rubber Soul*.

He seemed to have changed since moving in with his girl-friend during the spring term, and he grew more and more impatient with me that summer. I'd call him, and he'd give one-word responses to my questions. I tried harder, offering invitations to dinner at my place for him and Darcy. I could cook – people always liked that about me – but Max made excuses. The day I fell off the bus I called for the last time.

'Leigh Anne will be back in a couple of weeks,' I said, avoiding the subject of work and my horrible rooming search for the moment. 'We should all get together and see a film or something.'

'Yeah, well, I don't think so. I've graduated, and she's what – a senior? I can't be bothered with undergrads any more,' he said coldly. I was a year behind Leigh Anne at college; I took the hint and ended the call. I'd hung up without the sympathy I craved and went back to the classifieds. I may have lost my friend but I still had to find a place to live for the autumn term.

Potential roommates usually did some version of a double take when they met me. Opening your door and finding 29 stone of brightly eager college girl probably came as something of a shock. I applied for rooms in elegantly renovated triple-deckers, cockroach-infested artists' colonies and in detached quasi-suburban ranch houses. None of the people with rooms to let – not a single person from this wide spectrum of humanity I tried so hard to sell myself to – ever called me back.

Some of these people frightened me just a bit, too. In August, with my sublet about to expire, I scheduled an appointment to look at a room on the third floor of a converted whaling cottage in Allston. Arriving at the flat after a long walk from the tram stop, my round, flushed face bore a shiny glaze of sweat. I knocked on the purple front door, and was greeted by a thin, colourless person of indeterminate gender.

'Are you Rebecca?' The voice, a high-pitched soprano, told me I was probably dealing with a woman. A woman with a short, chartreuse Mohican who'd recently shaved off one of her eyebrows. She wore overalls and a black tank top; her bare arms were roped with a densely compact layer of muscle. Ronald Reagan smiled at me from her right bicep, his vintage Waffen SS uniform an odd counterpoint to his ocean wave of dyed black hair. Despite the stifling wet heat that day, my potential housemate wore combat boots and had a hand-knitted orange wool scarf wrapped around her neck.

An odour combining all the smoky, floral notes of rotten potatoes with the sharp, ammonia undertone of cat urine oozed out of the flat. I repressed the urge to gag, and thought fast. 'Have you ever read the Book of Mormon?' I asked. 'It's another, um, chapter thingy in the Bible.' I smiled as hard as I could, thinking it'd make me seem more holy. Scarf Lady slammed the door in my face, giving me the easy way out I wanted. Luckily, I hadn't given her a phone number or my last name.

In August I finally found Denise and her cheap, skuzzy brownstone in which she rented individual rooms through the university's off-campus housing office. Denise didn't live there herself, so my fatness didn't offend her so long as I had the money for the first month, last month and the deposit.

The flat was rented to four women, but Adia was the only one in residence that summer. Tall, stocky and shockingly pale, Adia was a business student at BU but worked at various temp agencies over the summer break. Adia's paleness had nothing to do with fashion trends or fear of skin cancer; she had albinism, the only pigment in her body coming from a pair of blue-tinted contact lenses. She never dyed her white hair: 'I've seen dyed hair on albinos, and it just looks stupid,' she told me. 'Fake and stupid.'

The quality of the furniture in the common areas of the flat relied heavily on the taste and personal habits of the people who'd left these sofas and tables on the pavement as rubbish. The sofa was a bilious green with a faded but recognisable floral motif and several rusty brown stains I prayed hadn't been left by decomposing corpses. And it clashed violently with the purple shag pile carpeting.

We worked at making it feel like home. We hosted a lot of dinner parties for our friends, many of whom actually seemed to know one another, and I threw together a birthday party for one of our other roommates just a couple of weeks into the term. I baked a cake and invited all my old dorm friends.

'This totally reminds me of a place in Glebe, a French bakery called Le Chocorêve. They had the best chocolate cake in Sydney,' Adia said, licking a dollop of icing off the tines of her plastic fork.

'You were in Sydney?' I asked. 'Was it some kind of holiday?' Adia had spent a term in Sydney through BU's study abroad programme. She'd worked for an international accounting firm, and had loved every second of it. She brought out the photo albums. We admired shots of her in front of the opera house, with a koala, smiling on the beach. After the second album of beach snaps, I knew where I wanted to spend at least one of my remaining terms. The study abroad programme also offered journalism internships, which I knew would appeal to my parents – they had this strange idea that I'd need actual experience in my field if I wanted a job after graduation.

I applied in October and, less than a year later, arrived in Australia. I had spent the summer working in Boston, then flew home to Toledo to spend a couple of weeks visiting my family before going to Los Angeles for my international flight. I didn't fly directly from Toledo to LA. You can't really fly anywhere directly from Toledo. Our tiny airport still requires most passengers to walk on the Tarmac and climb stairs to enter the planes. I took a harrowing ride in a tiny commuter plane, changing planes in Pittsburgh. I spent the four-hour flight to LA next to a little blonde girl holding a caged iguana on her lap. 'His name is Louis,' she told me. 'He eats lettuce.' Louis lay on the smooth floor of his plastic habitat. He was so still that I began to wonder if he might be an ex-iguana. Luckily, he blinked once, disproving this theory. The little girl fell asleep clutching the clear plastic iguana cube. She never told me her name.

The Los Angeles airport presented an overwhelming combination of strange people and noise, the entire open terminal bathed in sunlight. I bought postcards, and dashed off a quick note to Leigh Anne. A woman walked by as I sat writing, leading a ten-year-old boy on a leather leash. 'I met a girl with an iguana and saw a lady dragging her child around on a lead like a cocker spaniel,' I wrote on a postcard adorned with the Hollywood sign. 'Amazing the strange creatures some people keep as pets,' I added.

After a 12-hour flight, we landed in Sydney, two days after our departure from California. I crossed the international dateline, the Pacific Ocean and half a dozen time zones. I'd lost a day to gain this new continent and celebrated by sleeping for about 16 hours.

The university leased a hotchpotch of houses, hostel suites and flats for the hundred or so college kids in the Sydney programme. Rented buses collected us from the airport. In the student-friendly suburb of Glebe, Glebe Point Road runs the entire length of the neighbourhood, its pavements lined with chip shops, bookstores, cafés and bars. It dead-ends into Broadway, a central street that takes you to the heart of Sydney in one direction and to the University of Sydney (a.k.a. 'Sydney Uni') in the other. My bus let me off in front of a tiny yellow house on Lombard Street, directly behind Glebe Point Road, which was to be my address for the next four months. I climbed the steps to the house, dragging my huge suitcase behind me and struggling for breath. As I fumbled with the keys, the door flew open.

'Rebecca? It's you! Or do I call you Simone de Beauvoir?' Jean-Claude stood in the entrance, naked except for a red beach towel. I knew him slightly as he'd lived in BU's French Language House with Leigh Anne the year before. He liked to answer the phone because he could ask nosy questions about who was calling and why they wanted to talk to Leigh Anne. Jean-Claude always wanted to know everything about everyone, and asked in the bluntest possible way. I'd taken to giving the French author's name when he asked who was calling, just to annoy him.

'No. You can call me Rebecca, of course. Have you been here long?' I asked. Jean-Claude helped me drag my bags into the house, and kissed both of my cheeks, surprising me as much with his affection as with the sandpaper of his stubble.

'I've been in Oz for a month. Backpacking. Hostels. Men. The men here – very good,' he said. 'The women are great, too,' he hastily added. At 22, Jean-Claude still officially described himself as 'bisexual'. He always had at least one gorgeous girl hanging about. Not that anything ever happened with them. Once he brought a stunning redhead home, only to ignore her for two solid hours when a prospective boyfriend called. I nodded, trying to seem nonchalant. I'd known a lot of gay people, especially for a girl from Toledo, Ohio. One of my favourite high school teachers, a guidance counsellor and a lot of my mother's friends had been gay men.

'Have you met our housemates?' I asked.

'No. You're the first. I'm sharing with some guy from NYU. He's coming tomorrow, and I already grabbed the top bunk. Isn't that too much? Bunk beds? How funny.' Jean-Claude hadn't shared a room before, as far as I knew. His parents owned flats in Brussels, Paris and New York and had holiday homes in the south of France and Switzerland. Until I patiently explained basic hygiene concepts and laid out the eating habits of indigenous insects (such as gigantic flying cockroaches), Jean-Claude hadn't even understood why we should put the lid back on the peanut butter. 'At home, the maid does it,' he explained.

'Yes, well, the maid lives in Brussels, and she should never be confused with me. So you'll have to pick up after yourself,' I explained. Something about Jean-Claude's own bluntness allowed me to speak to him this way. I felt no need to feign politeness with him, as politeness wasn't something he himself pretended (or attempted in any serious way) with anyone. I felt strangely liberated by this, and enjoyed Jean-Claude's company a lot more than I ever thought I would. It helped that he had courtly, European notions about paying for things (and a ton of his parents' money). He could be generous in ways that had little to do with cash: Jean-Claude organised a birthday party for me in Sydney, also buying a chocolate cake from Le Chocorêve for me.

After a few weeks of classes, I still hadn't made any friends among my fellow Americans. I sat home alone one Saturday night. Jean-Claude had rented a car and gone to meet friends in the Blue Mountains. I sat on the grey vinyl sofa in our living room and watched a made-for-television film. As the female lead fought off a would-be home invader/future ex-husband, the phone rang.

'Rebecca? I'll be home in ten minutes. I still have the car. Want to tour around a bit?' Jean-Claude didn't have to ask twice. I was off the sofa and waiting for him on the front porch before he had a chance to say goodbye. Jean-Claude screeched to a halt in front of the house, and we were quickly away. We drove up to a famous waterfront restaurant, and walked along its dock. We went and looked at Sydney's famous Gap, a curving cliff overlooking the Pacific, and headed back towards the city. We drove over harbour bridge. The windows were down, and a cool wind lifted my hair. The opera house glowed brilliant white against the dark night sky. I leaned into the open window, trying to improve my view of the city skyline but the seat belt strained a bit against my abdomen so I gave up on the view, falling back into the compact car's bucket seat.

We got back to the house, and Jean-Claude went to unpack. 'I've got a surprise for you,' he said, pouncing on me and pinning me to the sofa. 'I got jelly penis in the mountains,' he said, laughing. Thankfully, this wasn't a slang term for a trendy new venereal disease. Jean-Claude had obtained a ten-inch-long translucent rubber cock. We were both hysterical on the sofa as I was trying to fend off the jiggling red rubber sex toy when our housemate Tammy walked in.

'Rebecca, Jean-Claude, I'd like you to meet some friends from church. We thought you might like to pray . . .' Tammy trailed off, her expression one of shock and revulsion. Two chubby church ladies stood at her side, their mouths gaping and Bibles clutched to their ample chests. All three turned and walked out of the room without another word. Jean-Claude and I lay still for a moment, frozen in the positions the Witnesses had found us in, then we laughed so hard I fell off the couch and lay gasping on the ugly grey rug.

'We're going to burn in hell,' I said, giggling. Jean-Claude didn't disagree. Tammy stopped trying to name-drop The Lord into casual conversation after that. Jesus can forgive almost anything, but I guess a rubber penis in the face is kind of pushing it.

Jean-Claude never seemed put off by my body. Not that he had any sexual interest in me, but he'd jump on me and give me kisses on both cheeks. He also asked me uncomfortable questions no one else would. 'How did you get so fat?' he asked once. I couldn't provide an answer. I got flustered and upset and avoided him for days afterwards. He hadn't asked unkindly; he genuinely wanted to know. But, at 22, I still wanted to pretend I wasn't fat, wasn't different from anybody else. Jean-Claude's question unsettled me because it ruined my denial.

The day I got back from Byron Bay, he asked about my sex life. 'So you're a virgin, right? That sucks, I think,' he said while snuggling up to his new boyfriend, a hunky blond hairdresser from Paddington in the southeast of the city. Guy ignored the virginity talk and nuzzled Jean-Claude's ear. 'I really want to know. Have you had a man, Rebecca?'

'Yes, of course,' I lied. 'In high school. There was a guy.' I tried to look worldly, but the flame-scarlet blush made it a hard sell.

'Okay. Sure. You were probably thinner then, no?'

Jean-Claude and Guy retired to the bedroom, and I sat on the sofa and lamented my unwanted purity for a while. Then I went to Le Chocorêve and bought a croissant.

Given my size, men rarely approached me. In Sydney, my sole would-be suitor had been a drunk, toothless, homeless guy who tried to pick me up as I waited for a downtown bus. I passed on that opportunity (I'm not a fan of body lice), and devoted myself to a hopeless crush on one of the regular employees at the radio station I interned at.

2SER-FM was a community station on the top floor of a huge skyscraper on Broadway. I did the four o'clock news every day, calling politicians, activists, entertainers and sundry persons of interest for quotes that I'd edit into my stories. Community radio doesn't take itself especially seriously. After almost four months at 2SER, I had the run of the place, and sometimes actually got to edit the news when my boss was away on station business. One day in December, my colleagues and I decided that a charity programme using Fokker aircraft was of vital importance to our listeners.

'You've got to read it, Rebecca,' Janine told me. Janine, an Aussie journalism student, was my partner in crime that day. 'It's the accent. If we say "Fokker", it sounds, well, like something you do with a guy in the backroom at the pub.' Janine – tall, blonde and stacked – was a very popular girl. We worded the story so that I said 'Fokker' or 'Fokkers' at least 20 times in less than a minute. As soon as our producer turned the mikes off, the three of us gave in to the fit of giggles we'd barely held back on the air.

The broadcast had contained remarkably little actual news. The other major story of the day had outlined a shocking new study about the deadliness of Ayers Rock. Apparently, climbing a 90-foot-tall monolith in 100-degree heat could cause heart attacks in fat guys. This revelation cost the Australian government a million dollars in scientific grant money. 'I would've told them that for just a hundred grand,' I solemnly informed my colleagues. I'd read the story with utter seriousness, following it with the Fokkers to create a ten-minute broadcast I could never use in my resumé reel.

The producer, Johnno, wore round granny glasses and had

a giant white man afro in a lovely gingery colour. A classic geek, he had a wry, sardonic sense of humour and was at least six feet tall (if you counted the hair). I followed him all over the station like a kitten, finding excuses (like the chronically broken photocopier) to seek him out. He tolerated this attention cheerfully, totally oblivious of my infatuation.

As my time in Sydney ran out, I couldn't find a way to make this crush into anything more substantial. Johnno liked me, and even seemed to flirt a bit, but I had no experience and even less innate skill when it came to dealing with men. So I got slightly tipsy at the station Christmas party. We all assembled at the Rose Hotel in Ultimo, a suburb close to the station. I talked Johnno into buying me a drink, and all seemed well. We sat with Janine, who kept telling the same dirty old hippie (complete with a dozen 'Free East Timor' buttons and some serious body odour issues) to piss off. I admired her directness.

'What an idiot,' she said, right in front of the guy. 'Mate? How many times do I have to tell you to fuck off before you actually go away?' After another ten minutes of abuse, he finally took the hint and departed. I sipped my Strongbow and tried to bat my eyelashes at Johnno.

'Have you got something in your eye?' he asked.

One of our colleagues, a movie enthusiast named Colin, came up to us.

'Rebecca. Great fucker story! What journalistic integrity you've got,' Colin slurred, staring at my chest. Then he grabbed the back of my head and kissed me, his mouth tasting exactly like ten bottles of Tooheys Old Dark Ale. ''Night, Becca!' he said, staggering out of the door. Johnno looked on, aghast.

'What cheek! Some guys, they just do anything they like,

don't they? Some of us spend weeks, months even, pretending we know how to fix the copier, and others, others just take advantage. Unbelievable.' I know this should have been some sort of subtle cue to me, but the alcohol and my usual lack of sexual confidence made the meaning unclear.

Johnno walked me out of the bar at last orders, and we stood together and said awkward goodbyes for at least ten minutes. I watched him as my cab drifted away from the kerb. He stood there, watching me leave, and gave a sad little wave. I never saw him again.

When I tell them now, people in the US can't believe that I went to Australia. Sometimes, I barely believe it myself. I weighed about 29 stone. Usually, this would mean finding a sofa somewhere to become permanently stuck to, not a trip halfway around the world. I take some pride in having gone, in the ravines I trekked, the rustic creeks I swam in, the 12-hour train trip I took to Byron Bay all by myself. There's a sadness, too, at the many missed opportunities. I often wonder about Johnno, if he might actually have liked me despite my fat body and general awkwardness.

After a brief stopover in Hawaii, I flew home to Toledo. I found the city buried under a rough blanket of dirty old snow. I spent the Christmas break ignoring my father, going to films with my sister, and calling Adia for news and gossip from BU. Though Tammy wrote me off as a Satanist and never spoke to me again, I heard from Jean-Claude a few times after we graduated. I got an e-mail from him about a year after my weight-loss surgery. He'd read a magazine story I wrote about losing 14 stone, and offered his usual sensitive response. 'No offence,' he wrote, 'but you were huge!' And I was – it's a fact –

but only, really, on the outside. The big confidence I projected was all for show. Most of the time, I felt terribly small and insignificant, unable to carry out even the most basic of human transactions. I think of the shy kangaroo sometimes, and wonder if I shouldn't catch another plane Down Under sometime.

11

LOBSTER GUTS AND DAD'S WEED

The bong stood proudly in the centre of the marble coffee table, its clown's head logo smirking at me contemptuously. Empty Pop Tarts wrappers littered the dusty hardwood floor. The bay window was wide open, and I seriously considered hurling the three-foot glass pot pipe into the street two floors below. My roommate Nina and her drug-dealing boyfriend slept peacefully in her bedroom, safe from my fury. All my Pop Tarts were gone, the flat was freezing, and the place smelled like my parents' bedroom after a holiday weekend.

I hadn't planned on living with a wispy blonde princess whose circle of friends seemed to consist mostly of stoned idiots, but here I was. I blamed Adia, my parents and the entire Thai nation (whose famed 'stick' brand of weed left my roommate and her friends delirious, ravenous and intent on my Pop Tarts). Adia had moved out of our old flat while I lived in Sydney, finding a place a long, inconvenient bus trip away from campus. I couldn't live with her because of the distance, so Adia had found me a sublet instead.

Whatever gratitude I felt to my old roommate for finding

the flat dissolved about five minutes after I met Nina. 'Charmed, I'm sure,' she said, extending a translucent hand for me to shake. I could feel sharp edges of bone in her fingertips. Nina weighed 7 stone and wore a pink silk teddy and matching ruffled underwear. As I counted the vertebrae in her neck, I decided that if this was Victoria's Secret's target demographic, their stuff would never be for me. Not that it ever was.

Nina introduced me to the other three housemates: Jenna (the drunk Italian girl who wandered around nude), Mary (the self-appointed house mum) and Allegra (blonde, Brazilian, aristocratic and terrifying). Jenna drank all my cooking wine if I left the bottle in the shared refrigerator, and I learned that she wasn't a natural redhead about an hour and a half after meeting her for the first time. Mary hid the frying pan from me because she didn't think I knew how to wash it. Allegra had the room next to the flat's only bathroom. She went to bed at 9pm every weeknight and, if you used the toilet after that, she'd appear from the darkness, the door to her room opening silently inwards as you passed in the hall. Then she'd hiss loudly, her eyes glowing in the dim light.

Nina seemed to spend most waking moments purging, smoking up or screwing. She wore clothes only when outside the flat; at home, her wardrobe consisted entirely of poorly fitted lingerie with bra cups designed for women with actual breasts. She ate only when she was stoned, and never bought any food, preferring to take my Pop Tarts.

No matter how high she was, though, Nina never took anything from Allegra. Marijuana may soften the edges, but in Nina's case, it never touched her survival instinct. Allegra's restaurant leftovers sat untouched in our fridge, safe inside their tinfoil trays, and Nina's intestines stayed on the inside of her body (though you could sort of see them through her skin when the light hit her the right way).

Adia felt a little guilty about my living situation and extended an open invitation to her own rented accommodation. She lived in a seventies townhouse on a bus line that only seemed to run in one direction, so I took taxis out to visit, and caught the bus home. The situation at Weed Central meant that I spent a lot of time at Adia's. I soon learned that Nina had a finely tuned sense of morality. Anyone who disagreed with her right to smoke weed or prance about in her undies, or who confronted her over the theft of the last two frosted cherry Pop Tarts, was clearly not a good person. She also viewed leaving dishes in the sink as a crime on a par with serial murder. She always assumed that I'd left the dishes, probably because I was the only woman in the flat who knew how to operate the oven. To Nina, I was the fat girl, and that automatically made me a slob. I worked hard at ignoring her, but we usually ended up arguing over the provenance of the dirty plates. Neither of us ever gave an inch, but Nina had her own sneaky way of meting out punishment; whether she was punishing me for being fat or for imagined crimes against the communal kitchenware remains a mystery to me.

Returning from class one afternoon, I noticed half a dozen filthy plastic dishes piled directly in front of my bedroom door. On this mound of cheap white dinnerware stood a primly folded greetings card. An insipid white kitten stared beseechingly at me from the glossy paper. I picked it up and flipped it open: 'Rebecca, I decided you needed an actual INVITATION. Wash your fucking dishes. Love, Nina.'

She dotted the I's with tiny hearts, including the one in 'fucking'. None of the plates were actually mine as I'd spent the weekend in Pennsylvania at a quiz bowl tournament and hadn't so much as touched any dishes in the flat in days. So I dumped the reeking pile of plates in the kitchen sink and went off to find a cab to Adia's. I only had about five dollars to my name – enough to cover the fare if I didn't tip – but figured that blowing my tiny cash reserve probably beat going to prison for choking Nina to death with her favourite purple thong.

My mother listened patiently when I called to complain about Nina. I worried that I'd talked the topic to death, when she surprised me by bringing it up herself one day. 'When we come to Boston for graduation, there's something special your roommate could do for Dad. You know, the roommate in the underwear?' Mum paused to let this sink in. Horrible pictures danced in my head as I pondered the unthinkable. Mum wanted Nina to sleep with my father! I thought about how I might say no and still get the après-graduation dinner Mum had promised for me and my friends at Legal Seafood. After another minute of silence on the line, I finally worked it out.

'Oh! You want Nina to get Dad some weed.' I'd never felt so relieved about my parents' ridiculous drug habit. Weed was so much better than Nina sexually servicing Dad on my graduation day. I could live with Nina selling my father some nice, wholesome pot grown in the soil by honest, tropical peasants. At least my parents rolled their joints like civilised people. I would have died of shame if they owned a giant bong with a clown's head on it.

'Are you crazy?' Mum shrieked so loudly I had to hold the phone away from my ear. 'I'm on a cordless! Anyone could be listening. Anyone! I don't know what you're talking about. I would never do anything illegal. But if Nina has any . . . stuff . . . we could give you money for it.'

The day before I graduated from college, Mum gave me 20 dollars so I could buy their marijuana. Nina never showed up at the corner bar to sell it to me, so my sister and I were forced to use the drug money for spring rolls at Quincy Market.

For the millionth time, I thought it was a pity I hadn't been able to continue to rent the room I'd had over the summer before I left for Sydney. My previous roommate, Jill, had had a bottomless supply of pot. She also worked at Legal Seafood as a waitress and occasionally brought me home pints of their famous clam chowder. Some people favour a post-work martini. Jill, a 28-year-old bottle blonde who stood about four foot ten in heels, preferred to wind down the day with a four-inch joint. She'd sit in the darkened kitchen of her small, beautifully appointed Brookline flat and blaze up, inhaling deeply. Her tense shoulders would relax, and she'd start to look like a human woman instead of a tiny, anxious troll in waitress clothes.

One night I wandered into the kitchen to make cocoa while she was winding down, and slowly lost track of what I was doing. 'Jill? I've boiled some milk and I can't remember why. Any ideas?' I asked, totally enveloped in a thick cloud of pot smoke.

'None. I'd offer you some of this, but you really don't need the munchies, if you know what I mean,' Jill replied, taking another long drag on the joint. Weed made Jill more honest and less polite than when she was straight. She'd sit at the table getting high while lecturing me about my poor diet. 'Do you read labels? I mean, do you care what you're putting in your body?' Jill would say, lit joint clamped firmly between two fingers. She daintily tipped ashes into a cut-glass dish her grandmother had given her as a housewarming present. Jill shook her head, clearly disgusted by my sloth and total dearth of healthy living habits.

Jill never dieted but weighed about 6 stone. Her job required a high level of physical activity, and she had weed for dinner. Both of these things helped her maintain the lithe, lightly muscled frame of a healthy 12-year-old boy. With her tightly permed hair and the androgynous waitress uniform of black pants and a white dress shirt, she looked like a tiny, angry elf. The restaurant clientele rarely helped her mood and even giant cash tips failed to cheer her as it was a high-end restaurant and they were therefore expected. 'You wouldn't believe the crap I have to deal with,' she said, taking a long, cleansing drag. 'People are morons. There's this woman who comes in at least once a week. She dresses like a total whore – blouse open practically to the waist, short skirt, fishnets. Different guys always buy her lunch, but she always gets the same thing. It's disgusting.' Jill finished the joint and ground it angrily into the glass dish.

'So what does she get?' I asked. I loved Legal Seafood, especially the chowder and their deep-fried shrimp. I couldn't imagine eating there once a month, let alone once a week. As a poor college student, I was lucky when I could afford McDonald's or a pizza.

'You'd think she'd get a nice salmon, shrimp, clams … the chowder. Everybody loves the chowder. I've worked at Legal for three years and *I* still love the chowder. But no. She gets something so disgusting it isn't even on the actual menu. It's a special request order, which means it's not only disgusting, but a flaming pain in the ass.' Jill lit a second (slightly smaller) joint. Clearly, the stress of reliving the whore's lunch order was getting to her.

'So tell me. What does she order?' I asked, gingerly perching on the edge of one of Jill's delicate kitchen chairs. I usually avoided sitting in the kitchen because I feared the shame and expense of damaging her spindly, thin-legged seating, but I'd been standing for a good ten minutes, and my feet ached from the strain.

'She gets a gigantic bowl of lobster guts. Cooked lobster guts served in the shell,' Jill shuddered and took a hit off the joint, its end glowing a bright cherry red. 'She slurps it all down, the whole green mess, without ever touching the silverware, and when she's finished, she piles her dishes and all the empty lobster shells on the floor. I hate that. I hate having to stoop and pick up her dirty mess. It's really demeaning.'

'Lobster guts are green?' I asked.

Jill nodded silently, her blue eyes wide as she mentally relived the horror. All of a sudden, my tough garden gnome of a roommate looked like a sad little girl. The white dress shirt gaped a bit at the collar as she slumped over the table, and I could see the curve of her collarbone, that hollow at the base of her throat.

I could understand why Jill needed all of that weed, but I still couldn't remember what I'd been doing in the kitchen. Maybe some cocoa would help? Handily enough, there was hot milk in a pan on the stove. I added cocoa powder, vanilla, sugar and a pinch of cinnamon to the pan, brought it back to a nice simmer, stirred thoroughly and poured the resulting mixture into a hand-thrown ceramic mug Mum had bought me on Cape Cod. Jill declined my offer of hot chocolate, opting instead for half a tin of Pringles and three or four tiny fistfuls of pistachios. Sated, she retired to her bedroom, her black cat Charlie following close at her heels.

By the time I came back from Sydney, Jill had rented out my old room, relegating me to weed central. Nina eventually took to stacking plates in my bed – which is where I found a bunch of dishes one day when I got home from Adia's. The kitten on the card was chocolate brown this time, obviously an ominous sign, and I didn't bother to read the note. I stole five dollars out of Nina's laundry bag and caught another cab to Adia's.

Nina's boyfriend practically lived in our flat. Kenny had an endless supply of weed, a bunch of stupid friends who came over to steal my food, and a pager that never stopped buzzing. He was a short, greasy creature showing early signs of male pattern baldness. He had lots of clients and a product that pretty much sold itself. I wondered about turning him in to the police after my strawberry Pop Tarts went missing; it wasn't that I thought they'd investigate grand theft Pop Tart, but the weed would probably have garnered some official interest – his personal supply alone was probably enough for a conviction. I really wanted to call the police, but I couldn't quite pull the trigger. For a start, I worried that Nina and Kenny would work out who'd turned them in, and bury me in an empty car park under a pile of white plastic plates. The card would feature a jet-black kitten with a sad, knowing expression in its wide green eyes.

I've lived with friends and I've lived with enemies. When I arrived at Boston University as an 18 year old, I chose a dorm room in the university's specially designated writers' corridor.

Our floor in Shelton Hall, formerly a Sheraton hotel, built in the 1940s, boasted the room where playwright Eugene O'Neill was staying when he died. My dorm room had views of the Charles River from its huge, square windows. I don't miss my fellow writers' corridor denizens. We were all precious, pretentious, obnoxious, spoiled children, but I like to think I had a little something extra, a little soupçon of humanity under the college-cool façade I tried (and utterly failed) to create for myself.

After the dorms, I lived with Adia, then Jill, then with Jean-Claude in Sydney before winding up back at square one, living with people I hated. When graduation time came, I felt relieved to be moving home for the summer.

My family arrived for my graduation in shifts. Andrea and my father flew in from Toledo as Andrea's school year hadn't ended and she could only stay for the weekend. My mother and grandmother drove from Ohio – a 12-hour trip – in a rental car roughly the size of the *Titanic*. I stayed with my family in a chain hotel in Cambridge.

My mother had many bitter complaints about the accommodation. 'Front desk? I'd like to report that I found a condom – a *used* condom – in the phone book. What do I want you to do with it? I want you to come get it. And I want another phone book. No, I don't need more condoms.' Mum somehow got through this important phone call without swearing. She saved all of that for the ceremony itself.

Each school and college at BU held its own graduation, and one for the College of Communication (known as COM) took place in a park by the river. Because COM was one of the largest schools in the university, the crowd was enormous, and my parents, grandmother and sister had to watch me receive my diploma (actually, the empty cardboard tube that would have held my diploma if I hadn't owed the school 48 dollars in library fines) on closed-circuit video. Given the fact that my tuition had cost them an amount equivalent to a new Mercedes-Benz, my mother did a lot of swearing that sweltering May day.

My parents had still agreed to take Adia and me to Legal Seafood despite my failure to produce their drugs and, after a brief wait in the bar, a hostess led us to our seats. 'Hello! My name is Jill, and I'll be your server this evening,' the waitress said, her face frozen into a tight, nearly genuine-looking smile.

'I can promise that we won't order lobster guts,' I told her. I hadn't met up with Jill for some time, and it was good to see her. In turn, Jill was happy to see me as she could be reasonably sure of a good tip.

Despite the rental car's gigantic proportions, squeezing four of us into the back seat (when one of us was 29-stone me) had taken a lot of manoeuvring and tightly held breath. We dropped Adia at the townhouse after dinner. I saw her infrequently after that: she moved to California and later to Seattle. I know the distance didn't help, but when she stopped speaking to me, I felt certain my weight had a lot to do with it. She was living with a new boyfriend at the time, and I wouldn't have been a good house guest. After all, if they'd taken me out, they could never fob me off on any of their male friends. I felt like she had become ashamed of me.

I speculated a lot about Adia's sudden disappearance from my life. I wondered how she was and what she was doing. I

missed her keenly, especially after my father died. I knew Adia
for only two years, but her drive and confidence had a strong
influence on me. I still seek out strong women as friends,
hoping some of their toughness and self-assurance will rub off
on me.

I never saw Nina after graduation. I like to imagine her
working as a dishwasher in a truck stop, her greying hair
permanently stuck to her forehead from the kitchen steam. I
hope the diner is in the Arizona desert, and that she has to
subsidise her meagre wages by turning tricks with long-haul
truckers in their overheated cabs. Actually, Nina probably
makes a six-figure income and has a rich husband and two-
point-five perfect children, but I dare to dream.

I left Boston in a giant rental car with all my worldly goods
crammed into the boot. I watched the city vanish as we sped
down the Mass Pike at 80 miles an hour. Wedged tightly into
the back seat next to an enormous box of books, I spent the first
four hours of our drive wondering what I would do at home
with my parents for an entire summer. I decided I could always
close my eyes and think about Sydney or Boston, that I'd read
novels and watch television, and I'd survive it. And if my new
college failed to impress, I could always bide my time and live
inside my head. I'd survive that too. I knew that neighbourhood
better than any other and I wasn't afraid to live there alone.

12

GRAD SCHOOL DROPOUT

The ugly school mascot had feet of clay, literally. It was a terracotta statue of a Greek warrior. Because the university especially valued anything to do with cars, parking and traffic flow, the statue stood in the middle of a roundabout. One day I asked a young quiz bowl teammate what would happen if I made a fantasy I had a reality.

'If I smashed Sparty with a sledgehammer, would anyone care?' I posed the question before practice one April evening about six weeks before I concluded my graduate school career – not with a degree, but with about 60,000 dollars in student loan debt. Much as I wanted to be a nice person, my bitterness oozed out a little at the edges.

Jamie, a 20-year-old biology student, flinched slightly at the very idea of my proposed desecration before giving me a very serious answer. 'Jeez, Rebecca, no one would do that,' he said, frowning. His dark brows retreated from his funny little widow's peak as he grimaced at the thought of Sparty in a billion pieces, the rough clay chunks killing traffic flow and snarling dozens of American-made cars into epic gridlock. 'If you went after Sparty with a hammer, a mob would form pretty much instantly and they'd beat you to death on the spot.' Jamie looked both satisfied and discomfited by his answer. He knew with absolute certainty that killing Sparty's theoretical attacker was the right thing to do, but he seemed bothered by the idea of broken statues and violence.

He worked through this contradiction while I pulled our buzzer set out of its cardboard box and began untangling its many snarled cords and cables. The team met once a week in a classroom attached to a college dormitory. The dorm, a red-brick square whose interiors boasted acres of dirty grey linoleum and thousands of off-white acoustic ceiling tiles, housed several of the young players I'd recruited when I formed State's first ever quiz team. The room held three or four long tables, a blackboard and a bank of fluorescent lights.

I hated State, I hated Sparty and I didn't like Jamie all that much. A sheltered kid from a conservative family, he'd never cooked a meal or done a load of laundry in his life. His mother fetched his dirty clothes once a week, returning a couple of days later with a neat pile of freshly washed and folded shirts, trousers and unmentionables. She drove an hour each way to provide this service, and Jamie's notions of appropriate female behaviour differed vastly from my own. Despite that fact, he was a teammate, not a terrible person and still looked a bit upset, so as Jamie and I set up the buzzers at two opposing tables, I tried to put him at ease.

'I would never hurt Sparty,' I said. 'I was just kidding. Sparty is an art treasure.' In truth, I felt a little ashamed of my snobbish loathing of the thing. Sparty wore little underpants because Midwestern college students would probably die if they saw a terracotta cock. All the innocent, corn-fed undergrads adored Sparty, a beloved symbol whose origins practically reeked of wartime patriotism – clay had been used to build Sparty, conserving metal so that America might better defeat Hitler.

'Yeah,' said Jamie, his relief almost palpable. 'You're right. Everybody loves Sparty! Well, everybody but those A-holes at the U,' he added, referring to the more selective public university an hour south that was State's sworn enemy. Graduates of that august institution included all sorts of Nobel laureates, a star of *The Brady Bunch*, one of the great heroes of the Holocaust, and Madonna, whereas State probably did something tremendous for cattle breeding. Also, State made and sold chocolate-flavoured cheese in its campus dairy shop. I thought about this disparity for a minute and regretted not studying harder in Boston.

When I'd arrived at State as a 22-year-old graduate student, my father drove the U-Haul, my mother came second in the convoy in their car, and I followed behind both of them in the 1986 Chrysler LeBaron I'd recently received as a belated graduation gift. My father took the wrong exit, and my mother pulled over to the side of the road, gesturing wildly for me to follow suit. I pulled behind her onto the hard shoulder. The sun hung low in the pale, cloudless sky, scorching my shoulders as I walked over to her car. The electric window glided down, allowing a lurid stream of cigarette smoke and obscenities to escape.

'Fuck! What the hell does he think he's doing?' Mum's question was rhetorical. We couldn't have asked him if we wanted to. Mobile phones hadn't yet caught on for the mass market and neither of my parents possessed one. I shrugged.

'Dad knows where we're going. He's got the address. It's not like there's anything we can do about it,' I said, as traffic whizzed by at about 90 miles an hour. My new state of residence had just adopted a 70-mile-an-hour speed limit. This wasn't nearly fast enough for its crafty natives, most of whom drove like a pack of meth-crazed weasels. 'I can't fix Dad's sense of direction by getting hit by one of these nutjobs. We've just got to go,' I said, pressing myself into the side of her car as a huge truck roared by.

When we arrived at my new apartment building, Dad had yet to turn up. He had most of my things in the rented truck so we stood outside in the car park with nothing to do. My sister finally spotted him driving away from the complex and ran out into the road to flag him down. He pulled into the car park, parked the truck next to Mum's new Buick, barely said hello to us, and celebrated his safe arrival with a cigarette. His faded, tattered jean shorts hung low off his bony hips, which seemed even more ridiculously frail when you compared them with his bloated gut. Dad carried every extra pound around his abdomen and had the shape of an extremely thin, eight-months-pregnant woman.

Sated, he dropped his spent cigarette on the black tar of the car park, crushing it out with the heel of his trainer. 'Let's get this over with,' he said, opening the back door of the U-Haul. He struggled with the attached ramp for a few minutes. He couldn't get it to extend out of the truck and finally gave up in a huff. 'Well?' he demanded. 'What do you want?' he snarled in Mum's general direction.

Mum gave him a look – she gave him *the* look – and set my sister's current boyfriend, Rob, and her best friend (and future boyfriend) Shane to work on the ramp. The boys managed to pull it free, and it hit the asphalt with a loud clank. Shane and Rob were 16, skinny, and eager to earn the ten dollars Mum had promised them for helping with the move. The boys began unloading the cars and the rented truck. Andrea helped too, carrying all the heaviest pillows and tea towels down the short staircase to my garden (really a basement) flat. I carried a box of dishes, castoffs from my mother's kitchen. Just carrying this little box left me panting at the bottom of the staircase, the heat and my excess weight taking their toll. I gently lowered it to the floor. Shane and Rob eased a sofa down the steps, and I got out of the way so they could manoeuvre it into the flat.

I practically fell onto the sofa as soon as the boys put it down, relieved at having somewhere to sit, and a little ashamed at needing to after such a short interval of work. I sat back against the gold chenille cushions (another hand-me-down from my parents) and tried to breathe like a normal person. I had spent a lot of time in my teens and twenties trying to do things like a normal (thin) person would. Whenever I had to climb stairs in front of people, I'd grasp the rail and struggle slowly upwards, trying to pace myself so that I wouldn't be uncontrollably out of breath by the time I reached the landing. If I could get up the stairs without sweating heavily and gasping, I could pretend I was just like everybody else.

And it worked. Unlike a lot of fat women I've known, I felt little shame about my size in the course of an average day. Without an actual mirror in front of me, I was easily able to lose myself in the fantasy that my body wasn't a problem. When confronted with a too-small chair or an unexpected flight of stairs, however, the pretence of normality vanished instantly. It wasn't my size that embarrassed me; rather the limitations my size imposed. Having to force myself into chairs that bruised my hips or trip wheezing up a single flight of stairs put me squarely into the reality of my strange and inconvenient body. I suffered these indignities and then quickly and purposely forgot about them.

The apartment building had white columns and a concrete porch. I could hear cars whizzing by as I stood in front of my window. My view was a thick ribbon of grey concrete and the bottom of a column. Peering out across the floor of the porch, I noticed several black handprints smudging the column's white paint. The bedroom view showed part of a retaining wall and the roots of an oak tree. The kitchen had no windows at all, just tiny appliances crammed into a linoleum square about half the size of my car.

Mum walked into the kitchen carrying a shower curtain. She surveyed the interior and shook her head. 'You should think about getting some throw rugs,' she suggested, lighting a cigarette off one of the stove burners and using the sink as an ashtray. Her thick thighs rubbed together, and she had a rash across the tops of her legs. She had a bad hip, and I could tell it ached from the way she braced herself against the worktop. My sister lay on the floor, her waist-length brown hair fanning out to one side. The tiny air-conditioning unit puffed out a thin stream of cool air. Andrea waved one pale arm and Rob dropped to a crouch by her side.

'I'm hot,' Andrea said. 'Fan me!' Rob shrugged, pushed his shoulder-length blond hair out of his eyes and immediately set to work. He found a square of cardboard in the box of dishes and flipped it back and forth in front of my sister's flushed, sweaty face. My father grunted and took the cardboard away, directing Rob to some more useful task. Andrea finally stood up and went to help the boys move my bed frame.

I sat on the sofa and wondered what I would do when everyone left. This flat was the first place I had ever lived in by myself. I looked forward to the privacy and to not having to argue with roommates about their drug use, but worried about being on my own in a strange town. I only knew one person at State, and I'd never had an easy time making friends. I thought forming a quiz team would be a good way to meet people. Before classes had even started, I collected paperwork from the university's activities office so I could organise the group.

My single contact at State was a veterinary student I'd met through another quiz bowl friend. Mary had needed a lift to Pennsylvania for the Philly Experiment masters tournament, and we made plans to rent a car together. Mary and I exchanged dozens of e-mails before the tournament and she had seemed bright and funny when we'd spoken on the phone. Despite that, I never told her how fat I was.

Other troubled people can hide their problem areas. The nascent junkie wears long sleeves to cover his track marks. Bulimics wear bulky sweaters and lie about having a stomach bug. My deepest flaw, however, is never a secret. When you are heavily overweight, you can't hide it with a sweater. It's always the first thing people notice about you. The summer I met Mary, I was 22 years old and probably weighed 32 stone. Though I wore long T-shirts, futilely trying to camouflage my vast stomach, nothing could blunt the impact of seeing me for the first time. I dreaded meeting new people, especially people like Mary who only knew me from funny e-mails or as a sweet voice on the phone.

Mary planned to stay overnight at my house so we could leave for Philadelphia early the next morning. The trip takes nine or ten hours, and we wanted to be underway by 7am at the latest. 'Rebecca! Door!' my father shouted from his upstairs bedroom. Mary had arrived and I went to greet her. I took a deep breath, opened the front door, smiled brightly and hoped for the best.

The young woman standing on my front porch looked a little stunned. She'd just driven three hours on a hot day in an old car with no air conditioning. It was very humid, especially for early June, and her long, reddish hair had puffed into a frizzy corona. She wore shorts and a T-shirt; she was tall but short-waisted, and her knobbly arms and legs were tanned darkly under all of her freckles. Mary stared at me, mouth agape, for what felt like hours. She finally shook my hand and walked past me into the house, mumbling a shy 'Hello'. I showed her the basement guest room, and she carried her rucksack down the stairs. Despite the phone and e-mail contact we'd already had, seeing my body had turned Mary back into a stranger.

As I sat on the sofa in my newly rented apartment, I wondered if Mary would really do all the things she'd promised on the phone. Would she show me around town, go to the cinema with me? I doubted it. Despite my impending solitude, however, I felt glad to have the flat. I'd spent the summer before grad school looking at rentals with my mother. It had taken two or three trips to find a place I could afford that wasn't also a filthy hellhole over a crack den. When we finally found my garden level shoebox, I was determined to make the best of it. I picked a shower curtain with a tropical fish pattern and bought some second-hand pieces of furniture. One Sunday, Andrea and the boys helped me strip and paint these cheap wooden treasures on my parents' drive.

We had a guest that night. A guy from Michigan's quiz team, a postgraduate student a year or so older than I was, had seen my posts on a quiz bowl website. In desperate need of a quiz bowl girlfriend, he called me out of the blue one day after finding my home phone number in State's online directory. I'd never met him, and felt flattered by the attention. I didn't think the phone call would lead anywhere, and had no idea what, if anything, to tell him about my size. I never talked about my weight with anyone; I had no idea how I would break the news. Even I barely acknowledged the fact of my obesity, despite the years I'd spent lugging all the weight around, the teasing I'd endured at school, and the random catcalls from strangers in the street. I thought about asking one of my BU teammates to e-mail the guy a description. They knew what I looked like, and could give my new suitor a clue, but I abandoned this insane idea. We had a lot in common. Maybe that would be enough.

I never tried to lead Dave on, and I hadn't sought him out. I just lacked the capacity to type out the words 'I'm fat' in an e-mail, and I certainly couldn't say them out loud over the phone. I couldn't say it at all, not even to myself, because that would mean I wasn't normal. None of the things I'd accomplished – the travel, my honours degree – would matter if I talked about my weight. I'd worked towards most of these accomplishments for the express purpose of proving I was just like normal people. Why spoil it by talking about my fat?

So on the phone I talked to Dave about films and quiz bowl tournaments, and hoped he'd surprise me by finding me acceptable. Dave had invited himself over that Sunday after-noon. He'd initially wanted to drive me around Toledo, so I might give him a tour, but I'd worried that he might be driving a small car or that the seatbelt wouldn't fit. Instead I'd invited him to help us paint furniture, and he'd accepted. I wore jeans and a tie-dyed T-shirt, combed out my curly hair and even applied make-up. My sister could scarcely believe this effort.

'I hope this guy is cool,' she said, looking a little worried.

'I hope so, too,' I told her, blotting my lipstick on a McDonald's receipt I'd found in the bottom of my make-up bag. I checked my reflection in the mirror, baring my teeth to practise the smile. I spritzed myself with Givenchy and went out to the driveway to set the scene. If Dave drove up and saw me industriously supervising Andrea, Shane and Rob, he'd under-stand what a capable person I was. Given all the work I put into looking neat and presenting a pleasant picture it seems a touch ironic that I didn't know what Dave looked like at all either. I knew that he'd seen *The Princess Bride* and *Better Off Dead* hundreds of times; we could both recite lines from these films from memory. I knew he was studying engineering, and that his family lived in Virginia. He liked the sound of my voice on the phone. My mother had high hopes.

'There's a lid for every pot,' she told me. 'Maybe this Dave is your lid.'

'Why am I the pot in this analogy?' I asked. We stood in the kitchen, my mother frying ground beef while I sliced onions for chili.

'You be the lid then. You know what I mean.' She stirred the browning meat with a fork and took the pan off the heat. I went outside to check my crew's progress and to wait for Dave. He arrived promptly at six, and I pretended not to see him driving up in his tiny Japanese hatchback. I set the stage, calling out orders to the crew. 'Shane, can you move the desk a little to the right? We don't want the neighbour's sprinkler to hit it,' I asked, in a tone of voice I imagined to be light, bright and girly. Shane rolled his eyes and snorted, but did as I asked. My sister sat cross-legged on the driveway, painting an old end table. She had turquoise paint on her knees, and had pulled her hair back into a messy ponytail held together with a green rubber band from the morning newspaper. Rob offered to go and fetch her a drink, and she nodded. Shane rolled his eyes at this, too, but I was the only one who noticed.

Dave got out of his car and waved as he started up the steep incline of the drive. A sandy-haired guy in his mid-twenties, Dave seemed to possess every single trait of the classic trivia team geek: he wore glasses and high-waisted shorts, and was tall and thin with a terrible haircut. He wore a golf shirt and carried a cheap bottle of red wine.

'Rebecca? Great to finally meet you.' Dave had a huge grin on his face as he addressed my sister. The moment stretched out forever, as we all stood immobile on the drive. Andrea had her hands on her hips as she frowned in confusion. Shane's eyes darted nervously from me to my sister and finally to Dave. I didn't move at all; a smile was frozen on my face.

'Actually, I'm Rebecca,' I said finally, stretching out a hand for him to shake. He didn't stop smiling, but disbelief, disappointment and sad acceptance registered on his face in the instant it took us to exchange a limp handshake.

'It's great to finally meet you,' he said, sounding almost sincere. I let myself enjoy the fantasy, and set him to work sanding a bedside table. My father came out to say hello. I worried that he'd make some snide remark, but he seemed genuinely happy at the idea that a man might be interested in me. After an hour of painting, sanding and small talk about quiz bowl, Dave, the kids and I headed inside for dinner with my parents. My mother, ever the subtle social engineer, seated Dave next to me.

As we ate, Andrea, Rob and Shane jostled each other and told jokes no one over 16 could understand. I felt really old watching them. At 22, I felt like I'd never really been young – definitely not the way my sister and her friends were. People saw all the fat and made assumptions. My parents treated Dave like a minor celebrity. He was the first guy who'd ever come to see me, and their fantasies about his intentions were even more ridiculous than my own had been. After he mistook Andrea for me, I knew he could never be anything more than a friend. At least I told myself I knew that, but as he helped me load the dishwasher after dinner, we finished each other's sentences, and I felt a tiny spark of hope.

"'Hello. My name is Inigo Montoya . . . '" Dave began, handing me a plate.

"'. . . You killed my father. Prepare to die,'" I finished, my Spanish accent at once flawless and utterly ridiculous. Dave smiled and nudged the dishwasher shut with his hip. After my parents had retired to their bedroom and my sister and her friends had settled into the basement room to watch a horror film, Dave and I talked for a couple of hours. We stood in the dining room, which was barely large enough for a table. I stood next to the basement door, and Dave leaned against the wall next to the kitchen. We had a long, funny conversation facing each other across eight feet of space. Neither of us made any move towards a more comfortable room, and, eventually, Dave realised how late it had got and told me he had to go.

'I'll see you at a tournament sometime this autumn,' he said, just before climbing into his car. I never really talked to him again. He found the quiz bowl girlfriend he wanted. I don't know how he met Lisa, a postgraduate student from another neighbouring university, but they were a solid couple by the time the first autumn tournament rolled around. He always seemed to have one arm wrapped around her narrow waist, and he also liked to pet her spectacularly awful perm. They shared a loveseat in the student lounge as they waited for the next round of the tournament to start. Lisa lay with her head in Dave's lap, and he stroked the tight, oily curls like you'd pet a poodle you were about to have put down.

Despite my jealousy, I felt a little bit relieved. The idea of someone putting his hands on me in that way made me very uncomfortable. When people were close, I couldn't pretend I wasn't fat. Their proximity, the way they related to my body – these things shattered the façade of normality I hoped to project.

I failed miserably as a graduate student. None of the promised journalism internships materialized, and all the classes seemed to involve the running of cable television stations. After the first month, I knew I'd probably never finish the degree, but I didn't know what else to do. Given my size, I knew it would be very hard for me to get a job, and I couldn't go home. I never wanted to live with my father again. I went through the motions:

attending classes I couldn't comprehend; going to quiz tournaments with undergraduates who rejected all my social invitations; adopting a cat from the local animal shelter. I even organised a tournament at State to raise money for the team's travel expenses. The event went off without a hitch.

At five o'clock the next morning, as I lay in bed with my new cat trying to groom my forehead, licking me with his rough tongue and tapping my face with one white paw, I heard my mother's voice on the answering machine. Half asleep, thinking I might be dreaming, I listened as she said that my father was in the hospital, that he'd had emergency surgery, and that he might not live. All through that winter, my mother, sister and I kept a vigil at Toledo Hospital. My father had had an aortic aneurism, a slow leak in the huge artery that curls around the heart and runs through the torso to supply the body with blood. Surgeons repaired the leak then took him in for a second emergency operation to repair it again. My father lay in the ICU for months, drugged, delirious and hallucinating. He even told my mother he dreamed I'd been raped. The hospital released Dad to a rehabilitation centre in January, and he came home in March. My father had never looked old before the aneurism. After his recovery, he rarely left the house. He'd sit in a chair in front of the television, quietly angry as each long, empty day wore on.

The rehab centre called one day. They'd misplaced Dad's glasses, but insisted he come there in person to look through all the pairs in the lost-and-found before they would pay for new ones. I was home for spring break, and I drove him across town to the rehab centre, wedging myself tightly into his old Japanese car, tilting my seat back as far as it would go. Dad wanted me to wait in the car park, but after almost an hour I grew impatient and went inside to look for him. A woman at the reception desk told me he'd gone to the claims office. I followed her directions and soon realised that the place was a long, long walk from the centre's main office. When I finally arrived, I saw Dad slumped over in an office chair, a box of glasses on the desk in front of him. The man behind the desk shook his head, frustrated.

'Mr Golden, we need you to be absolutely sure none of these are yours,' he said. My father didn't speak. He frowned at the floor and shook his head. The hospital rep wouldn't take no for an answer. He smiled ingratiatingly across the desk and tried again. 'C'mon, now! Be a good sport for me and look through the glasses one more time,' he added, pushing the box towards my father.

'Excuse me,' I said, leaning heavily on the door frame and glaring in at him. 'Dad looked once, and that's enough. He's just had surgery. You lost his glasses, and you can pay for new ones. We're going home.' I helped my father from his chair, and we walked out of the hospital. He couldn't remember how to get back to the car. Despite my own slow, heavy pace, he had a hard time keeping up and I had to stop and wait for him. We drove home in silence.

Dad died that summer. While in the hospital for a bowel impaction, he developed pneumonia and then an antibiotics-resistant infection. The drugs necessary to keep him breathing destroyed his kidneys, and the hospital, wanting him out of their intensive care unit, suggested we take 'comfort measures'. This meant that they moved him to a normal room where the nurses wouldn't give him pain medication unless he asked, and he couldn't ask because he couldn't talk anymore. They put him on a morphine drip, inducing a sort of coma. He had no awareness of our presence at all. My mother found him shortly after he died. His eyes were open, and he was covered in his own vomit.

I felt guilty immediately after he died. I'd gone back to State to start packing up my flat to move to the new one I'd signed a lease on. Hours after arriving, as I sat on the floor surrounded by packing boxes, the phone rang and my mother told me the news. My father would have died exactly as he did, no matter where I'd spent that afternoon. I knew that I couldn't have kept him alive by loving him more. I know all this in some logical way, but the part of me that finds fault – the part that starts the endless self-justifying arguments in my head – disagrees.

The last memory I have of Dad includes the sweaty confinement of rubber gloves on my skin as I grip his thin hand. I remember the smell of the hospital, a revolting miasma of human decay, bodily fluids and floral disinfectant. I remember the closed casket embossed with the Star of David and the way one Christian uncle wore the yarmulke like a baseball cap.

Everyone in the family had heard him talk about me. Dad once tried telling my aunt about my wish to be the fattest girl in school, his favourite putdown in front of company. She told him he should be ashamed, that I was a good, beautiful girl. But no one seemed to think I mourned my father enough. At the funeral and at the house afterwards I felt their eyes upon me, judging me because I hadn't cried. Rob, still dating my sister despite the gruelling time we'd had when he helped with my move, had wept openly. I stood silently beside him, numb to all of it.

I had lost my father years before that funeral. I'd done the mourning already, done it alone. Part of me didn't believe he could die. He'd taken up all the air, light and space in our house when I was a child. I didn't know how someone with such a huge presence could dwindle away to nothing, to the festering contents of a simple poplar box.

My return to campus did little to ease my mind. Some days, I didn't get out of bed at all. I'd stare at the ceiling, consider attending class and then will myself back into sleep. I had no friends at State. I couldn't even call Leigh Anne because she'd gone to France for a year to research her doctoral dissertation. Mary avoided me outside of quiz team meetings, and even during those she seemed offended by my very presence. I never actually told her that my father had died, but other team members knew, and I assumed word had got around. After the first couple of weeks, I just couldn't stand telling people about it any more. I didn't have the words.

One day after practice, Mary asked me to stay for a private chat. I can't remember what complaint she had that evening. My grief and confusion were so profound, so complete, that nothing else really touched me. I nodded as if I'd heard her and went to the ladies' room. I threw up explosively, my dinner of fast food cheeseburger and fries splattering all over the green walls of the stall. I cleaned up as best I could, wiped my mouth with a rough brown paper towel and drove home to my empty flat.

Most evenings, I'd drive around town with no destination in mind. Sometimes I'd see a film, trying without success to lose myself in someone else's fantasy world. Other nights I'd eat at restaurants I couldn't afford just so that I might talk to another human being. I practically lived at the local chain bookshop. I'd sit for hours in its faux living room, reading books I also couldn't afford and hoping one of the other patrons might talk to me.

In May, I dropped out and moved back to Toledo. I had no degree, no job and was tens of thousands of dollars in debt. I got two things out of graduate school: I can use newspaper design software, and I still have the cat I adopted from the animal shelter. Nevertheless, I had no idea what to do with my life. I began applying for jobs at newspapers, being interviewed for positions that wouldn't pay enough even to cover the interest on my loan. That spring, I moved in with my mother to wait for my future to start.

13

SELLING MYSELF BY THE POUND

'm a thousand feet above Detroit with two dozen other unlucky Toledoans and we've all found religion. The plane is shaking like a wet dog. I hear 'Oh, God!' and 'We're crashing!' and a chorus of 'God damn it's so loud and fervent that I imagine my mother might be on board. My hands clutch the parts of the armrests not blocked by the overflow of my belly and I wonder what I could possibly have done to deserve this. Apart from applying for a job in Iowa.

The newspaper offered plane tickets and one of its staff to fetch me from the airport just days after I sent them a CV and clips of my reporting work. The editor who spoke to me on the phone seemed eager and enthusiastic. He went for the hard sell, telling me all about the many wonderful riverboat casinos and McDonald's franchises his small town had to offer.

'We're right on the Illinois border, so if you ever want to go and watch triple A ball in Rockford, you're just minutes away,' he told me. I pretended to care and accepted his offer of the airfare and a free stay in a cheap chain motel. Since you can't fly anywhere directly from Toledo, and I hadn't been able to talk the editor into booking my flight directly from Detroit and letting me drive there, I climbed into a tiny plane euphemistically described by the gate agent as 'non-jet equipment'. Minutes later I found myself wishing I'd paid more attention to the pre-flight safety lecture.

The plane dropped quickly at a sharp, downward angle. People all around me screamed and crossed themselves. The moment opened wide, swallowing me whole. Frozen in my tiny seat, the metal armrests biting into my tender, doughy thighs, I thought about the many disastrous jobs and bad interviews that had led up to this hellish plane ride. I know I should have spent the time regretting other poor life choices and the vagaries of fate, but after nearly a year in my mother's basement, thoughts of the job market filled all the available anxiety space in my head.

I prayed then, for the first time since my stint in Catholic school. I prayed that I'd get this job in Iowa and finally move on with my life. The plane's gyrations ceased to upset me. At that moment, living and dying weren't as important to me as getting a job, any job, so I could recapture my self-respect and go back to thinking of myself as normal. I felt strangely calm, and the plane finally settled itself. We landed in Detroit, and I waited for my connecting flight to Rockford.

With two hours to kill before my flight, I pulled out my portfolio and looked over my clips. The job in Iowa required both features writing and newspaper design. I write great covering letters and my CV, which I designed myself using news design software, was a thing of beauty. Nowhere in my covering letter did I use the word 'fat'. Where would I? Nor did I mention my physical condition on the phone.

I sat in the old terminal at Detroit Metro watching planes through the two-storey windows and wondered what I might say.

'I've got one of those glandular problems. Normally, I'm not at all this fat. Mostly.'

'I know I seem really big, but it's all water weight – from *female* issues.'

'I'm sorry I'm so fat. Please hire me.'

I rejected all of these statements. I had no metabolic disorders and I didn't have any female issues – all the densely packed fat I carried around my midsection totally inhibited menstruation. Waiting in the airport as a 27-year old job seeker, I realised I hadn't had a period in at least ten years. I didn't miss it. I had no romantic notions about the beauty of menstrual flow and the ripe, earth-goddess fertility the whole reeking, bloody mess supposedly represented. And I definitely wasn't sorry I was fat. I didn't enjoy it, and I often wished I was thin, but I didn't feel guilty about my weight. It was my body and my business, I told myself.

At this point in my fat woman career, I weighed nearly 36 stone. I didn't know this, and I wouldn't realise it for another six months or so. I had some vague awareness of my uniqueness. People reacted to me with shock, and I noticed the stunned disgust on their faces. I knew I couldn't drive my sister's Mazda; I couldn't fit behind the wheel, not even with the seat all the way back. I didn't fit into booths at restaurants. The flight attendant on the non-jet death trap discreetly handed me a seatbelt extension as I boarded. I needed one in my car, too. I had to stop wearing trousers in graduate school – I caught a glimpse of myself in a ladies' room mirror and saw how the trousers clung to the ponderously drooping swell of my belly. The fat around my hips and on my stomach stretched my skin into a great, white lump that hung nearly to my knees like 7 stone of rancid bread dough. The front panel of my trousers captured the fat, bunching it so that I seemed to have a second pair of buttocks instead of a waist and a stomach. I first noticed this at a quiz tournament and felt relieved to have a bag full of clean laundry in the boot of my car. I fetched a skirt during the tournament's lunch break and never wore trousers in public again.

Skirts and long shirts themselves couldn't hide the sheer size of my body, but they blunted the edges just enough for me to pretend normality. I'd look in the mirror and see myself as tall and rectangular, my body reduced to large coloured squares. An outsize men's T-shirt in slimming black. An A-line skirt, also black, down to my ankles. Double-wide shoes, usually black, always ugly. This was my look for nearly ten years. I seldom wore make-up. Sometimes, I'd leave the house in a gigantic T-shirt and an ugly prairie skirt without a bra. Given the limitations I faced in terms of clothing and shoes, I didn't think this mattered. I didn't think a bra or make-up made any difference. Despite my insistence that everything was fine, that I was normal and that the shining beauty of my soul would surely, certainly land me a job, it is hard to pretend every minute of every day. I gave up on beauty. Most days, I would have given anything if I could just be average, anonymous. I wanted to walk down the street and not feel all eyes upon me, not have my head full of a million imaginary conversations in which I told these rude, staring people to mind their own business and leave me alone.

In the airport, I shook my head to clear it. This wasn't helping. I had a job interview to prepare for, and worrying about my wardrobe wasn't useful. I flipped the pages in my portfolio and saw the greyhound staring out at me, its black eyes wise and sad. The dog adorned the last features page I designed in Illinois. The dog's image sold the story beautifully, and my editors had complimented me on the design.

After leaving grad school, I'd spent almost eight months attending interviews before landing the job as a copyeditor at a small daily paper in Illinois. By that point, I would have gone to the moon for a job in my field, and desperation clouded my judgement. Rentals in the area were insanely expensive, so I lived out of my car for nearly five weeks. I finally found a flat in DeKalb, a college town half an hour's drive from work. I didn't have any furniture. I bought a bed and watched television in my empty living room, lying flat on the floor or propped against an oversized pillow.

Apart from my work colleagues, all of whom were at least ten years older than me and loaded down with spouses, children and obligations, the only people I had any regular contact with were waitresses in local restaurants and the boy who sold tickets at the discount cinema. Sometimes I shopped late at night, just so I could talk to the cashier at Giant Eagle. My work hours alone made meeting new people difficult. My day began at 4pm and ended shortly after midnight. I drove home in darkness to an empty flat, wondering how I might become a better copyeditor and get a new job somewhere less bleak.

I didn't last long in Illinois. I made clumsy mistakes and hadn't yet learned to just shut up and do my job. Fat women are supposed to know their place. We aren't supposed to display anger or use sarcasm. If we want to keep the low-paying job in the coldly expensive town in the middle of nowhere, we must be perfect in every way and perfectly, cheerfully silent. Pretending to be normal meant I sometimes made mistakes that a real girl would. This had doomed me at the paper, leaving me with nothing – no redundancy pay, no health insurance, no savings. I moved back to Toledo to live with my mother and sister. My mother tried to be kind. My 17-year-old sister was still angry that I'd taken the job and felt like I'd abandoned her. I eventually went back to DeKalb alone to pack up what little I had in my apartment.

After Illinois, I moved into Mum's basement and lined up job interviews at newspapers all over Ohio, Michigan and Indiana. I put together the best CV and clippings package I could, given that I hadn't even lasted a year in Illinois, and drove for hours to interviews. One of the jobs, at a paper in a rustbelt town in eastern Ohio, seemed promising. The editors put me up at an old hotel in the quaint city centre, and I spent my 26th birthday in the hotel's basement restaurant. A group of office colleagues seated at the next table enjoyed a raucous party while I choked down my iceberg lettuce salad and the dry clump of beef in my overcooked cheeseburger.

The next morning, I tried out for the job by helping to proof the paper's afternoon edition, editing stories about local fires and wire copy about a terrible incident unfolding in Wyoming. A college student in Laramie, Matthew Sheppard, had been beaten unconscious, tied to some fence rails, and left to die alone in the cold. One of the staff made a gay joke, and the newsroom churned with laughter. I knew that I didn't want to work with any of those people. I finished a full day of editing and design, and one of the paper's senior reporters escorted me to my car. I could tell from the sad, pitying expression on his face that, whether I wanted to or not, I wouldn't receive an offer. I told him a lie about my many other prospects. We shook hands, and I drove back to Toledo, at 80 miles an hour all the way, feeling the whole time like I was making an escape.

The second flight, from Detroit to Rockford for my latest interview was easy and uneventful. When I arrived, I saw a teenage boy holding a sign with my name scrawled on it in black felt tip. He cheerfully shook my hand and escorted me to the car park where his father, the editor, waited in the family's people carrier. The boy, a thin 13 year old with reddish hair and a gap-toothed smile, threw my luggage into the car and started to take his seat in the back. His father shook his head, indicating that the boy should sit in front. The boy looked confused, and his father made no explanation. He'd correctly guessed that I couldn't fit into the car's seatbelts, and didn't want to chance a ticket by letting me ride upfront unbelted.

During my interview in Iowa, I had to ask for a chair without arms as I wouldn't fit into most of the newspaper's office furniture. I flew home knowing I would never hear from them again. After driving five hours for another job interview, during which I had to go to a local hospital and urinate into a little plastic bowl to prove I wasn't a drug addict, I started to look for clerical work closer to home. No one in Toledo would hire me. I wrote stories for the local weekly paper, thinking they might eventually hire me for a staff job. I wrote an art column; I interviewed any celebrities who happened to be passing through Toledo; I wrote stories about war protests, the local hospice, public education and Toledo's reaction to the September 11th attacks. My stories won awards, but the paper still wouldn't put me on staff. I'd arrive for work meetings totally out of breath from climbing the steep staircase, and the publisher – a thin 40-something brunette who favoured glasses with fashionably skinny lenses – would look at me as if I were something she wanted to scrape off her shoe. When the paper finally had an opening for an arts editor, I'd been writing for them for nearly five years, but she hired someone with no credentials – a local cover band guitarist whose sole journalism clip was the angry letter to the editor he'd once written. A few months later, I quit.

Needing some way to pay my bills, I took a job doing phone customer service for a national cable internet provider. I worked from 5pm until 4am four days a week in a huge call centre located in a crumbling shopping centre on the south side of town. OmniCorps employed six hundred Toledoans who worked around the clock to make sure people in Texas and Colorado never lost the ability to surf porno sites or send e-mail. Nine months into my 18-month tour of duty at OmniCorps, I took the cubicle next to a guy, and listened as he instructed one of our many technologically challenged customers in the fine art of modem repair.

'Ma'am? Is the modem plugged in? You needed the socket for vacuuming? I see.' He hit the mute button and turned my way. 'Idiot sub,' he said. 'Sub', short for subscriber, was what we called the customers. I nodded in agreement. He hit the switch again and continued the call. 'Ma'am? Plug the modem into the wall socket. Why? Well, much like your toaster, the modem requires electricity to function. Yes, that's why the lights weren't blinking. It's working now? Great. Thank you for calling.' He disconnected the call and flung his headset onto the desk in disgust. 'These people are all morons. I've got to quit this job before the brain damage is irreversible,' he told me. 'By the way, I'm Bill.' We traded life stories between calls from subs. It turned out that Bill was also an aspiring writer. He'd seen my byline in the weekly and wondered if they might use him for freelance projects. I told him that they'd use anybody with opposable thumbs and internet access. Bill ended up working for the weekly for three or four years before catching on with a bunch of nationally prominent magazines. I like to claim credit, but Bill was pretty tenacious.

I made other friends at OmniCorps. Karen had four children and a shifty, brooding (soon to be ex) husband. She showed me snapshots of her daughter Rachael, and I commented on the family resemblance. 'Rachael's my foster daughter, but everybody says she looks like me,' Karen said. Karen moved to Detroit shortly after giving birth to her oldest child. Armed only with a baseball bat and a terrifying facial expression, she had once fought off gang members who threatened her family. After being subjected to a special talk by management, I turned to Karen, knowing I could count on her tough-minded kindness.

'The supervisors said someone complained about my body odour,' I told her. 'I wouldn't even sign the paper saying we'd had the meeting. I wash every day! I don't know what else they want. My clothes are always clean. I don't know what they're even talking about.' I felt tears form in my eyes, and struggled hard to keep them back.

DeDe, the girl who'd complained about me, was a pale, bony thing with long, white sticks for arms and legs. She liked to wear tube tops to the office, and would shrug on a sweater to avoid being caught breaking the dress code whenever she thought she saw a manager approaching. DeDe had spent the last week making veiled comments about my supposed smell to colleagues, hoping I'd take the hint and sit somewhere else. 'Can you smell that? I didn't know fat had a smell. So gross. Somebody needs to go and sit next to her own team,' DeDe said, giving me a pointed look. Then she'd shrugged and changed the subject to a lighter topic: her most recent abortion.

'I told them I wouldn't sign,' I repeated. Karen drew me into her arms and let me cry on her shoulder. The embrace surprised me. I couldn't believe that anyone would actually want to touch me. I stopped sitting by DeDe, though it meant I had to sit further away from the ladies' room and the break room. My skin rubbed raw between my thick thighs, and my back and ankles ached constantly. Even so, I preferred a longer walk during break time to listening to DeDe talk about how much my body disgusted her.

I'd visited a doctor about my backache. Standing on his scale, I learned that I no longer weighed 26 stone, which was the last figure I'd been told. At the age of 28, I weighed 37½ stone. I filed this information away in some dark place at the back of my mind and tried hard never to think about it. People like DeDe made denial impossible, however, so I avoided them. Their hostility and barely hidden rage at my offensive body frightened me. If I never looked them in the eye or spoke to them, I could still pretend I wasn't that fat. I continued to cling

– though more weakly than ever – to the idea that I was still somehow a normal human being.

My grandmother tried to raise the subject of weight one day. I often visited her when I worked for OmniCorps and the weekly paper. We'd sit in her kitchen and talk about the news. She told stories about her days as a nurse, or about crazy things my grandfather had done. Sometimes we'd sit quietly in her den, a strange semicircle of a room with tall, narrow windows overlooking a tree-lined street. We'd watch *Jeopardy!* or *Everybody Loves Raymond*. Grandma loved that show, for some inexplicable reason.

'I was reading about gastric bypass in the paper,' she told me one day, her tone cautious. 'Do you think that's something you'd ever consider?'

'I don't know,' I answered, noncommittal. 'Maybe. I don't know if my insurance would cover it.' I changed the subject, and Grandma let me. She never pushed her opinions on anyone, and had brought up surgery only because my continuing weight gain terrified her. Life at 37 stone is full of physical pain and good reasons to feel sad. However, I didn't pursue surgery then, even though my grandmother would have supported it, because the only thing that made my life possible *was* my denial. Acknowledging the fact of my enormousness would have shattered me. Despite the threat to my health and the social limitations it imposed, I still wasn't ready to do anything about my weight.

When OmniCorps finally fired me (trying to start a union there probably wasn't the best idea), I felt relieved. After the firing, I had a bout of sciatica – a nerve condition that causes back and hip pain – and was bed bound for nearly a month. I couldn't do any writing, and the sheer agony of sitting upright made driving a car impossible. My mother thought I should take on freelance assignments and work through the pain. She still expected me to unload shopping and carry baskets of laundry from the basement; with degenerative arthritis herself and could no longer do these things without help. 'You're ruining my life!' she screamed at me through my closed bedroom door. I called my sister, hoping she'd come home from college for a weekend to help me. I felt helpless and worthless, lying in cold, dirty sheets with the phone pressed to my cheek. My sister refused to come home. She had to study, she said. In the state I was in, I believed she didn't come home because she thought I'd brought the sciatica on myself. I was fat, and I deserved what I got because of it. I tolerated the pain and boredom for over a month before my doctor finally prescribed cortisone. The sciatica disappeared completely. I went back to my freelancing, though still barely making enough money for the monthly payments on my used car.

Despite all of these close calls, my dire career situation and the shame of being a 30-year-old woman living with her mother, I still did nothing about my weight. All the little reprieves – the successful cortisone treatment, my freelance pay cheques, birthday money from a kindly aunt and uncle – allowed me to continue life as usual, safe in the cocoon of denial I'd spent three decades creating for myself. It took a family tragedy and another harrowing bout of sciatica to finally wake me up.

14

DEATH AND CHEESE FACTORIES

I had a new bathing suit, maps printed from the Internet and serious reservations, few of which had anything to do with the cheap motel we planned to visit. On that hot, humid August day, two hours in my dying Lincoln with sporadic air conditioning and my mother's chain-smoking seemed like solid clues that the trip was a bad idea. People over the age of 12 (I was 32 and Andrea was 25) should never attempt long road trips with their mothers.

A mobile phone rang in the back seat. I looked over my shoulder and watched as my mother fished the phone out of her bra. 'Oh, Bander boy, who's a good doggie? Who gets a treat? That's a good boy.' Mum spoke thickly guttural baby talk to the Canadian dog on the other end of the line. Mum's friend Arlene, a woman she'd met playing cards on the Internet, called just so Mum could talk to the dog. The sound of my mother's voice as she offered treats long distance began to become distorted inside my brain. Each cooed word, each unanswerable question separated into high-pitched syllables. I cringed and slunk lower in the passenger seat, shoulders hunched tightly as

I put my hands over my ears to block out the noise. I thought about yanking the steering wheel so that we'd ram the truck in the next lane at about 80 miles an hour. I begged my sister to make a pit stop, and we cruised into the car park of a McDonald's near Rockford, Illinois. I ate a double quarter pounder with cheese in about 12 seconds flat. The grease, fat and insipid white bread had their usual calming effect on me, and we soldiered on into Wisconsin.

Driving along the main drag of Wisconsin Dells, we saw upmarket hotels advertising indoor water parks, and cheap motels with gaudy, brightly coloured animal statuary as their gimmicky calling cards. A frog the size of an SUV guarded one outdoor pool. The pink paint had chipped off the amphibian's plaster tongue, and the tiny swimming pool stood empty, despite the unrelenting heat. We passed hotels with safari themes, restaurants offering prime rib specials, and cars full of other tourists. We stopped at a light and I waved to a little boy in the next car. He stuck his tongue out as his father hit the accelerator. Their car screeched off and the smell of burning rubber hovered in the air. I wanted to roll the window up, but the air conditioning had shut itself off again.

At the edge of town, a sprawling gambling complex made primarily of turquoise stucco caught my eye. The Ho Chunk Casino was named after an American Indian group, not the fat whore I'd originally imagined. When I'd planned the trip, I thought Mum might enjoy losing money there, but as we drove by, she complained about the epic size of the place, its lack of motorised scooters – my mother didn't like to walk as she'd had a hip and two knees surgically replaced – and the reputedly 'tight' slots at Indian casinos. The Dells also had a state nature reserve with a tranquil blue lake, rolling hills and beautifully manicured hiking trails, but we as a family preferred air conditioning and cable, and stuck to the city and its unsubtle entertainments.

We passed theme parks, their rollercoasters towering over the street. Happy screams echoed across the Tarmac but these attractions didn't tempt us. The only member of our party who could actually fit into the rides, my sister Andrea, had just driven us six hours from Chicago. After we checked in, she planned to go for a run and then spend as much time as she could by herself. We pulled into our motel, tired and anxious from the long, hot drive, and I felt guilty about having manoeuvred everyone into taking the trip at all.

The motel had threadbare green carpet and faux wood panelling in a variety of ugly colours. It had an indoor pool where I tried out my new swimsuit, a tasteful navy halterneck with no back and zero breast support. The suit did nothing to flatter or control my figure, but I had bought it because it was the only one I could find that fitted my 37 stone. The skin on my back rolled from the neck of the halter to the top of the swim briefs in one vast, undulating, pasty wave. My breasts pointed aggressively south, and my arm flesh oozed in pale stalactites over the gathered elastic. I didn't care. I wanted to swim, and I reasoned that my ugly halterneck suit would offend other bathers far less than my naked body.

That evening, though, there were no other bathers. Floating alone in the motel pool, I thought about the last few hellish weeks. My mind drifted to the hospice bed, my grandmother tiny, still and pallid, lost against stark white sheets. I'd asked for the Kaddish, the Jewish prayer for the dead, despite my agnosticism and the fact that my parents raised me as a

Catholic. Something about the rhythm of all those Hebrew words I didn't understand, dedicated to a god whose existence I personally couldn't vouch for, gave me odd solace. My grandmother believed in God and I hoped for her sake that heaven was real.

I'd stood at the head of her bed and talked. I needed the sound of a voice, even my own, so that the room wouldn't seem so still and sterile. 'We're all here, Grandma,' I said, patting her foot through the blanket. She hated having her feet covered, but was long past complaining. Her blood pressure had slowed to almost nothing, and she hadn't opened her eyes or spoken in nearly two days. 'Uncle Drew is here, and Uncle Mike. Amy, Aunt Barbara, Aunt Tish. My Mum. We're here and we love you very much. The nurses here are really nice. You'd approve.'

Grandma lay still and silent, her breathing slow and shallow, her pale-lashed eyes firmly closed. I wished she could talk to us. She'd spoken to me the day before she fell into the coma, when she was still at home. Aunt Tish had ordered a hospital bed to be set up in Grandma's den, the room in which we'd spent so many afternoons together watching *Oprah*. A sofa crowded up to the side of that bed, the rest of the furniture pushed together in a tight, awkward jumble. I'd stood up to leave, leaning down to kiss my grandmother's papery cheek.

'Your shirt is pretty,' she'd said, smiling up at me. I wore an oversize knitted top with a pattern of red roses ordered from an online catalogue.

'It's new,' I'd replied. 'I love you, Grandma.' We had never made a practice of saying this, but ever since Grandma's last hospitalisation for pneumonia, she always told me she loved me whenever I left at the end of a visit.

'I love you too, Becky,' Grandma had said.

She'd lost so much weight over the previous five days. During my visit, she'd shuddered in her sleep, the bed groaning with every movement. When she woke, Grandma told one of my aunts that she wanted to sit next to Bob, a high school boyfriend she broke up with in 1943.

Three days later, we moved her to the hospice. The redbrick building, surrounded by freshly turned soil, seemed naked as it waited for proper landscaping. After Grandma settled in and a nurse brought me a copy of the prayer I'd asked for, I gave Grandma's hand a squeeze and left her alone so that my mother and her two brothers could say goodbye in private. I took the computer printout with its English phonetic rendering of my Hebrew prayer and went to the family lounge, a lavishly appointed space complete with a huge fireplace and a big-screen television. My cousin and I worked on a jigsaw puzzle while our parents kept vigil over their dying mother in a room down the hall. The puzzle would make a picture of a flower-filled meadow, assuming all one thousand pieces were still in the box.

We left for the evening around 11pm, and at midnight, one of the nurses called. 'Mum?' My mother sat in the darkened kitchen of our shared home, staring blankly at the computer monitor. The ambient glow from the screen made her face into a greenish Halloween mask. 'Grandma's gone. I'm so sorry.' My mother nodded, wiping a tear away. I poured her an enormous glass of rum and left her alone with her friends online. I tried to reach my sister and got her voicemail.

*

Spring bled into a humid, colourless summer. My relatives discussed who would take what, dividing all of Grandma's things like rival patrons at a garage sale. I got her dishes, Fiestaware from the 1930s in turquoise and orange, butter yellow and pale green. Every time I set the table for a special meal, I'd think of her.

I also got a painting by my great-grandmother. The tiny watercolour showed a road stretching towards the orange glow of sunlight. Dawn, sunset, both, neither? No way to tell. Grandma had hung her mother's watercolours all over her house: a horse-and-buggy scene over the fireplace in the living room; bluebirds and robins in a tidy little row over her upright piano; the winter scene in her den by the window. I couldn't stand the negotiations about possessions. I stayed home alone, often falling asleep on the sofa with the television on. I dreamed of my grandmother telling me that everything would be okay – I didn't believe it – until the phone woke me up, and she was gone again.

In August, my aunt organised an estate sale, and I helped empty my grandmother's house of all the things that weren't on offer to the public. The work of emptying cupboards and sorting through old photographs exhausted me. Most of my excess weight settled around my midsection, and the hot folds of fat-filled skin sweated and itched despite the glacial air conditioning. I pieced through Grandma's costume jewellery, looking for makers' marks that might indicate value. I emptied a cupboard that reeked from a long-dead cat's indiscretions, and found grey wool cloaks lined in scarlet silk, presents my grandmother Lois and her older sister Jean had received when they graduated from nursing college. Aunt Jean had served in the Army Air Corps, tending wounded in the South Pacific during the Second World War; Lois had worked at St Charles Hospital on the south side of Toledo. Because she was tiny, my grandmother was often sent to accident sites where she'd crawl into the wreckage of broken cars to tend victims trapped inside.

Grandma had saved all the cards and letters I sent her: ten-year-old postcards from my term in Australia; hand-painted Christmas and Easter cards; letters from my college days in Boston. She'd saved a thank-you note for a visit she'd made to my school English class to speak about treating shell-shocked soldiers after the war, about ration books and painting lines up the back of her calf to simulate a stocking seam. I'd forgotten she was coming and skipped school that day, but luckily she had a sense of humour about it.

No souvenirs exist to mark all the times Grandma visited or picked me up from school. She came to all my junior high school quiz team games, sitting proudly in the front row, happy to claim the fat girl in the plaid shirt with the mismatched socks. No keepsakes mark the afternoons we spent together playing with her kitten or watching *Oprah*. I also found an audio tape of Grandma playing the piano, a tape she recorded a few months before entering the hospital with pneumonia. She'd been a child prodigy and had performed concerts as a little girl. She could sight-read music and loved old show tunes. Before emphysema tethered her to an oxygen tank, she'd performed at local nursing homes, playing songs from the roaring twenties for people old enough to be her parents.

Her funeral was small, just family and an elderly minister who'd attended high school with Grandma more than 60 years before. The cemetery, set among the corn and soya bean fields of Fulton County, Ohio, stood next door to a simple white church with a small steeple.

I knew we should have music at the service, since music meant so much to Grandma and my friend Sue, a local music writer, recommended a guitarist. He played Grandma's favourite song, which had been a comfort to her as her illness progressed:

> *But come ye back when summer's in the meadow*
> *Or when the valley's hushed and white with snow*
> *And I'll be here in sunshine or in shadow*
> *Oh Danny boy, oh Danny boy, I love you so.*

When the guitar player finished, I stood, tugging at the hem of my shirt so the roses would all line up evenly. I read from a David Barker poem in a little green autograph book Grandma had been given for her seventh birthday:

> *Life is fleeting as a shade,*
> *Make your mark.*
> *Marks of some kind must be made.*
> *Make your mark.*

'Grandma made her mark. As a nurse and in her life, she helped almost everyone she ever met. She helped me. I loved her a lot. I'll miss her forever.' I went back to my seat and held my sister's shoulder as she cried.

We ended up in Wisconsin not long afterwards as I'd thought it seemed like a good place to go to forget the sad jumble sale we'd made of Grandma's things. I wanted to forget the petty family arguments over this ornament or that piece of furniture; the estate sale where strangers picked through Grandma's linens and beaded necklaces; her empty house, stripped naked, awaiting a quick sale.

After a night of swimming and recovering from the long drive, we took a boat tour of the Dells, waiting an extra 20 minutes at the landing for a boat with seats wide enough to accommodate me. My mother sat on a bench by the water, complaining about the long walk and the heat. The boat, a thick white wedge with a green awning, pulled away from the dock, and we glided to the centre of the river. The blue-green water, glassy and still, eddied around pine-topped stone islands with names like 'Sugar Bowl', 'Inkpot' and 'Lover's Heart'. A wholesome college girl narrated the trip, making sure to remind us that she worked for tips alone. I didn't leave the boat at any of its stops. The long drive from Toledo to Chicago and then to the Dells had left me with a stiff back, and my hip ached from sitting too long. Later that day, my mother, sister and I ate at a restaurant called the Cheese Factory. Andrea was still a vegetarian, and she offered me little bits of tofu from her plate. I ate a small pizza, drank glass after glass of Coke, and finished the meal with sweet potato pie and ice cream.

By the time we got back to Toledo a few days later, after a detour to Chicago and eight hours in the car, my hip and back throbbed, the pain so intense that I couldn't sit upright. Doctors diagnosed sciatica for the second time. A swollen disc in my spine pressed on the sciatic nerve causing pain in my hip and leg. Every time I tried to sit upright, it felt like someone had smashed my hip with a sledgehammer. For a while – a few days, a week maybe – I gave up trying to sit, and lay in bed crying. I slept only when the pain permitted, but dreamed of my death so often that I was afraid to close my eyes.

I spent nearly a month unable to sit or drive. I left the house only for visits to the accident and emergency unit, the only option for medical care for people with no insurance. Pregnant women get sciatica from carrying all that extra baby weight; I got it because I carried 14 stone of densely packed fat around my hips and stomach. The abdominal skin stretched, and my swollen gut hung heavily to my knees, putting terrible pressure on my lower back.

One night, I also woke up unable to feel the big toe and most of the front half of my left foot. I lay in bed, terrified, waiting for my mother to wake up so that I could ask her to take me to the hospital. A bald, gnome-like doctor diagnosed gout as the source of the numbness, wrote out a prescription and told me to avoid shellfish, green beans and mushrooms, foods I enjoyed, but which are rich in the chemical that brings on gout. I made a final trip to A and E after learning that gout doesn't in fact cause numbness; it causes agonising foot pain. Henry VIII had gout; one of my bald uncles had gout. Did I have gout? Maybe. But the numbness in my foot had nothing to do with it, leaving me to ponder all sorts of other horrible possibilities.

'I can't see a family doctor because I don't have a job, any money or insurance,' I told the blond male Barbie doll of an A and E doctor who wanted to know why I was wasting his time. After three weeks of sleepless nights, of days spent lying awake in dark rooms, the pain, numbness and exhaustion had taken their toll and I couldn't have cared less about this pretty man's opinion of me. 'I'm fat. Huge. You can see that. My whole life, people have told me "You're fat, you'll get diabetes and they'll cut off your feet." Well?' I spat at him. 'How about it? I can't feel my foot. I don't want to lose it.' I glared at him, too angry and tired to cry. After a moment of stunned silence, the doctor gave a brief nod, pulled out a stethoscope and bent to take my left foot in both of his well-manicured hands.

'The pulses are strong and the temperature is fine. Your circulation is good,' he told me. 'I'm sorry that I can't tell you where the numbness is coming from. It could be the sciatica. It might be some other nerve impairment. You might want to have an MRI when you've got insurance again.' With that, he left the room. I was relieved that I'd keep my foot, if frustrated with the lack of a clear diagnosis. I left the hospital wondering what to do next.

Julie, my quiz team friend, drove three hours from Kalamazoo to spend an afternoon with me some days later. When she walked into my room, her hair freshly red from a recent henna application, I felt my depression lift a little. 'Honey, I think you need to try and walk. Why don't we take a stroll around the back garden?' I resisted at first, but her manic cheer won out. I stepped barefoot into the garden. I stood still for a minute, enjoying the sunlight, the fresh air and the distant birdsong. I made a slow circuit of the garden with Julie walking close behind me. I moved unsteadily, my balance thrown by the numbness in my foot. We stayed outside for a long time. Feeling the grass underfoot and the sun on my skin made me feel really awake for the first time in weeks. That night, I dreamed about Grandma again. 'It'll be okay, all okay,' she said. 'You'll make this right.'

The next morning, I phoned Social Service agencies and charities until I finally found a psychotherapist who worked on a sliding scale. I called the Social Security office to apply for disability status, and this eventually led to health coverage. Strangely enough, I had no idea of my exact weight at the time. I hadn't visited a doctor's surgery in five years. I knew I weighed over 36 stone; and I knew I needed to take serious action about my weight if I wanted to survive and enjoy any kind of quality of life.

Everybody always wants to know why I didn't diet before this. I did. But not often and never for very long. As a teen, I'd wanted to lose weight as a means of obtaining revenge on my many high school enemies. I wanted to walk into school after a summer of magical weight loss looking like Olivia Newton John at the end of *Grease* (minus the cigarette and unfortunate perm). I'd be miraculously hot, and I'd rub it in everyone's face. Bee Gees music would swell, and I'd fly off into the clouds with the cute guy from my English class.

At 16, I researched dieting at the library. After amassing a pile of medical texts nearly two feet high, I went to work on my plan of attack, but what I learned derailed the diet train before it ever really left the station: that most dieters regain all the weight they lose (and more); that a portion of the weight you lose is actually muscle; and that yo-yo dieting is worse for you than just being fat. The human body isn't really designed to lose excess weight. Because of all our hunter-gatherer ancestry, our bodies try to hold on to every ounce in order to stave off starvation. When you diet, the body interprets the reduction in food intake as starvation and slows the metabolism to conserve calories. You feel tired and ill and, eventually, you give up. My research provided logical reasons for me not to try harder to lose weight. I also lived with my father (as teenagers do, barring death, divorce or joining the circus), and eating whatever I wanted was pretty much the only way I could rebel that wouldn't end with him hitting me, shoving me into a cupboard or telling me how useless I was.

So by the time I left for college I weighed 26 stone. At that point, losing ten pounds wouldn't have made much difference to my overall health or appearance. In my late teens and twenties, inertia, depression and a personal metabolism tailor-made to pack on bum fat all combined to make dieting seem like a huge waste of time. Also, I loved food. A lot. I loved the sharp, sweet sting of Coca-Cola and biscuits I baked myself fresh from the oven. I loved fast food, ice cream and chocolate. And I saw no reason not to indulge myself.

By my early thirties, I'd had two bad bouts of sciatica; I couldn't find anyone willing to hire me, no matter how well qualified I was; I lived with my mother; I never dated; and I avoided restaurants with booths and riding in small cars. My body limited activity so severely I felt imprisoned by it. A simple trip to the shops exhausted me. The walk from the car park alone required several rest stops.

After that final bout of sciatica, after my grandmother's death and the depression that followed, I knew I had to act. More importantly, I was finally ready to do so. I could no longer afford the luxury of denial, and I made the decision that I wanted gastric bypass surgery. My grandmother had worked as a registered nurse for almost 40 years, and had had enormous faith in science and medicine. Not only had she been the person to mention it, but using surgery and the professional help of nurses and surgeons felt like something my grandmother would have wanted me to do. *And* it felt like the right thing to do.

I've read patients' stories on support sites for gastric bypass. A lot of people write in to complain that thin people (usually family members) mock them for taking 'the easy way out' and having an operation. For me, surgery wasn't an easy option but I wanted that initial period of quick weight loss because I had such a huge amount of weight to lose to really improve my health, and thought that I'd die long before I could lose the same amount of weight from a diet.

People have died having the surgery, of course. I thought about the risks for a long time before settling on a doctor. My chosen surgeon told me that the anaesthesia posed the greatest risk for someone my size so I decided to lose as much weight as I could on my own before the surgery. I began exercising six days a week so that my heart and lungs could withstand anaesthesia. I worked on core strength so that I'd walk more easily after the operation; walking a lot lessens the risk of a fatal blood clot.

I knew all the risks, and the risks scared me, but staying super-morbidly obese scared me more. Weighing nearly 43 stone as I did by this stage carried the risk of death (or of a paralysing stroke) with no possibility of improvement in the future. The surgery posed some danger, but offered the possibility of a decent life, of good health and of living to see 40. I weighed the risks and chose the operation.

I lost 3 stone before I had surgery, and more than 18 stone afterwards.

Unlike some of the women on the support site, I will never apologise for having had surgery. Whenever I see a ladies' magazine showcasing ordinary people who lost weight without surgery (through hard work alone!), I feel like flying to

California and putting a size ten foot in some editor's boney behind. People judge you harshly for weighing too much – and in America, a lot of people interpret 'too much' as anything over a size eight. But they also judge formerly fat people harshly for losing weight without struggling hard to do so in a conventional way. I'm always having self-justifying conversations with myself, but it's hard for me to care very much about the opinions of other people who use the term 'easy way out' derisively to describe weight-loss surgery and as a put-down to me for having undergone the procedure. If my house were on fire, I wouldn't walk from one end to the other to escape through a door. I'd take the easiest way out to save my life. I'd climb out through a window, and no one would criticise my choice.

I needed surgery to save my life. Through diet and exercise alone, I simply couldn't have lost enough weight sufficiently quickly to avoid an early death or permanent disability. People who have a problem with how I lost the weight mystify me. I wonder why they feel like they have a right to criticise my medical decisions. No one tells a cancer patient – even a heavy smoker – that having tumours removed via surgery is a cop out. No matter how I've struggled or what I've achieved, some people will always need to hate me because I'm fat, because I used to be tremendously fat, and because I lost weight without, in their minds, really 'deserving' to. Of course, most of the people who've asked me why I didn't just try Atkins and buy a treadmill aren't friends or family – those people who knew me when I weighed almost 43 stone could see that I had to do something drastic.

I wish my grandmother had lived to see how I've worked to

take control of my life. She would have felt such relief for me. Really, though, I wish that my grandmother hadn't died at all. I miss her funny hospital stories, her husky laugh and her common sense. I'd gladly sit through every single episode of *Everybody Loves Raymond* for another afternoon with her at her kitchen table. As I made my first tentative steps towards surgery, I knew my grandmother would approve. She valued the old-fashioned work ethic; she would never normally have advised a quick fix to any problem, given what a good, sensible, conservative farm girl she was at heart, but she had urged me to have this operation.

Four months after my grandmother died, I started seeing a therapist. A year later, I lay on a white-sheeted operating table and waited for my life to begin.

15

DISEMBOWELLED

The best thing about weighing 36 stone is eating whatever you want. You don't worry about gaining a few pounds. You know that it won't make a difference. You know that starving yourself to lose a few pounds won't make a difference, either. The futility of the situation creates its own inertia. When I weighed 36 stone, I thought nothing of drinking all the Cherry Coke I wanted. I ate triple cheeseburgers and apple pie and quiche Lorraine.

Weighing 36 stone should have meant that I had diabetes, high blood pressure and heart disease at the very least. I had none of the above. I drove a car. I worked. I never became permanently fused to a plaid sofa. Burly firemen never had to remove a picture window from my house so they could haul me away to the hospital. Still, I longed to do ordinary things. I missed having the ability to get up off the floor unassisted, to sit in booths at restaurants and to ride in Japanese cars.

After my grandmother's death, after the bad road trip and the last horrible bout of sciatica, I knew I had to do something about my weight. Not just for my friends and family, and not at all for the sake of the career I'd never really had; I just didn't want to die. I read somewhere that the life expectancy for someone my height (five foot seven) who weighed over 36 stone was 33 years. At 32, even after I recovered from the sciatica, I'd lie awake late at night with that in mind. I was afraid to close my eyes. If I slept I believed I might have that giant heart attack doctors had been threatening me with since I was a little fat girl.

I wish I could say that I decided on surgery, got some therapy and my life changed overnight, but nothing worth having ever comes so easily. In the weeks that followed my recovery from the sciatic attack, I alternated between terror and overwhelming sorrow. I had panic attacks over trivial things. If the cat got out, I'd cry for hours. If I lost my car keys, I couldn't function. I'd sit behind the steering wheel weeping, and then pound the dashboard in frustrated rage. I knew these reactions had nothing to do with the minor problems at hand so I called a local psychiatric clinic. Even with their sliding scale, I'd have to come up with 25 dollars for each counselling session.

I'd stopped writing for the paper and had no income so I asked my mother for the money. I probably should have felt guilty for asking, and, more importantly, for living with Mum rent free, but my attitude was pretty much 'you broke it, you buy it'. I didn't hold Mum responsible for every bad thing that happened during my childhood, but she was there and she was an adult. On an intellectual level, I know what utter bullshit this is, but in my heart, in my gut, I feel like my parents owe me a debt that can never be repaid. My father owes most of that, but he's dead and beyond collection. So I borrowed from my mother, I lived in her house, and, at least for the first few months of counselling sessions, I took the money she handed me every time I left the house to meet my therapist.

My therapist's practice used office space provided by the local Catholic archdiocese. The modern multi-storey building in central Toledo had a huge bronze statue of Christ affixed to its façade. Jesus hovered in mid-air, sans cross, but with a nail driven through both feet. When I arrived, I was greeted by Lorri, the receptionist. After a few visits, I realised that it was Lorri who had taken my initial call when I'd cried into the phone, telling a faceless stranger about my weight, my living situation, my joblessness. After months of weekly visits, Lorri started greeting me by name. She laughed easily at my jokes, and I started to feel a bit more normal, less depressed and slightly more like myself. My therapist, Cathy, would call me into her office, and I'd sit in a black office chair, trying to ignore the way the chair arms bruised my thighs.

Cathy was in her early sixties but looked decades younger and wore stylish, tailored clothing. During our initial sessions, she listened to me talk about my father, my grandmother's death and about how sad I felt all the time. She talked about me in the third person. 'But what does Rebecca do in that situation?' she might ask. I was evasive. I didn't intend to dodge her questions, but I wanted desperately to be accurate. No matter how angry I felt, I wanted to give all my childhood antagonists a fair and balanced presentation. I backtracked; I equivocated. A few months into the process, Cathy stopped me midway through a long excuse I was making for my father that involved the Depression, the Air Force and the socioeconomic conditions in Youngstown circa 1930. Cathy put up a hand to stop me, and gave me her best clinical assessment of my case history: 'You had a shitty childhood.'

I couldn't disagree, but I felt like accuracy was important, that I wouldn't be helped if I wasn't totally honest. 'Parts of it were good. We went on vacations,' I said, immediately realising how ridiculous I must have sounded.

A few months after I started therapy, my application for government disability was rejected. I found a lawyer to argue the appeal, and filled out a physical functionality report as mandated by the state. In this document, I enumerated the many ways in which my obesity was disabling me: 'I can't climb a flight of stairs. I can't step up onto the wide, flat porches of many suburban ranch houses and some office buildings. All my weight pitches me forwards, and falling at my size would be catastrophic. If I broke a bone, I might never recover. I don't fit into any chair that has arms. I have infections underneath the skin on my calves. I sleep uneasily, sometimes staying awake for 36 hours at a time before passing out from sheer exhaustion. I cry uncontrollably at the slightest provocation.'

Reviewing this form before posting it off to the lawyer, I felt deeply ashamed. I felt like the sort of dog you have put to sleep. Nevertheless, my only hope for having surgery lay in this disability programme so I mailed the form. If I qualified, the government would provide me with health insurance. Surgery still wouldn't be a given; the government insurance would have to grant approval for that, something they only do in the most dire, life-threatening cases. And, despite my mobility problems, my depression and the pain in my lower back, ankles and knees – despite my extreme obesity – I didn't have diabetes, a heart condition, high blood pressure, asthma or blood clots. I realised I might actually be too healthy to qualify for gastric bypass surgery.

Six weeks after submitting the appeal, my lawyer called to tell me I'd been approved. I set up an appointment with my family doctor and she referred me to a pulmonologist to confirm if I had sleep apnoea as she suspected. Apnoea happens to some fat people because all the weight on the chest and neck can disrupt the breathing during sleep. You wake dozens of times each hour without realising it, and feel tired all the time during the day. Having apnoea would strengthen my case for surgery. *Not as good as being diabetic*, I thought, *but I'll take it.*

When I scheduled these doctor visits, I knew I weighed at least 36 stone. I didn't have a specific number. My family doctor's scale stopped at 25 stone, so she never even attempted to weigh me. In the pulmonologist's office I found out. In the five years that had passed since I'd had an accurate weighing, I'd gained almost 3½ stone. The electronic scale read 40 stone, the number writ large in neon green lights. That sort of number comes as a huge shock. You try to deny its significance. If you're me, you leave the doctor's office, head directly to Wendy's and buy a Classic Triple, large fries and a Cherry Coke. You eat this meal in your car, and you cry like a little girl.

When I had found out I weighed 37½ stone, I managed to slide into denial about it. I did nothing about my weight. But something about this new number, 40 stone, disturbed me profoundly. I couldn't put any positive spin on that number. I also couldn't bring myself to ignore the weight any more. The weight was killing me, but so was my silence about it. Pretending to be normal wouldn't keep me alive. I finished my cheeseburger and started researching gastric bypass surgery in earnest.

None of the bypass surgeons in Toledo was willing to accept government health insurance. I researched the fatality rates of various surgical practices in other parts of the state and settled on one that had had only one death in two thousand cases – the national average for the operation is one death in every two hundred surgeries – so I liked my chances. I had a lot of time to think about surgery. The earliest pre-op appointment the centre could offer me was three months after the date of my initial call. When the day came, my mother and I drove three hours south to a glossy suburban office park wedged delicately between Cincinnati and Dayton. We drove through Dayton on the way there, and I thought about my father. We'd buried him in a military cemetery in Dayton, though I'd never seen the grave – I'm just not a cemetery person. I don't think Dad's spirit resides in a poplar box under a stone with the Star of David carved into it, and I can't see myself talking to Dad's tombstone. I've had conversations with him in my mind, for all the good they do. I wish I knew more about him, but talking to the still ground and putting a rock on the grave won't answer my questions.

The evening before my 7am appointment, Mum and I stayed at a ramshackle hotel in Middleton, a down-at-heel dormitory town slightly closer to Cincinnati than to Dayton. We had a terrible dinner in the hotel dining room, retiring early in preparation for the long day ahead of us. In the morning, it rained heavily, and the rutted grey streets were slick and shiny with water. My left knee ached and I could barely fit into Mum's car, a mini-SUV with narrow front seats. My knees wedged into the hard plastic dashboard, and the seatbelt didn't fit at all.

'Where the hell is this place? Damn it! We're going to be late, and they won't see you and all this will be for nothing.' My mother, on the verge of tears because of the rain and the bad directions, burst into an angry fit. The combination of her tension and the heavy smell of cigarette smoke made my head hurt. I didn't want to deal with any of this, not on the day of my first surgical appointment, but I knew I needed to calm Mum down and direct her or we'd both die in a ditch on the side of the road.

'Look, the map is pretty simple. We'll be a little late, but the appointment is supposed to last all day, so I think we'll be okay,' I said, trying to sound calm and to keep the irritation out of my voice. 'I'll call the centre and let them know we'll be a little late. It'll be fine,' I promised. Mum stopped sniffling and nodded. When we finally arrived, Mum parked in the space closest to the door. I went in alone while she smoked her final cigarette of the morning. The waiting room – a square, white-painted space with many artificial plants and a small stereo system on a wrought-iron table – was ringed with chairs. The chairs had no arms, and were at least twice the size of any office chair I'd ever seen. I presented my insurance card to the receptionist.

By the time my mother joined me, I'd already spent half an hour filling out forms, including a huge multiple-choice test. One question asked about my belief in God. I deemed this irrelevant and left it unanswered. After separating for a few minutes while a nurse drew my blood, weighed me and took a 'before' picture, Mum and I reunited in an office where we watched an orientation video about the surgery. I met with the staff shrink, and he asked me questions about food and my expectations for the surgery. After receiving a food journal from the staff nutritionist and discussing exercise with a physiologist, I finally met the surgeon.

Dr Warwick was a tall, shockingly thin blonde. She wore subtle gold jewellery and elegant linen trousers under her white coat. She spoke with a slight accent, and one of the nurses told us later that she had emigrated from Russia. Her hands were long and graceful, and when she touched me her fingers were dry and cool. As she entered the room on our first meeting, she reached into her pocket and pulled out a plastic cup the size of a shot glass.

'After surgery, this is what your stomach will hold,' she said. She explained that a gastric bypass would involve creating a tiny pouch out of my stomach, sealing the pouch off from the remaining stomach, and bypassing an area of intestine that normally absorbs fats (and also many of the nutrients in food), then connecting the new pouch to the intestine. For 18 months or so the small pouch and malabsorption would allow me to lose weight. My body would catch on to the scam eventually, weight loss would slow, and I'd have to rely on good eating habits and exercise to maintain a healthy weight. Some post-operative patients can't eat any sweets; some can't eat fats; others react badly to spicy foods. In addition to the possibility that I would never eat chocolate again, however, there were more serious issues. I could develop a leak in the new pouch. I could have a pulmonary embolism. I could die.

The doctor examined my stomach. I stood before her with my shirt raised to expose my abdomen. She lifted the heavy fold of skin and pressed the space between my hips. She nodded, and asked to see my legs. I lifted my skirt, staring intently at the wall as Dr Warwick squeezed my calves. I endured this silently, feeling like a horse during a veterinary examination. When the doctor finished, I took a few minutes to rearrange my clothes.

'Have you ever operated on anyone my size?' I asked.

'Yes. I feel that the best way to help is the operation. It's the fastest way of getting the weight off. We also bring in a second surgeon from our Chicago practice. We want to do this quickly, so you're not under anaesthesia any longer than necessary. Surgery will take an hour, hour and a half at most,' she said.

After six hours of tests and meetings, my mother and I finally left for home. During the long drive, I thought about the risks of surgery and decided I still wanted to have it. Surgery is risky. Weighing nearly 43 stone is risky. But surgery offered potential rewards I'd have a hard time achieving on my own – at least in a very timely fashion. My surgeon had only had one death, and I had none of the risk factors that usually result in complications. I wasn't diabetic or over 50. Still, I knew I wanted to prepare for the operation. I wanted my heart and lungs to be in the best possible shape so that I could mitigate the risks of anaesthesia or of having a blood clot.

I joined a gym and stuffed myself into my backless, braless swimsuit so I could do water aerobics and swim laps. I cut out fast food and fizzy drinks completely. I started losing weight, dropping over a stone the first month that I went entirely without greasy cheeseburgers and Coke. I still ate dessert and had the occasional bowl of clam chowder or a chocolate bar but I wrote down everything I ate, and found myself eating fewer fatty or sugary things. I don't know if I had any more willpower than before; I just didn't like to write 'enormous slab of chocolate' in the journal. My surgeon's nutritionist would review the book at our next visit, and I didn't want to lose my shot at being a model patient.

My first water aerobics class took place at the YMCA gym on

the south side of town. The building, a utilitarian concrete square with a flagpole as its lone adornment, had an indoor pool. I wore my swimsuit under my clothes so I wouldn't have to change in front of the other women in the changing room. The pool had wide plastic steps down into the water, necessary for me since I couldn't climb ladders. I arrived early, stashed my clothes in a locker, and negotiated the slippery hallway leading to the pool. The water felt good against my skin that hot July day, and I was glad to be indoors swimming. The other women in the class arrived. Many were over 60 but a few were my age. There were no men. Our instructor welcomed the group; most of the women seemed to know her already. Terry was small and had short hair the colour of old straw. Her age was hard to determine, but I thought she might be in her late thirties. I noticed that the skin on her heavily muscled thighs hung a bit; one of the other women later told me that Terry had had a gastric bypass herself and once weighed over 21 stone.

'Okay ladies, here we go. Remember, don't look down – there's nothing there we need to see!' Terry said. The women laughed at this joke. We laughed at it class after class, as it was always true, and always delivered in Terry's brusque, drill sergeant manner. Terry made us jump for the better part of 45 minutes. We also did thigh exercises she called 'crabbing', crouching low in the water and tapping our feet rapidly. Every time Terry yelled at us to 'Crab it!' she got a chorus of groans in reply. We did sprints, running on the spot for two minutes at a time. We moved into deeper water and did crunches, floating on our backs and bringing our knees into our chests.

Every class ended with stretching. During my initial classes, I couldn't do some of the stretch moves. I couldn't clasp my hands behind my back. I tried to grab my elbows while lifting both arms over my head, but the heavy layer of fat over my biceps took up so much space that I couldn't hold the position my classmates achieved with ease. I couldn't grab my ankle and pull my foot up to my rear. I made do by pressing my foot against the side of the pool and leaning into position. We finished each class by raising our hands over our heads, inhaling and then exhaling deeply as we brought them down. We applauded Terry and ourselves, and then headed for the changing room. I never used the showers at the gym. I'd change while hiding my body behind an enormous bath sheet and drive home with the windows open so that my hair could dry.

My food journal included spaces for me to record the length of each workout and the pulse rate I achieved. I recorded every detail of my food regimen, describing the preparation and ingredients used for each meal. I took the vitamins my surgeon required. Andrea visited for a few days and bought me a red plastic water bottle. The bottle held a litre of water, and I used it to measure my liquid intake; I still have this bottle and try to remember to fill it, though I now prefer coffee. As the summer before surgery progressed, I finally worked up the courage to talk about the operation with Terry.

'I drank Pepsi – regular Pepsi – right up till midnight the day before surgery,' she confided as we stood hip deep in the shallow end. 'But I was great about exercise. I'd do ten aerobics classes a week.'

The pool was a simple rectangle in an enormous, echoing room with cartoon characters painted on the concrete block walls, encouraging us to embrace the YMCA's many wholesome values. The water temperature fluctuated wildly. Some days, the pool heater failed us, and we froze for the first few minutes of the workout.

We'd swim across the deep end, each of our exercises named after an animal of some sort. 'If I ever teach the class, I think I'll just make up random names for the moves,' I told a classmate one day as we lunged from side to side trying to approximate the motion of a clock pendulum. 'Forget about the frog move. My class would do the Crunchy Un-boned Real Dead Frog.' My workout friend laughed and we switched to Rocking Horse, flailing backwards and forwards so hard we couldn't keep up a conversation.

I still weighed over 36 stone, but I found that my energy level increased after a couple of months of regular exercise, no fizzy drinks or fast food. I could run two or three errands without getting tired. I spent a lot of time in my car driving to the pool, savouring the time alone. My mother had a big presence – a big, loud, swearing, complaining, demanding presence – and the pool and my car felt like a quiet sanctuary. I found myself going to classes four days a week and trying to swim laps on the non-class days.

I told my therapist Cathy about the gym, about the other women and about my irritation whenever I saw boys of a certain age in the changing room. 'Some woman had her 12 year old in there the other day,' I complained. 'The last thing he needs is to learn about female anatomy from me. His mother overheard me talking about her and she told a whole group of us that her kid would be molested if she let him use the men's changing room. I really wanted to tell her that there wasn't a chance – her kid was too ugly for that – but I just nodded and smiled.' Cathy smiled slightly at this joke. She knew I didn't really mean it, that I was full of tough talk. 'I know it's sort of mean – okay, very mean – but I'm not wrong about the kid being too old to be in the ladies' changing room, and I didn't actually say anything to the mother. Why is that? Why can't I ever tell people that they're overstepping?'

'Because you're polite,' Cathy said. She knew I had more serious things on my mind. The surgery practice had finally got permission to operate from the government agency overseeing my insurance. As the day of the operation approached, I felt more and more afraid. I knew that I would probably survive the operation, but nothing was guaranteed. I drafted a will and a note to my friends and family. I printed them out and left them where my mother or sister would find them if I died.

Weeks ticked by. I celebrated my 33rd birthday in October. By then I'd worked up to swimming half a mile every time I did laps – 33 lengths of the pool. I thought about the significance of each number before I began a length. Number 14 reminded me of Brendan Shanahan, my favourite professional hockey player. Number 18 was *chai*, the Hebrew word for both the number 18 and for life. I did the breaststroke and thought about the song 'L'chaim' from *Fiddler on the Roof*. Nineteen was for Detroit Red Wings' captain Steve Yzerman, another favourite hockey player. After 21, I thought about having a drink. Thirty-three, the final length, was my age, the famous age of Christ, a significant number, even for an agnostic. When I finally swam my first full mile, I laughed, gulping in bleachy, chlorinated pool water. Sixty-six reminded me of Mario Lemieux, who wore the number for the Pittsburgh Penguins ice hockey team.

*

The day before my surgery I drove to Middletown alone. My sister and mother were due to follow, but I needed to check into the hotel early so I could drink two bottles of foul-tasting carbonated bowel cleanser and then wait for the unpleasant results. After a few hours, I changed into my ugly bathing suit and went to the hotel pool to work out. I did water aerobics for an hour, lunging and jumping until I was breathless. My heart beat so hard I could feel blood rushing in my biceps. I got out and left a trail of wet footprints on the hall carpet as I walked back to the room. When Andrea and Mum arrived, my mother retired to the smoking room we reserved for her, and Andrea and I watched a film. I tried not to think about the operation, and Andrea didn't bring it up, either.

At six o'clock the next morning, we climbed into my mother's car and drove to the hospital. It was pitch black, a cold, wet morning. As we took the motorway north to our destination, we passed a monstrous sculpture of Jesus. The Lord, rendered in bright white resin, appeared as an angry, flailing torso. His head and shoulders erupted from the hard, cold ground and he flung his arms skywards as if to grab at passing planes *à la* King Kong. The church that erected this artwork also aimed a floodlight at it. Jesus glowed in the dark, his tortured face perfectly mirrored in the reflecting pond before him. The obnoxious religiosity of this highway oddity briefly took my mind off the unpleasantness to come.

It was still dark when we finally arrived at the hospital. My memories of the exterior are hazy. When I entered it the morning of my surgery, all the hard edges of orange brick and grey concrete were blunted by the dim light; when I left four days later, I was exhausted, drugged and eager to escape. I checked in at the admissions desk. A nurse handed me a gown, and I stripped off the men's turtleneck and flowered challis skirt I had selected especially for the occasion. I folded my clothes and put them in a plastic bag provided by the hospital. My mother and sister filed into the room and sat by the bed as the nurse numbed my left hand with lidocaine and inserted an intravenous tube. My surgeon stopped by to visit, her blonde hair windblown and her cheeks flushed from the cold. She was wearing a leather bomber jacket and a smart wool skirt. She introduced me to the anaesthetist and to her colleague from Chicago who was going to assist.

The anaesthetist, a bald Texan with a tenor drawl, walked next to me as nurses wheeled me into the operating theatre. The lights were bright, as I expected, but the room itself was tiny, white and nothing at all like the operating theatres I'd seen on television. Because of my weight, I had to move from the trolley to the operating table myself. Scooting from one bed to the other is the last thing I remember. I fell down a deep, black hole.

Consciousness returned in fits and starts. I felt light burning against my eyelids but struggled to wake. Coming around took all the energy I could muster. It felt like swimming up from the bottom of a very deep pool. I opened my eyes and saw a nurse at the foot of my bed. 'You're so beautiful,' I told her, my voice thick and muzzy. I knew I hadn't died and felt incredibly happy about that fact. I waited for terrible pain in my stomach, but none came. Someone I couldn't see wheeled my trolley to a lift and then into a hospital room.

My mother and sister arrived. Mum had orders for me right away. 'You should hit the morphine as much as you can,' she told me. 'Shouldn't you be breathing into your spirometer?

You know you've got to do it a hundred times an hour. You don't want to get pneumonia,' she instructed, shaking the little plastic gadget that would measure the volume of air my lungs were inhaling and exhaling. Andrea said she was hungry, and I gave my sister a grateful look as she steered Mum off to find a restaurant.

My room had a view of the back of another building and a tiny, hilly patch of snow. I occupied the lone bed. Nurses and aides darted in and out of the room, checking my IV, adding medications, taking my temperature. I still didn't feel any pain. My midsection felt separate from the rest of me, alien. I pulled up the neck of my gown and saw the incision. An eight-inch line of surgical staples divided my torso. I had a drain stitched into the skin on the left side of my incision. Its clear bulb filled with blood and one of the nurses suggested tucking this bulb into the pocket of my gown. Another tube drained greenish liquid from the part of my stomach that was sewn off from the new pouch.

Lisa, my day nurse, was tall and plump with curly black hair and rosy cheeks. She held my arm as I struggled to stand. I felt a little dizzy, but I worked through that feeling and shuffled out into the corridor. I clutched my IV pole for support, and managed to make it all the way to the nurses' station before tiring. Blood clots are a potential complication of surgery, and I needed to move around to keep up my circulation, so Lisa and I eventually walked a full circuit of the floor. Andrea came back alone, my mother having returned to Toledo, and we walked three more circuits together. After surgery at 10am and a long day of walking and puffing on the spirometer, I finally found myself alone around 8pm. As I sat staring out of the window, surprise and delight at being alive suddenly overwhelmed me. I sat in the darkened hospital room crying silently into my plastic cup of ice cubes.

By day two, I'd walked ten circuits of the floor. I still had the bag of stomach contents to contend with, and the surgical drain hung off me like a giant blood-filled yo-yo. That evening, I had a coughing fit that brought on a bout of nausea. I was afraid of straining my stomach or the tender, sutured skin on my abdomen and I paged the nurses' station. The night nurse who came rushing into my room wore the traditional cap over her stiffly sprayed bouffant. She drew her lips into a disapproving line as I begged for a new anti-nausea patch. She told me that it wasn't nice to disturb 'Doctor' at home. I insisted that she call my surgeon and I struggled not to vomit, tears trickling down my cheeks.

'Honey, you just need to relax and trust God's grace to get you through this,' the nurse said, crouching in front of me and taking my hands. I was too exhausted to fight with her over religion, but I still wanted a new patch.

'Call my doctor. Call her now!' I insisted. The nurse stood suddenly, leaving the room without another word. She returned ten minutes later, slapped the patch on my neck and punished me by making me use the itchy inflating leg pillows that kept my legs up to avoid blood clots. My doctor had given permission for me to sleep without them because I was walking so much, but the nurse insisted, and I just wanted to sleep, so I didn't fight. In the morning, a tech woke me to draw blood from my wrist, and the night nurse came in half an hour later to force me to the toilet.

'If you don't make some urine for me, I'll have to catheterise you,' she threatened, smugness wafting off her like the stench of rubbish off a landfill, so I got up and used the toilet. When Lisa relieved Nurse Wretched later that morning, I was very glad to see her. Lisa was like a mother from a storybook, with her round pink cheeks and soft, comforting figure. We talked about the surgery and the things I did to prepare for it, and she made jokes about my blood yo-yo.

On day three I got to shower. Standing under the hot spray, I looked at my wound through its protective shield of plastic film, and the scar was an angry red slash. I turned off the water and threw on a clean gown.

On my last day in the hospital – four days after the surgery – I walked down the corridors, putting in ten circuits, ten times past the nurses' station where my caretakers snacked on Doritos and chocolate biscuits. I admired the knitted Christmas stockings and paper decorations lining the corridor, but I made Lisa take the candy cane off the door to my room.

My sister drove me back to Toledo, a three-hour drive in the snow, stopping every hour so that I could walk around in petrol station car parks. I barely remember the drive. I drifted in and out of sleep as my sister steered my old Lincoln through the wet, blowing snow.

During the summer when I was exercising and writing in my food journal, surgery had seemed like a destination, like the end of something. After arriving home and settling into my recovery, I had to rethink this notion. Surgery wasn't the end of anything. As I started dropping weight and moving out into the world, I knew that surgery had merely started something, acted as the catalyst for all sorts of changes in my life. And the more I changed, the more people around me – my mother especially – seemed to stay exactly the same.

16

MUM GONE WILD

My mother left her vibrator on the kitchen worktop one day. I saw it lying there, pink, shiny and with a hook at the end like a classic Roman nose. This wasn't the first time I'd seen the thing. A year or so before, I'd noticed my grey tabby Bertie rolling on my mother's bed, playing with a new toy. Looking closer, I discovered the adult nature of the toy and had to take it away from the cat. I had covered my hand in half a roll of toilet paper, extricated the device, and dropped it into the drawer of Mum's bedside table. I thought about doing that again, but then I noticed the webcam Mum had installed next to her desk in the kitchen. A horrifying picture formed in my mind.

Mum was 62, retired and had artificial knees and a replacement hip. She chain-smoked while playing countless games of euchre, pool and Scrabble online, and had assembled a rogues' gallery of Internet buddies. One of these friends lived in some godforsaken part of Alberta, claimed to have psychic visions and once tried to talk Mum into taking in a man she'd accidentally married.

'Arlene had a vision,' Mum explained. 'There was a dragon in her bed. A couple of days later, Bob showed up. They'd been chatting online for a couple of months, and he decided he had to drive all the way from Cleveland to be with her.' Mum said this in a matter-of-fact way, as if marrying some unemployed foreigner you met the day before the wedding was a prudent and reasonable thing to do. When the visions went awry six months later, Arlene tried telling Mum that the goddess wanted Bob to drive to our house from Alberta and live in our guest room.

'I don't know why I should tell her no,' Mum said, brow wrinkling in obvious confusion.

'How about because you don't know this guy from a hole in the ground?' I suggested. My mother nodded. She turned Arlene down, but felt guilty about it. As if allowing the husband of someone you'd never actually met to live in your house rent free was something she ought to have done, was obligated to do.

My world contracted dramatically that winter. I'd sit on the sofa eating tiny spoonfuls of chocolate-flavoured liquid protein. Eventually, I managed to lick peanut butter off a spoon before finally moving on to soft foods. In the early days after surgery, exhaustion tempered every social interaction. I didn't want to talk to friends on the phone. Talking tired me. I didn't want to drink the protein, but couldn't find the energy to argue with my mother about it.

Mum and I drove down for a post-op visit with my surgeon. I hadn't needed my feeding tube at all in the two weeks following surgery but I hated having to clean the oozing wound around the rubber tube, and the strange feeling in my stomach whenever I flushed the tube with water. The medical adhesive I used to tape dressings around the wound tore my skin, and every night while I slept my stomach would swell, pushing the tube outwards and ripping the tape. Dr Warwick refused to remove the tube, however, and I was too exhausted to disagree.

Mum and I left the surgical centre, and I had my first solid food – a scrambled egg at a country-style chain restaurant on the road outside Dayton. The egg made me feel swollen, bloated and sick. While my mother enjoyed a postprandial smoke, I went outside alone and sat on one of the restaurant's rustic benches. My breath formed little clouds in front of my face in the freezing air as I listened to the buzz of traffic and struggled not to vomit.

When Mum first started dating men she met online, she believed everything they told her and allowed these creepy strangers to dictate the terms of the relationships. When one net suitor wanted to drive four hours for a visit on New Year's Eve, Mum agreed, even though I'd had surgery less than three weeks before and couldn't leave the house. Given the selection of men available online, I was afraid the guy would kill me in my sleep.

When Mum told me about her plans, it upset me. The last thing I wanted to do was fight with my mother, but the idea of having a stranger in the house made me nearly giddy with anxiety. I asked Mum to call off the visit, but halfway through my reasoned explanation of stranger danger, I realised I was crying. I couldn't continue. I shook my head over and over again, and Mum stared at me.

'What? Why are you upset? Don't I deserve a little fun after this last month with your surgery?' Mum asked.

'I guess so. I just don't want anyone to see me like this, and

I can't leave,' I said. 'We don't know him, either. He could be a rapist or a murderer for all you know.' Mum made a face. I may have been overcautious. Most men on dating sites aren't rapists or serial killers, but parts of me were stapled together, and I had a rubber tube hanging out of me, creating an open wound that bled and wept and stank of antiseptic and dying skin. I'd never felt weaker or more exposed in my whole life. I wanted to feel safe in my house and I wanted everyone to leave me alone.

My mother wouldn't listen to me. I tried again to tell her how all this made me feel, but she walked out of the room before I could finish, installing herself in front of her computer and refusing to discuss her plans any further. I called my sister, and Andrea also tried to make our mother understand why I didn't want this guy in the house; Mum finally agreed to put him up in a motel. On New Year's Eve, Jim – a tall, white-haired ex-hippie with a gibbous pot belly – stood in our family room and stared at me. I wore a tatty old nightgown and my posture was stiff because of the tube sewn into my abdomen. I stared at the television but Jim didn't take the hint. He wanted to make conversation.

'I heard you had the gastric surgery,' Jim said, absent-mindedly scratching his gut. 'I saw stuff just like that in 'Nam,' he added. I nodded again, wishing Jim would go away and leave me alone. I didn't reply to him, but inside I fumed. ''Nam? Really? Gastric bypass must have been huge over there,' I thought.

Jim and my mother went out to dinner and then back to his motel room to sleep off all the alcohol. I spent New Year's Eve alone. Julie and her husband Rick called at midnight. I felt a little better after hearing their voices. 'It would've been terrible if you'd come through surgery only to have some nutcase from the net smother you with a pillow,' she said. I agreed wholeheartedly. My mother didn't seem to have the common sense or healthy fear of strangers you'd expect in a six year old. I sipped my liquid protein and thought about how much happier both of us would be after I moved out.

I'd actually recovered from surgery when I found the vibrator lying on a swatch of shiny purple fabric in the kitchen. I'd been hoping to have some turkey breast for lunch when I spied the ten-inch plastic phallus and inexplicably lost my appetite. While I felt fairly certain that her artificial hip and knee joints would prevent Mum from twisting herself into the necessary position for a live web sex show (her office chair has wheels and you'd need to be fairly flexible to use it in that way), I knew I couldn't take any chances. I had to have a Very Special Talk with Mum about the dangers of web whoredom, and I had to do it over pancakes.

The next morning, we shared a table for two at the Original Pancake House. Mum loved the bacon there, and I hoped the folksy setting would put her at ease. Surrounded by homespun angels, large-scale portraits of enormous apple pancakes and rough-hewn (purely decorative) signs advertising charmingly quaint prices for coffee, I broached the subject.

'Mum, I found something of yours on the worktop. Something long and pink. Something battery operated.' I said this with my eyes fixed firmly on a plate of scrambled eggs and toast. My mother thought about it for a second before catching on.

'Oh, that! I forgot all about it.' She sipped her coffee and shrugged.

'Yes, well, I um, er . . .' I fought to spit it out. 'You're not doing live sex shows on the Internet, are you? Because people can forward that stuff all over the place.' I said this in a quiet voice, but not so quietly that I'd have to repeat myself.

My mother laughed, a great smoky cackle. 'No! Of course not. I would never! I was taking pictures of it for a friend. I used some purple silk as a backdrop, you know, so it'd look professional,' she said.

'I see. Okay. Well that's . . . interesting. As long as you're not making pornography. Taking pictures for a friend is better, sort of,' I said.

'I sent it to a guy I've been talking to in Arkansas. He used to want to date me, but now he thinks he's gay. He had a threesome with some other guy and the guy's girlfriend. Then he e-mailed me pictures of his penis – it's huge! – and asked if I might want to do something like that.' She said this in the same bright tone she might use to recommend a good cleaning lady.

'You wouldn't really do that, would you?' I asked, dreading the answer.

'No! Of course not!' she said, scandalised. 'Why? Would you?' Mum peered at me intently, eager for an answer.

I gave it some thought. 'Not with two guys from Arkansas,' I replied. Times have changed. Senior citizens are having threesomes and e-mailing each other rude pictures. I knew I should celebrate Mum's liberation, but I couldn't help but be bewildered, and just a touch creeped out, by all of this.

We finished brunch and left the restaurant. Later, Mum called me over to her computer. She opened a file and I found myself looking at a photo of a 50-year-old white guy with a steel-grey mullet. Mr Mullet leered, the pink tip of his pointy tongue visible through his pursed lips as he aimed his enormously swollen penis at the camera. He held the great purple monstrosity with both hands, hoisting it up so that his protruding stomach didn't block the shot. Mr Mullet wore black ankle socks and had a large, pink scar on his left knee. The picture wasn't sexy. It reminded me of holiday photos of some fat suburban neighbour – the kind where a Hawaiian-shirted insurance salesman with a thick stripe of zinc oxide on his nose poses with the three-foot marlin he caught in Florida. I stared at the picture, shocked into silence by all the lurid trashiness.

'Well?' Mum asked. 'What do you think?' She looked at me expectantly. I struggled to seem cool and unaffected.

'I think you should forward it to Andrea,' I said. I share everything with my sister. I'm considerate that way. Besides, Andrea lives far away in Texas and she has the luxury of distance.

'Okay. I'll title the e-mail "What do you think?",' Mum cackled. She hit 'send' and the deed was done.

Before her hard drive crashed (in protest, I imagine), Mum had amassed a large file of pictures sent to her by random men from game and dating sites. Most of the pictures included only the nude torso, or a close-up of genitals. I shudder to imagine what Mum sent them in return. My mother was a good 3½ stone overweight. Her short hair was dyed an almost natural shade of brown, and her face showed signs of her age. Short and busty, she favoured trousers and flower-print blouses. In short, she looked like someone's mother.

I tried to pretend that men sending her these photos was funny rather than disturbing. 'I swear, these guys are the result of brother/sister marriages,' I told Julie during a trip we took to Canada shortly after I found the vibrator. We walked the streets of Niagara Falls, Ontario, a brisk, cold wind whipped at our faces as we looked at the falls, and I told Julie all about the guy from Arkansas and his major endowment. I put on my best southern accent, pulling out all the stops to sound drunk, horny and well-hung. Both of us fell into fits of giggles. Julie was lucky. Her mother was 89 and didn't own a computer. If she wanted to, Julie could pretend her mother had never seen a penis, let alone collected a file of anonymous dick shots. Without a job and an income, I continued to live with my mother's odd habits every day.

I resumed my writing career about eight months after the surgery. I published articles on Salon, and in *The Times* and in *Eve* magazine. My routine had changed drastically in little more than a year. I exercised frequently, swimming laps at the YMCA or using the treadmill. I went out to clubs and tried to meet more people. I planned that my time with Mum would end soon – I'd get a paying job, get off disability and move into my own place. While I was sure we'd both enjoy the privacy, however, I knew my mother would miss the company; she had never lived alone. She grew up in a tiny flat in east Toledo and shared a bedroom with one of her brothers till she was 15. After leaving home, she lived with college roommates and finally with her husband and her own children.

At 35, I realised that I was far too old to live with my mother. My cats and I needed our space, and we needed that space to be far, far away from Mum, her boyfriends and her constant commands and complaints. I loved my mother and I enjoyed her company, but I enjoyed it more when we lived apart. I could think of her as a peer or a friend rather than as the person who still told me to clean my room and take out the rubbish.

'How did this towel get on the floor?' she asked one day as I tried to compose an article on my laptop. I'd just settled into my writing project and didn't feel like having a conversation about bathroom linens.

'I don't know. I think it must have been those God-damned toilet gnomes again,' I said.

Sometimes I felt like I'd never actually grown up, as if I was about 16 years old on the inside. I'd make flip remarks, rebelling against the authority my mother should have relinquished years ago. It didn't help that I gave her that authority by living in her house. Everything I did – leaving a bill by the letterbox, leaving a glass in the sink, taking a phone call from someone whose voice Mum didn't recognise – merited the same sort of investigation as the towel on the floor. Nothing I did went unscrutinised, un-commented upon. Sometimes the pressure of all this observation forced me out of the house. I drove around aimlessly, wondering where I could go to avoid home. I spent hours in the local chain bookshop, drinking coffee and reading magazines. I ate dinners out when I couldn't really afford to. I spent my nights online, looking at ads for flats and plotting my escape.

I discussed my mother in therapy. Cathy, my long-time shrink, asked me what I wanted from the relationship then lapsed into shrink-speak. She suggested I needed to establish boundaries – 'mutually respected boundaries', actually. I thought about it for a minute, sitting in the black office chair, the arms of which no longer pinched my thighs. In the 18 months since surgery, I'd lost 14 stone, and furniture no longer represented an obstacle to daily life.

'What I want is what I've always wanted,' I told her. 'I want my mother to be an adult.'

'Yes, of course you do, but . . .' Cathy trailed off, inviting me to finish the thought.

'What I really want is for the past to be different, to have had a better childhood,' I told her. 'I still wonder why she couldn't keep my father from hitting me. I blame her for some of the weight.' We took a minute to consider this. 'I just want my own life,' I said. 'You'd think Mum would want that for me, too.' I twisted my hands together, fingers circling fingers, pulling hard against the knuckles. I tapped my foot and looked down at the dingy grey industrial carpet. I hated complaining about my mother. It made me feel like a bratty teenager, or like the ungrateful bad person I suspected myself to be.

I was in limbo. I thought about the future every day, looking at ads for jobs and flats and even postings for used furniture. I wanted to move forward so badly that the present didn't seem entirely real to me. This disturbed me more than anything else. One of the first things I realised after starting therapy was that saying 'I'll be happy when I'm thin' or 'I'll be happy when I move out' was really holding me back.

Mum suggested that I stay on with her after my second planned surgery, an operation to remove a large apron of hanging skin from my midsection. She thought I should stay on after I began working again too. 'You can help with some of the bills,' she said. I shrugged, not wanting to start a fight, but not at all interested in another second of the world's longest childhood. I stared out of the window and thought about moving. Then I went to the pool and swam: half a mile, a thousand metres, a mile. My shoulders ached, and I thought about the furniture I'd buy for the new flat.

17

SHOPPING AROUND

I used to have a sort of uniform. I wore a men's extra-large T-shirt and a long skirt. The skirts came from a website specialising in large sizes. The T-shirts were from a men's catalogue whose other offerings included jumbo-sized hunting camouflage and logo T-shirts proclaiming the wearer a 'Big Daddy'. My extra-wide shoes came from catalogues or from the men's section of the local discount shop. I never wore trousers. I lost the first 3 stone while preparing for surgery, but I didn't buy any new clothes. I still weighed over 36 stone and didn't see the point of buying new things before the operation.

After surgery, I slowly resumed my life. It took a while. I had the feeding tube to contend with, and the fatigue. Following a few weeks of bone-deep exhaustion – it hurt to be awake – I discovered that the low-fat milk I'd been drinking gave me 'dumping syndrome'. Dumping syndrome is a major pitfall of weight-loss surgery: all the sugar in whatever food you've just eaten dumps directly into your blood. You feel like you're dying, like every bit of energy has been sucked out of your body. The food that causes the dumping syndrome differs from person to person. I could eat chocolate, the occasional biscuit or half a piece of cake, but I couldn't drink milk unless it had been heated. It's a tradeoff I gladly accepted. I missed cereal with milk, but I'd have missed chocolate more.

The surgery changes how you eat. I am lucky, I think, because I can now eat nearly normal amounts of food – normal for a very thin person with an average appetite. I cook a lot and occasionally bake. I still like food and have to mind what I eat so, if I bake, I give a lot of the product away. I've adapted the way I cook. I like to grill using fresh herbs, and I do a lot of stir-fry, fake Mexican things. I make chicken soup in the winter, skimming the broth so it's low in fat and calories. I feel like I can eat as much as I like – I just like eating a lot less food than I used to.

After I stopped drinking milk, my recovery moved along at a much quicker pace. I still had the feeding tube, though, and because my surgeon's office was a six-hour round trip from home, I went to a local hospital to have it removed. I checked in early in the morning and spent half an hour refusing to take a pregnancy test. I resented the nurses for not believing me when I told them I absolutely couldn't be pregnant. Unless a star had risen in east Toledo, the chances of conception were nil. I didn't date. I never had, really. Aside from barely remembered drunken encounters in college, my experience with men and dating was practically non-existent. I hated the idea of a pregnancy test – it reminded me that I was single and involuntarily celibate. I refused the test again, and when I reminded the admitting nurse that I'd just had an operation, during which I couldn't have been pregnant, she finally conceded the point.

I stripped off my clothes and put on a hospital gown. I had a few extra minutes to wait before we moved to the operating theatre. When Lisa, my day nurse, had removed my drain just before I left the hospital in Middletown, it didn't hurt very much or for very long and I didn't want medication I didn't really need. So, though the doctor had planned to sedate me, I asked him not to. Then they wheeled me into the operating suite to yank the tube.

The operating theatre at my local hospital was tiny and drab with grey-green walls. The doctor – a bearded East Asian with a softly lilting accent – pushed aside the gown to reveal my stomach. I wanted to close my eyes and wait for it to end, but curiosity proved stronger than embarrassment. I watched closely as the doctor used a huge syringe to deflate the balloon holding the tube in place. He gave the feeding tube a couple of medium-hard tugs before deciding it wasn't going to move. He decided then that the best way to work out why the tube wouldn't move was to do an endoscopy on me. He would shove a thick, black cable the diameter of a human finger down my throat so that he could see the inside of my stomach. A nurse sprayed my throat with lidocaine. It tasted like cinnamon-flavoured embalming fluid, and I gagged, struggling not to vomit. The lidocaine worked quickly, numbing my mouth and parts of my lips. My tongue lay on my soft palate like something alien, or a huge chunk of rare beef.

I was wide awake as the doctor began threading the cable through a plastic frame between my teeth. 'Breathe through the nose,' he told me, jiggling the cable to improve his view. The advice didn't help; I couldn't breathe. The rigid cable tore at my throat, gagging and suffocating me as the doctor slowly advanced it. I vomited. My heart beat so hard and so fast I could feel blood burning through my biceps. Four nurses struggled to hold me down as I thrashed on the table, desperately trying to breathe.

After five minutes, the doctor removed the tube. I lay there gasping while a male nurse patted my shoulder and made jokes to try and calm me. The doctor hadn't been able to see the feeding tube with the scope so he got on the phone and called my surgeon in Dayton. I heard her voice on the speaker, telling the doctor that the feeding tube was in the old stomach, the part stapled off from the pouch. The pouch is the part connected to my oesophagus, throat and mouth, so an endoscopy to view the feeding tube had been futile. When the new doctor asked my surgeon how to remove the tube, she offered her best technical expertise. 'Pull harder,' she said, before hanging up on him.

The doctor gave the feeding tube a hard yank. It came out, splattering him with stomach contents and bile. I lay there surprised for a second before saying the first horrible thing that came to mind. 'I'm pretty sure I don't have hepatitis C.' The stunned doctor wiped at the green stomach goo on his forehead.

My mother drove me home from the hospital. We'd been on the road a good ten minutes before I could tell her what had happened. The next evening I went to water aerobics for the first time in four weeks. Dr Warwick had forbidden any exercise for the first two weeks after surgery, and the tube had prevented me from using a swimming pool. Terry, my instructor, asked about the surgery, and my classmates welcomed me back. I made it through the 45-minute class, though I felt totally spent after we finished our closing stretches.

As I changed in the locker room, taking care to hold a towel over the fresh red scar, a woman from class asked about my progress.

'I lost 3 stone in the first four weeks,' I told her.

'Don't worry,' the woman said, 'Slow loss is probably a good thing.'

Slow? Losing 3 stone in 28 days seemed pretty quick to me. My weight loss came in fits and starts after the first month. I kept up my exercise, but only weighed myself every other month or so. I still weighed too much to use a household scale. I was able to use the one at the local hospital, but it was on the other side of town, and I had other things I wanted to do with my time.

After I lost the first 11 stone, six months after surgery, I started looking for clothes that fitted me. I still wore the oversize T-shirts, but they hung on me and felt old and shabby so I found myself shopping, even though I couldn't really afford new clothes. The first new outfit I bought, a linen skirt and knitted top in chocolate brown, made me feel pretty for the first time in years. When you weigh as much as I do and as much as I have, finding stylish clothes requires patience and ingenuity. I couldn't just go to the high street for clothes; I had to go to fat women's shops. I wrote a piece for a ladies' magazine. In it I'd written about Andrea and the editors wanted me to pose for pictures with my sister for the piece. They wanted the two of us together, dressed identically.

'Rebecca? We'd like you to take another look at the article. Did you and your sister compete for men? Readers will want to know,' an editor asked.

'We're seven years apart so it never really came up,' I said. 'I'm sorry about the outfits. I don't wear trousers. I can get a black skirt and a white blouse, though,' I offered. My editor agreed. The magazine stylist suggested the Gap, and I had to explain to her that, though I'd lost a huge amount of weight, I still wasn't thin enough to shop there. Andrea flew home from Texas, and we went to a hair salon together to be made over to ladies' mag specifications. My sister ended up with a pouffy bouffant, her long chestnut hair stiff with hairspray.

'Hug her tighter, Rebecca,' the photographer instructed. I clutched Andrea from behind and could feel the tension in her shoulders. She doesn't especially enjoy prolonged hugging. The photographer played a dance mix CD but I had to stop the proceedings when Nine Inch Nails' 'Closer' came on. No one wants to hug a sibling while Trent Reznor sings about fucking you like an animal. We smiled and pouted at the camera, and I employed expressions I'd learned from years of watching *America's Next Top Model*. I tried for 'fierce' and ended up looking violently constipated. Andrea looked like she'd just been forced into an arranged marriage – in prison.

The shoot moved locations, and Andrea and I strolled along the promenade at a riverside park. The photographer wouldn't let me wear my glasses – the magazine stylist had deemed them 'too mumsy' – and I couldn't see anything. I liked the new outfit, though – the white blouse and long black skirt flattered my figure. It wouldn't occur to me until weeks later when I read my much-altered article and saw the pictures the magazine selected that the matching outfits were supposed to create a kind of sight gag: fat sister, thin sister, marching side by side. I can imagine that the photographer might have hoped to capture the shocked stares of onlookers, but the early hour had thankfully prevented a crowd from gathering to witness our free show.

Despite this forced performance, I still enjoyed shopping and found that I could fit into trendier clothes. Although I continued visiting plus-size shops, I now shopped at plus-size shops for younger women. I went to Lane Bryant and to Torrid (which I promptly christened 'The Fat Whore Store' because of its wide selection of low-cut tops and short skirts). One day at Lane Bryant, a miracle occurred: I found a bra that fitted, and suddenly I had cleavage. I bought a black knitted top with a deep V-neck and wore it out of the shop, my giant men's T-shirt stuffed in the shopping bag. A man looked me over as I passed him in the mall. His eyes lingered on my chest, never moving higher. I smiled, and quickened my pace.

My mother noticed my new interest in clothes and accessories and bought me my first Coach bag. The tiny red leather bag, a birthday gift, went perfectly with the new knitted top and a flowing, red-and-black patterned skirt I bought. I soon had another Coach, courtesy of a cousin who'd bought a large periwinkle tote and never carried it. She gave it to me to clear space in her wardrobe and I loved it at once, much as mothers love new infants. I breathed in its rich leather smell and held it close to my heart.

I also decided that shopping for bags and clothes online worked well, so why not shop for men? I placed an ad on a free dating site. After six months, I still hadn't found any men I wanted to meet in person. I exchanged e-mails with a guy in Ann Arbor for a while. After a couple of weeks, I forwarded the link to his dating site profile to Andrea for her advice.

'Did you notice that he lists corsetry and "boobies" as hobbies?' she asked.

'No,' I replied. 'He lists a good hundred things under

hobbies. I thought he chose so many things as a joke.' After exchanging more e-mails with the would-be suitor and learning that he did indeed expect me to strap myself into something heavily boned and uncomfortable, I deleted him from my contact list forever.

After losing 14 stone, I began shopping in earnest. I found fuzzy sweaters in the winter, and revelled in the luxury of wearing a new coat. I hadn't been able to fit into a winter coat for at least ten years. My new black quilted jacket had a slightly Asian sensibility. I felt chic wearing it as I ran errands around town. I felt more than chic in fact: I felt normal. When you weigh as much as I did, you naturally attract stares. In the winter, wearing short-sleeved T-shirts had made me feel not only fat and freaky, but also like some sort of beggar. Now I found winter-weight skirts and tights that hid the cellulitis scars on my legs.

Having acquired clothes, I sought out new (and old) places to wear them. After too many visits to count, I considered myself a regular at a Toledo drag bar called Caesar's. Kenny Rogers immortalised the place in his song 'Lucile', about a wife who leaves a pathetic farmer husband and a houseful of brats for the high life of boozing and whoring in town. Kenny hadn't been to Caesar's in a while; I would surely have noticed an ageing country star amid the Abercrombie-wearing gay boys and plaid-swaddled lesbians.

After losing more than 16 stone, I still went to Caesar's because it had always been a safe place for me, somewhere I could dance and sing karaoke without having to worry about men commenting on the size of my ever-dwindling (though still considerable) bum. The bar was a live-and-let-live sort of place, and I fitted in there as well as anyone. Better than some. The male stripper who showed up whenever one of the drag queens called in sick was a prime example. He chose 'Don Cherry' as his stage name, totally unaware of the red-faced, white-haired former ice hockey coach who would probably strangle him for taking the liberty. Don wore plaid shirts and got naked after flopping around the raised dance floor that served as the stage. He called this break dancing, but it looked more like an epileptic fit. He never removed his black socks.

After he danced, Don would wander around the bar in his thong man panties ('manties') trying to elicit tips from people too drunk to reject him. He tried his shtick with me because I'm unfailingly polite. Don't get me wrong. I'm a horrible, horrible person. I love making snide comments about people, especially naked people with huge, pendulous testicles, but I prefer to do this behind their backs. Though I have a black and oily heart and will almost certainly burn in hell when I die, I usually mind my manners in public. Don observed this one night and leaned over me to compliment my pretty name.

'It's in the Bible,' I said, hoping he'd respect my invocation of the deity and go away. He failed to take the hint. 'Maybe you should try the karaoke,' I told him.

'Naw, I can't do no karaoke. I'd humiliate myself,' Don said without a hint of irony. I wanted to tell him that that ship sailed the minute his drawers came off to 'Umbrella', but words failed me. Doug, a guy I'd met earlier that evening, cemented his place as my new gay boyfriend by getting me out of there. He grabbed my hand and announced that the two of us were going outside to smoke. Ohio had passed an anti-smoking law, so we had to go out the fire door and smoke on the pavement, far away from

Don Cherry and his puffy undies. I took the excuse, even though I don't smoke, and Doug had to suck menthols for two, just like my mother did during her pregnancies.

Caesar's on a Saturday night presented a different, more elaborately made-up face. Men in women's clothing danced and lip-synched. Britney Spears was heavily represented in the stage show, as was Madonna. My favourite acts, Miss Lotte Bootée and Miss Rubee Roxx, had radically different styles. Rubee, an avant-garde vixen who hosted the club's fetish night, pulled off spectacular numbers to Marilyn Manson and Cyndi Lauper, while Lotte loved her pop stars.

'If it ain't Beyoncé, it don't exist to me,' she told me as she downed her sixth vodka and cranberry of the night. 'What's that dead raccoon just walked by?' she asked, attention diverted by a passing rival's bad weave. 'I don't care if she hears me!' Lotte bellowed, shrugging off all attempts to shush her. 'I'm a 21-stone man in a dress. Bitch says "boo" and I'll punch her in her face.'

Lotte embodied class. She carried the weight well, her impossibly voluptuous figure accented beautifully by her tight miniskirts and low-cut tops. She looked like someone's tough mama, only super glam, or like Beyoncé herself, give or take a few stone. Her confidence was magnetic, her stage act a sensation. Gay boys in tacky logo T-shirts, and crew-cut, flannel-draped lesbians, lined up to give her money, pressing crumpled notes into her plump, golden hand. An old straight guy in a sharkskin suit dropped a fountain of cash, flicking note after note onto the stage. Lotte mouthed a sultry 'thank you', her full, pouty mouth shimmering with cherry glitter lipstick. I saw Lotte without any make-up just once: oddly enough, she seemed smaller and less real with a bare face and in men's clothing.

Lotte was a mere slip of a 24 year old. On her birthday, as she downed yet another pink cocktail, I told her that she was just a baby. 'You could be my granddaughter if we lived in Mississippi,' I said, alluding to the ten-year age gap.

'You could be my grandma, cousin and probably my sister all at the same time,' she agreed, signalling for another round.

I made other friends who were regulars at the bar. Samantha, 27 years old and six feet two, had red hair and a lot of attitude. She told me what drugs to request before dental surgery, and threw back shots like a champ. Andrea, her roommate, had huge dark eyes that she accentuated with black liner and with expertly applied eye shadow. She sat at the bar sketching animé characters in an artist's tablet. Andrea never sang karaoke. She watched and clapped and would drive you home if you were drunk. Samantha gave orders and made off-colour jokes. I thought of her as bold and brave until some drunk decided to set the stripper on her. Samantha and I once went into the men's toilets together. She needed the facilities and someone had vomited in a spectacularly smelly way in the ladies'. I guarded her cubicle and was caught totally off guard when Don Cherry came in. He started to take something out of the manties, and I pounded the cubicle door, desperate to collect Samantha and flee. She opened the door, and gave me a puzzled look before spotting Don next to the urinals.

'Oh. Hey there, Don,' she said, totally unfazed. I took this as my cue and ran for the door. Samantha came out a few seconds later, clearly upset.

'Why'd you leave me? Don just tried to kiss me! I told him

I'm married, but it didn't even slow him down,' she said, gulping at her drink.

'I'm so sorry!' I said. 'I thought you were brave. If I knew you were just like me only taller, I'd have stayed.' Don came over to us and started touching Samantha's hair. Terry, the DJ, called me up to sing, and I grabbed Samantha's arm.

'C'mon – I'm doing Melissa Etheridge, and you can be my pretend lesbian girlfriend,' I said. She nodded gratefully, and practically ran to the stage. Don shrugged and walked across the room to do a lap dance for an old man in a three-piece suit.

I spent a lot of time with Samantha and Andrea. We shopped together and sang together, and the two of them advised me about men. Despite their best efforts, my man search was on hold as I needed more surgery. Although I still walked around the shopping centre (for exercise, primarily, as I was chronically broke), I hadn't bought any clothes for a while. I was waiting for my appointment with a plastic surgeon who would, I hoped, chop off the giant apron of mouldering skin from around my abdomen. It hung to my knees and often became infected from the constant rubbing. It ruined the line of my smart new outfits, and it had to go. I had a feeling the man shopping would proceed after that as well, though I wasn't in any hurry.

My new body with its cleavage and nearly normal girl shape surprised me every time I looked in a full-length mirror. I wondered about the delicate girl staring back at me. I could see collar bones and the tall column of her neck. Her ankles tapered as ankles ought to do. This new body scared me just a bit. I felt feminine for the first time in years, but also more vulnerable than ever. The novelty of men staring at my breasts had worn off, and I now crossed my arms over my chest as I walked through the shopping centre.

I hoped my insurance would approve the plastic surgery. Given the scarring I'd have and the other areas of sagging skin on my body, the best I could hope for was to look better in clothes. Still, looking better in clothes meant shopping for clothes. If all went well, I'd be wearing jeans before my next birthday.

18

FORTY POUNDS OF FLESH

I prepared for naked picture day carefully, selecting a new bra and making sure to shower the morning of the appointment. I rubbed satsuma body butter into my skin and wore a white cotton skirt and a black wrap top that gives the illusion that I have a waist. I wore make-up and perfume. I stood in front of the full-length mirror in my bathroom trying to fold the elastic waist of the too-large skirt so that the hem would line up evenly at mid-calf. I wanted to make a good impression on the new plastic surgeon.

'It's just like a date,' I told Samantha as we sat in the waiting room. We'd driven for two hours from Toledo to Cleveland, the trip fuelled by far too many Americanos from Starbucks. Samantha looked up from her copy of the last Harry Potter book and considered this.

'Really?' she asked, raising one copper brow purely for effect.

'Well, it's like a blind date with a much older married man who will only touch me with rubber gloves on,' I elaborated. I tore through my red Coach handbag in search of lipstick. I'd lost most of the initial coat to the rim of a Starbucks cup and wanted to reapply before my meeting with Dr Jordan. I reviewed the health form the receptionist had handed to me when I registered. Had I ever had a venereal disease? I ticked 'no', signed and dated the form and waited for the nurse to call me.

My first trip to Cleveland for plastic surgery purposes hadn't gone nearly as smoothly. Three months before my visit to Dr Jordan's spartan office, I'd had an appointment at a swanky hospital in the heart of Cleveland's revitalised city centre. I'd got lost and had to call the surgeon's office for directions. 'I'm passing Orange Street,' I told the assistant who answered my call.

'Whatever you do, don't turn there,' she advised. 'That's a really bad neighbourhood.'

I struggled not to laugh. Bad neighbourhood? The most dangerous thing that would ever happen to me in Cleveland would take place in the clean new hospital where the assistant's boss would take a very sharp knife and slice me open from hip to hip. The surgeon probably wouldn't steal my car afterwards, but cutting me was definitely on the agenda. I found the street I needed to get to the hospital, thanked the assistant and hung up.

I locked my car and crossed a huge metal-and-glass walkway from the multi-storey car park. I walked a good quarter of a mile across tasteful new carpets to get to the wing where the surgeon had her offices. I passed white-coated doctors and tried not to make eye contact. Though I'd lost nearly half my body weight, I still wasn't thin, and I always felt like I should reassure medical types. *Don't worry*, I want to tell them. *I've already had the gastric bypass!* I'd found the surgeon's waiting room, checked in and handed my clipboard of medical forms to a sleek blonde sitting at an enormous polished reception desk. The surgeon I met that day actually looked like a model herself. She was nearly six feet tall, slender and had a perfect pale complexion.

A nurse escorted me to the examination room and I stripped in front of a huge bank of windows while watching a group of workmen climb scaffolding attached to the building across the street. A tiny card on the sill assured me that the windows were tinted on the outside and that no one could see in. As I stood barefoot in my bra and panties, I resisted the urge to dance in front of the windows by focusing instead on tying the hospital gown. I was struggling with the back fastening when the doctor walked in unannounced.

'Don't worry about fastening it – I'm just going to pull it open again anyway,' she said bluntly. The doctor lifted my gown and then the heavy skin apron that hung from my hips to my knees. She moved my underwear aside to evaluate my groin. I stared at a spot on the wall and waited for her to finish. This doctor made little empathy gestures – the head tilt, the arm pat, the concerned nod – in a studied way. She took a medical history after allowing me to put my clothes back on, and then told me I'd have to return in the morning for nude photographs.

'We need them for the insurance,' she said, arm pat, head tilt. 'Can you stay in town overnight?'

At 10am, I returned to the fancy hospital and waited outside the plastic surgery photo suite with two other women, one young and blonde, the other middle-aged and African-American. Neither appeared scarred or mutilated in any obvious way. A tech wearing blue-green scrubs opened the photo suite door and called the blonde forward. She reappeared seconds later, rearranging her sweater. The tech gestured the other lady forward, and I stared at an enormous bank of cabinets, wondering about the files inside. They must contain thousands of pictures of small breasts, hidden penises, fat stomachs and horrifying scars, I thought. The tech reappeared. My turn.

'Take everything off but your bra,' she told me. I stood behind a curtain – briefly amused by this nod to modesty in light of the situation – and took off my enormous white granny panties. I'd decided not to buy new underwear until I'd had the apron skin removed. My bra, an architectural masterpiece in scarlet silk, contrasted sharply with the giant cotton briefs, and I felt glad, if only fleetingly, to have them off. My skirt and knitted top followed, along with my black slingback sandals. I folded everything neatly and arranged the pieces of clothing carefully in the order I planned to put them back on. I stepped past the curtain and the tech smiled encouragingly. 'Arms out, please. Face the butterfly,' she said. I turned right towards a bright transfer on the wall and the camera flashed.

'I'll need a copy of that for my Christmas card,' I told her. She laughed mechanically at my tired joke and told me to face the bunny rabbit. I turned. After a final turn towards the rain-bow, the tech asked me to lift the fat apron so that the insurance company could see how damaged and infected my skin was. I grabbed the hanging flesh and pulled it up, exposing my pubic area and the tender red skin of what should have been my waist. Flash.

'We're all done,' the tech told me. I moved swiftly towards my clothes. I knew I should feel *something* about this. Even people without 40 pounds of dead fat hanging round their middle feel strange about having nude photographs taken of them. I thought about calling my friends on the drive home. I buckled my shoes and picked up my bag. The tech wished me a nice day, and I drove home, disconcerted. My face wouldn't appear in any of the pictures, but I imagined insurance bureaucrats flipping through them, assessing my body, and felt a little sick.

Weeks later, the billing department in that shiny hospital discovered that they didn't take my insurance after all. All the naked pictures had been in vain. I called the insurance company direct and spent an hour on the phone before getting a referral to a Cleveland surgical practice. I called and made an appointment with the first surgeon who could see me, Dr Jordan.

Samantha continued to read Harry Potter, and I stared at my face in the compact mirror. I'd smudged the lipstick so I wiped it off with a bookshop receipt and applied more. A nurse called me back to the examination suite, and I followed her towards yet another electronic scale. I weighed 25 stone. Despite losing over 14 stone, I could still have qualified for a gastric bypass. I pondered this and dismissed it. My body, despite its many failings, could be so much worse. I had decent indentation above the fat apron. My breasts sagged, but not a lot more than those of other women my age. My face remained youthful, my cheeks round and unlined. From the ribs up and the knees down, I wasn't half bad. The nurse took my blood pressure (118 over 68) and my resting pulse (a low 60 beats per minute). She led me to the doctor's examination room, and he came in to introduce himself.

Dr Jordan had white hair and a tidy beard. The expression in his dark eyes conveyed intelligence, good humour and competence. He shook my hand and reacted so naturally to my questions that I forgot he sliced people open for a living. After discussing my weight loss and making sure I had realistic expectations of the surgery – that I knew I'd have a huge scar and would still be a fat girl when he'd finished chopping stuff off – Dr Jordan excused himself so I could put on a gown for the examination. He returned with the nurse, and I stood while he lifted the apron skin and peered intently underneath.

'I'm not sure how to ask about this,' I said as he knelt and assessed, 'but can you do anything about the pubic area?' I had a lot of excess fat and loose skin just above my pelvis. This embarrassed and upset me more than any other thing about my body. I hated the way the skin flopped over, the way the hair follicles clogged. My skin flaked around every follicle, rubbed raw by the constant rubbing of skin on skin. I wanted the apron gone, but I'd actually fantasised about chopping off the pubic fat myself, should insurance fail to cover the operation.

'Most definitely,' Dr Jordan assured me, gently releasing the apron. 'You're open and bleeding right now, actually,' he added, his face quickly shifting from a genial, matter-of-fact expression to one of real empathy as I began to cry quietly. He put a hand on my shoulder and told me it'd be okay, and I swiftly pulled myself together. I made a joke and he excused himself; I put my clothes on and went home.

A month later, I woke from anaesthesia at MetroHealth Medical Centre. I woke in fits and starts, struggling for consciousness. The bright light in the recovery room receded and then intensified. I became fully awake and my eyes focused on the first thing I saw: a grinning tissue paper jack-o'-lantern hanging over the foot of my bed – Halloween was a full month away, but hospitals always seem to decorate in favour of the most convenient seasonal festival. The walls in the unit were the brown of fallen oak leaves, and all the arches were pumpkin orange. They couldn't repaint every three months, I thought, as a warm serenity fell over me. My nurse, Dolores, a round, smiling woman with dark eyes and white hair, laid a reassuring hand on my forehead as she finished injecting morphine into my IV.

'Do I have a fever?' I asked.

'No,' she said. 'I just think it makes people feel better.' *She's right, it does*, I thought as I drifted back into sleep.

'Would you like to sit up a bit?' Dolores asked an hour later. I nodded, and she raised the head of the bed. Dr Jordan's assistant, Andrea, who had helped him place over five feet of sutures in me, stood to one side as he examined my wound and asked how I was feeling. When he left, Andrea stayed behind to reassure me.

'In two weeks, you won't believe the difference,' she told me, along with the fact that she thought they had removed at least 3 stone of skin and fat. I had no idea what the surgical site looked like. I was bandaged and a little high from the morphine, and had no desire whatsoever to move my body into a position that would allow me to see my new waist. Andrea left, and an orderly arrived. I found myself in a clean new room with faux wood floors and a rather nice view of the Cleveland skyline. *Maybe I should visit the Rock and Roll Hall of Fame tomorrow*, I thought, the drugs still very much in effect.

My nurse for the evening – a stout, 40-something with a fuchsia streak dyed into her short blonde hair – told me I wouldn't be walking after all. 'After panniculectomy, you need to lie in the deckchair position for at least 12 hours. The air cuffs will keep up your circulation, but you won't be walking till tomorrow morning.' I agreed that this was a good idea. Walking could wait. I switched on *America's Next Top Model* and drifted off during a catfight about pole dancing.

Early the next morning my surgeon and Andrea applied a new dressing to my wound. He helped me into a Lycra binder to keep the dressing in place and told me that I'd have to wear it for the next six weeks. Andrea taught me how to empty my two surgical drains – these were two clear rubber balls filled with my blood, hung over my hips, tethered to my body by tubing and black sutures. Each was pinned to the binder with a safety pin.

I stood up, nurse at my side, and stiffly walked to the bathroom. I didn't really feel any pain. I hadn't had morphine since early the previous evening, but the local anaesthesia at the surgical site seemed to help. I walked slowly out of the hospital room and made five slow circuits around the nurses' station. After checking out hospital breakfast (orange juice from concentrate, slab of French toast, 'coffee'), I changed into my street clothes in the tiny patient bathroom attached to my room. Careful not to disturb my drains, I pulled on a black flowered skirt and a form-fitting T-shirt over the architectural bra. I wore a pair of black sandals as the late September temperature in Ohio still hovered in the eighties.

'Looks like you're ready for the world,' my roommate told me, beaming. Dora, a white-haired black woman with many devoted relatives, smiled tranquilly at me from the bed across the room. She had been wheeled into the room just before I fell asleep to Tyra Banks, and I woke in the night once or twice when Dora moaned in pain. I agreed with her assessment. As an orderly helped me into a wheelchair and pushed me outside into the sunny car park where my mother waited to drive me home, I felt ready for just about anything.

Four days after surgery, I took a shower and saw my body in its new form. I took a long look in the full-length mirror in the bathroom. My overall shape had improved dramatically, though the first thing I noticed (aside from the line of staples and the great angry slash of the wound itself) is that a Georgia O'Keefe image seemed to have exploded where my vagina should have been. I looked like one of those exaggerated, anatomically-correct dolls they give little girls so they can show where the bad man touched them. I was cartoonish, extremely swollen, and I now had a waist. The apron was gone – incinerated, in fact. I stared at myself in the mirror for a long, long time before the pain asserted itself. I tried to apply a new dressing but I couldn't quite make the gauze cover the entire incision. I knew I needed help with this, but didn't want to ask. I crossed the hall from the bathroom into my bedroom and pulled on an old skirt and one of the men's oversize T-shirts I kept just for these occasions. Then I set my shoulders and called out to Leigh Anne.

Leigh Anne had flown in from Florida to help me after this operation. I had postponed moving from Mum's house so I could recover from surgery, but my mother and her bad knees would have had a hard time coping with my many post-op demands. When Leigh Anne arrived, I felt instantly at ease. She helped me cook; lifted all the things I couldn't; drove me to Starbucks (after three days without caffeine, I needed a Grande Americano almost as much as my pain medication). Leigh Anne let me rest and fed my cats. Now I needed her help with my incision, much as I didn't want to ask.

The incision stretched from hip to hip, riding low, skimming my pubis and the tops of my hips. I no longer had a navel, just staples, raw scabby skin and two balloons full of my blood. Leigh Anne stepped into the hall with me. I tried to apologise for asking for this help, for showing her more of my body than anyone without medical training should have to see, but she cut me off. 'I changed my grandmother's nappy. This is nothing, really,' she said. We worked together to cover the incision. I juggled the drains in one hand and tried to hold the end of the dressing with another. We struggled to put the binder back on, and finally, I was closed again – bound, covered, discreet. Leigh Anne wandered off to make tea, and I sat in a high-backed chair and trembled.

Two weeks after surgery, the swelling seemed a little better. I visited my surgeon, who removed a drain and answered my ridiculous questions. 'I felt something in there . . . in the groin area . . . lumps like undescended testicles.' I looked at Dr Jordan expectantly. He laughed.

'Those are internal sutures. You've got some swelling around them,' he explained as he patched the raw hole where the drain used to hang from my side.

'He didn't put any of *those* in while I was watching,' nurse Andrea said, grinning. The explanation satisfied me. I knew the strange, tender lumps under my skin were probably supposed to be there, but felt better knowing exactly what they were.

Since this second surgery my shape is now dramatically different, especially in clothes. I no longer have to arrange and rearrange hem lines because my body is even all the way around. I have an actual lap for the first time in at least 15 years. I feel tight at the waist, trim and sleek. I'm not a thin girl – I still weigh over 14 stone – but I'm not unattractive. Given my height and general proportions (not to mention the architectural bra), I am very nearly statuesque.

EPILOGUE

As I continue to recover from surgery, I spend a lot of time at Borders, a large chain bookshop attached to the shopping centre near my house. I've come to know the staff at the in-store coffee shop: Ellen, motherly and kind; Vanessa, the sassy girl whose hair changes colour with the seasons; Bret, a reedy 26 year old, who loves the Chicago White Sox and knows exactly which blends of coffee I prefer. Heather is tiny and barely out of her teens, but this doesn't stop her from offering romantic advice: 'Guys suck,' she tells me as she adds shots of espresso to my drink. 'You don't need a man to make you happy.'

And then there's the store manager, Vivienne, who's started to inspire some of my wardrobe selections. She wears short skirts and heels, her hair an unnatural but very fetching honey blonde. She has a sort of Mae West look, minus the feather boa, as she walks through the bookshop with clipboard in hand. I admire the clothing and the care with which she applies make-up: bright red lipstick and lots of mascara. Vivienne isn't a slender woman. Her body has no angles, only curves on top of curves. She carries her weight well, like a forties beauty queen:

plump, unashamed and confident in her intrinsic allure. Vivienne is my butterbabe role model. She's a big woman with no apologies, no concealment.

After having all the extra skin chopped off my abdomen, I find I can wear pretty clothes. I try on black flared trousers and pair them with a red print blouse. I display a bit of skin, my cleavage a fine combination of nature's bounty and a really good bra. I wear jewellery and make-up and carry a nice bag (Coach, whenever possible). I have work that I love, writing for magazines. I've just moved into my own house, and I feel as confident as I look.

The new house has come as something of a surprise. I always assumed that when I finally moved out of Mum's house, I'd live in a sad, boxy apartment over a nice, upscale crack den. My friend Bill's old landlord had a better idea.

'You'll love this house,' the landlord told me.

'I don't want a house. I don't want to shovel snow or do yard work,' I said.

'I'll do all of that. All you have to do is move in.' Clyde likes to tell you that he's blunt because he's from New York. He has a neat little moustache and the well-fed, well-tended look of a man who's spent his entire adult life as a member of the Chamber of Commerce. I'm loath to trust this type, but I gave in to the sales pitch and took a tour of the house. The green two-storey sits on a tiny plot in a part of Toledo called the Old West End. The houses here were built at the turn of the twentieth century. Some have bright new paint in period colours, neatly maintained porches and tidy landscaping, the hedges reduced to bare, skeletal limbs in the freezing December air. Others have clearly seen better days: the porches droop, the paint peels. The houses surrounding the green two-storey Clyde wants to rent to me all look well-cared-for. The neighbour on the left has a porch swing. I climb the stairs to the broad front porch and ring the bell.

Clyde welcomes me inside, and the first thing I see is an oak staircase leading to a landing. I step into the hall and notice a fireplace, casement windows and hardwood floors. Then I see the kitchen: granite worktops and brand-new appliances.

'When can I move in?' I ask.

'How about tomorrow?' Clyde replies. We settle on a date a few weeks away. The holidays are coming up, and I need to line-up a removals company.

While I prepare for the move, I work on my writing at Borders because it's quiet and my mother won't distract me. I note the many intriguing additions to Vivienne's wardrobe and think about asking her where she shops. In the new house, I'll spend less time in the bookshop and more time writing at home. I'll really start to live the new life I've worked towards for the last two years. My mother tries to talk me out of moving: 'That house is in the ghetto!' I resist: 'It's not! It's merely ghetto adjacent. Granite! Hardwood!'

Once I make the move, I continue to see Vivienne whenever I have a coffee at the bookshop cafe. I no longer spend so much time there, but I have found another purpose for the place. It's where I go on first dates. Dates with actual men.

Nearly two years have passed since a Russian surgeon disembowelled me for my own good. I've had so many milestones, tiny life events that my cohorts at the surgery support site call 'ah ha moments'. Seven months after surgery, I marvelled at having the ability to clasp my hands behind my back when I stretched after aerobics. After a year, I realised I could sit with my knees together, and that I could cross my ankles. At some point in the initial recovery, I learned to take extraordinary pleasure in the suddenly ordinary. Riding in a small Japanese car for the first time in ten years? That was a red-letter day for me. These little things are victories, but also the sort of clichés that abound in the world of gastric bypass. Everyone takes the same 'after' picture: they squeeze into one leg of an old pair of fat jeans and mug for the camera. It is my deepest struggle not to become a weight-loss surgery cliché, that and my continuing love of food.

One of the only good things about weighing nearly 43 stone is the sense of uniqueness it bestows. People had no trouble remembering me. I was a rare, elusive creature. But, day by day, as I dwindle down, I become more and more ordinary. Weight used to define me, even manufacturing my personality. My whole persona – the boisterous, obnoxious fat girl – lent me an aura of toughness. As the weight comes off, I find myself changing inwardly, becoming more feminine and more delicate in ways that both delight and terrify me. When walking down the street makes you an object of pity and disgust at worst, and unfettered curiosity at best, you need a certain amount of righteous hostility. But the battle armour doesn't fit any more, so I go out into the world without its reassuring heaviness. I have lost some of my dense outer layer of crankiness. These days, I'm a bit more open, a bit more hopeful in my presentation. I wear trousers or fitted skirts and try to rememeber the lipstick; I smile at strangers. While I love all the opportunities I'm finding and look forward to all the 'ah ha moments' ahead, I despise the idea of losing my big-girl righteousness as I lose the weight.

People like to tell prospective bypass patients they'll become a whole new person. This never appealed to me. I never hated myself. I hated some aspects of my body (breasts, for example, should point up) but never the inner person. But like it or not, that person has changed. Losing 21 stone will do that to a girl. As I move forward in a drastically altered body, the inner fat girl diminishes. Much as my body troubled me, I can't help feeling nostalgic about that girl. I hardly think about Cherry Coke and fast food any more, but that girl's scrappiness and general bad attitude saved my life a thousand times. I'm going to miss her.

ACKNOWLEDGEMENTS

I never would've written this book if Lauren Sandler hadn't pulled my essay out of a slush pile and put it on Salon. Thanks for your faith in my work. I also want to thank my tremendous publisher, Clare Hulton, for championing the book before it existed.

I want to thank my amazing friends and family for loving me before and after; Julie and Rick Stahlhut, Leigh Anne Eubanks, Michelle LaLonde-Reaume, Bill Frogameni and Kiki Hellman, Shane Jordan, Deb Garrison, Tish, Drew, Barbara, Mike and Amy Snyir, Frances Wexler, Karen, Robert, Nicole and Amber Woolley, Rachael Scheiber, Mike Wiseman, Jordan Lubetkin, Sharra Perry, Barbara and Richard Hobbie, Kerry Randall-Lewis, Scott Randall, Leslie and Jennifer Koehl, Monni Telfer, Akufo Opoku, Patty Murphy, Alana Woods, Jaclyn Angelle Stanley, Brandon Slotterbeck, Lynnh and Esther Keeling, Cathy Crabtree, Sue MacPhee, Rebecca Wood, Marc Grey and Jo Kozaczka.

Profound thanks to all of my doctors, nurses and counselors and their staffs: Kyra Schofield, Janis Zimmerman, Navin Jain,

Susan Federman, Roderick Jordan, Andrea Gallup, Lorri Esper, Lisa at Middletown Regional and Dolores at MetroHealth.

Everyone at Borders Toledo for watching me edit the book, providing an endless stream of Americanos and for all the good cheer I didn't have myself: Thanks you to Vanessa, Heather, Rachel, Bret, Ellen, Lori, Joyce, and John.

My amazing agent Joanne Brownstein and her lovely boss, Gail Hochman signed me before I'd written a single word. Thank you for your tenacity, wisdom and foresight. I'd also like to thank Miranda West, Rae Shirvington, Kirstie Addis and everyone at Ebury for their work in making *Butterbabe* the best book it could be.

Finally, I want to thank Catherine Carroll for listening to me at the worst time of my life and helping me find the tools to dig myself out. Without you, I really would've gotten stuck to that couch. Thank you for everything.